10 SIMPLE WAYS
TO BEAT STRESS FOR EVER

10
simple ways
to beat stress
for ever

Suzannah Olivier

CICO BOOKS
London

First published in Great Britain by
Cico Books Ltd
32 Great Sutton Street
London EC1V 0NB

Copyright © Cico Books 2002
First edition published as
*500 of the Most Important Stress-busting
Tips You'll Ever Need*
Revised edition printed 2006
Copyright © Cico Books 2006
Text copyright © Suzannah Olivier
2002 and 2006

10 9 8 7 6 5 4 3 2 1

A CIP catalogue record for this book is
available from the British Library

ISBN 1 904991 38 6

Edited by Alison Wormleighton
Designed by Jerry Goldie

Printed in Singapore by Tien Wah Press

For information about Suzannah Olivier
and her books visit her website,
www.healthandnutrition.co.uk

Contents

Introduction

Of course, the truth is that there is no such thing as truly stress-free living. Feelings of stress occur all the time. Viewed in a positive way, stress will help any organism, such as a plant or an animal, or a person, to adapt to their environment.

So what is this book about? It is about dealing with the daily stresses of life, small or big, to turn them to your advantage so that you grow and mature as a person. It is about self-knowledge and learning. This approach will allow you to brush off stresses and strains, putting them into context and dealing with them in a way that doesn't increase your stress levels. It will allow you to organize your thoughts, learn from your experiences and put them to best use to attain your dreams. It is about the future, and the present, that you need and want.

This is a book of ideas. The tips and exercises are easy to dip into so that they can be incorporated into your daily life without difficulty. The book starts with some pretty big concepts which have been whittled down to their essential components to make them ultra-usable. As the book progresses the concepts become less monumental and more personal, relating to the context of your daily life.

How to Use this Book

This is a highly practical book. I would strongly urge you to invest in an attractive spiral-bound notebook and a pen. Make sure the notebook is not too large – you want to be able to carry it around to use as and when you need it. On the other hand, don't make it so small that you can't fit anything on the page. One pen is sufficient, but it is even better to have available three or four pens in different colours. These are to highlight points you want to make to yourself. You will use your notebook in some – or all – of the following ways.

- Throughout this book there are exercises. Whenever you have the opportunity, please actually do the exercises instead of just reading about the principles. This will make the information come to life, personalize it to your own needs and help you to achieve your aims.
- You may want to make lists and mind-maps of goals (mind-maps are explained on pages 16–18).
- You can write down 'feel-good' thoughts that spur you on and unravel unhelpful thoughts that inhibit you.
- You can write yourself reminders of stages and steps.
- Above all, you can make this your very own book as a planner but also as a reminder, a memento and a souvenir of your journey.

Step 1

What Are your Priorities?

> ### KEY MESSAGE:
> ## The Difference between Need and Want
>
> Understand the difference between what you need and what you want. This will help you to sort out your priorities. For instance, you need to pay off your credit card balance but you want that new outfit. Put that way, it may help you to decide which is most important. On the other hand, you may want a holiday at some times of your life, while at other times you need to take a holiday.

In this chapter you can begin to unravel any stressful feelings you have by identifying your personal priorities and establishing goals that are not only inspiring to you but also manageable. If you are going to build firm foundations for the future, you need to know what you are feeling and what your needs are. This may sound incredibly obvious when put this way, but often we don't have a clue what we really want in life – which can be highly stressful. We can exist for many years on the cusp of anxiety until our health suffers or we find we start behaving irrationally. Now is the time to step out of that chaos, and to start to feel good about yourself.

Be consistent in your actions, but remember that flexibility is a great aid to achieving your goals. For instance, if fitness is your aim, consistency means doing something towards it regularly – say, swimming at least four times a week for half an hour each session. But flexibility means that if you injure your shoulder and you need to rest it for a couple of weeks, you take up brisk walking until it is mended. Or flexibility may mean that in the winter months when you are not motivated to swim, you go to the gym, instead of just giving up. In this chapter you will start to shape your dreams, but also learn to be flexible when necessary (which is most of the time).

Don't feel pressurized into setting some new goals. If you are content and your life is balanced, you may be happy at the moment to jog along. But you may still have some dreams that inspire you.

Setting Goals

Identifying priorities, goals and targets is all about having hope for the future, and the only way to realize your goals is to take action. You can dream for ever, but only by doing something will you succeed

Q: *Sometimes I think I don't know what I want. I know what I don't want, though – is that a good start?*
A: How you define your aims can mean the difference between failure and success. If you are always expressing your needs in the negative, this will only serve to tell you what you don't want. 'I wish I wasn't fat', 'I hate my job', 'I don't want to go on holiday there'. Express the same desires in the positive, and in the particular, and you instantly have a goal. 'I would like to weigh 60 kilograms', 'I will train to be a ballet dancer', 'I want to go to Timbuktu'.

Exercise: Identifying your Goals

If you have no idea what your goals are but you generally feel dissatisfied, do the following to help you identify them:

1 Jot down the main areas of your life that you want to change.

2 In order not to be overwhelmed, identify which is the most pressing or motivating aspect for you to work on.

3 If this does not come easily, place a number from 1 to 10 next to each goal to indicate its importance to you. For the top three, make lists of the pros and cons for each one and this should finally sort out your priorities. If you are still unsure, sleep on it for a night or two. It is amazing how things sort themselves out with 'Eureka!' moments as it all starts to crystallize in your mind.

4 Ask yourself, 'How will I know when I have achieved my goal?' Define exactly what your goal is. See, smell, feel and hear what it means. Visualizing it in an unambiguous way will make it more tangible.

Q: *Every time I try to tackle a job I get overwhelmed and end up just walking away from it because it all seems too much. It is easier to do nothing than deal with things head on. Also, if it doesn't work out I get demoralized.*
A: Taking one goal and dividing it into easy-to-attain chunks is a good idea. Whatever you want to achieve, set smaller goalposts along the way. Instead of focusing on a big leap of faith in the distant future, you can tangibly feel each milestone before you even get there. Create a detailed action plan, and do not fear failure. Getting imperfect

results when you work on something is just a way of learning lessons. Next time you will be wiser and more targeted in your approach.

Q: *I feel in a bit of a muddle and exasperated that I don't seem to accomplish anything on any given day. Do I really need goals or do I just have to get organized?*

A: Getting organized is a part of having goals. Are you doing what you want to do with your life? Do you feel good about most days of the week? If the answer is no, this could be a significant source of stress in your life. Identifying what you want to do is the first step. Goals can be small as well as big, and sometimes the small ones are easier to focus on initially, making you confident and motivated enough to go for bigger ones if you wish to. There can be as much satisfaction in sorting out a dusty, junk-filled cupboard, if that's your goal, as in finishing your first novel.

Exercise: Make an Action Plan

Here's how to create an action plan tailored to your own needs:

1 Pick your goal and express it specifically and in a positive frame (not 'I would like to' or 'I want', but 'I will' or 'I am').

2 Write down ten specific actions that would get you nearer to your aim ('pick up the phone and make a call' or 'write a precis of my book'). Don't think too hard about these steps, just be inspired and write down anything that comes to mind – you can add further thoughts and edit it later.

3 Put those actions in a logical order. Now write down everything you can think of that will help you ('I have a good telephone personality', 'I have some good contacts').

4 Write down everything you can think of that might hinder you ('I don't have a telephone', 'I don't yet know anyone in the business'). If you wish, you can use mind-mapping techniques (see page 16) for this. By writing things down they become clearer.

5 Finally, think of ways to overcome the obstacles and act upon the positive points.

Tips to Help You Achieve your Goals

- Don't procrastinate. People usually put things off for a number of reasons, such as not expecting to enjoy the task, lacking confidence in their ability to complete it or thinking the job can be finished more quickly than it can. Combat procrastination by focusing on the pleasure of completion. Reward yourself with a treat, like a nice meal or an evening out.

- The goals you think of can be for yourself, your family or others you are involved with. However, remember that while you have control over your own goals, other people's may not accord with yours, which means you may be disappointed. Listen to what it is that these people want and need, and resolve to help them towards their dreams.

- Prioritizing is another vital skill to learn. It's astounding how, when there is an important job to do, it suddenly seems so important to make the coffee, call your mother or take the dog for a walk. If you habitually procrastinate, get in the habit of making a daily plan.

Self-Determination

It is a fact that the people who feel most stressed are those who feel they have no control over a situation. For instance, you might think that high-powered executives with busy lifestyles would be most likely to feel stressed if their companies are in trouble because the need for troubleshooting falls to them. But, as it happens, it is often the blue-collar workers who are the ones susceptible to stress – they feel they have little or no influence over which way the company goes, and therefore over their job security. The most innovative companies recognize this and encourage forums for 'the workers' to participate in the direction of the company.

Of equal importance to being able to influence a situation is a feeling of being in control. One of the important things to restore in people who feel low or who lack confidence is their sense of having control over their lives – their feeling of self-determination. You may actually have a reasonable degree of control, but because you do not think you have choices and are unconfident about your decision-making abilities, you feel out of control, which can fuel depression and anxiety. (This sequence of events is referred to as learned helplessness.)

Q: *I keep trying to get control of different aspects of my life but I always seem to end up in the same place. How can I make changes?*
A: Keep a diary of problems that tend to recur in your life. This gives you the ability to root out the causes and be realistic about how to resolve them. If you are always late for work, figure out what your morning patterns are and what needs to change. If you

are always overdrawn at the bank, keep a record of your spending and analyse your spending patterns. If you regularly fall out with your kids, try to work out where your conversations tend to break down. By going through these exercises, you will regain control over the various threads of your life. Usually, attempts to change have only a temporary effect, as a result of failing to find an alternative way of behaviour. It is essential to replace old patterns with new ones and not just to eliminate them.

Q: *Making a list of my recurring problems just depresses me.*
A: Itemize your personal strengths as well – work on the list over a few days if necessary, adding fresh thoughts (see Mind-Mapping, page 16). This exercise will help you focus on your abilities and see yourself in a positive light. Your strengths could be anything, such as, 'I am highly organized', 'I have a good relationship with my colleagues/ family', 'I enjoy new challenges', 'I am outgoing and friendly', 'I am a good person'.

Q: *I'm not comfortable about being aggressive to get what I want.*
A: Nobody said anything about being aggressive – being assertive is not the same thing at all. Assertiveness can be perfectly healthy and can be thought of as a middle ground between being unhealthily passive and unhealthily aggressive whether at home, at work or at play.

Q: *So where do I start?*
A: If you find it initially difficult to take control of the major areas of your work or personal life, start small. The need to reduce these to manageable, bite-sized chunks comes up several times within this book, as it is so important. By working on small things and succeeding at making improvements, you can do wonders for your self-belief. You will realize that you are indeed able to make changes and positively influence your future.

Q: *It's all very well to talk about choice on a day-to-day basis, but what about the big stuff in life where you really are dragged along by circumstances?*
A: Believing that you can control your future is the best way to achieve self-determination. These words will sound hollow to a person in the throes of a difficult situation, but for the most part we really do have the ability to determine our fate. For instance, if you are about to be fired you have the choice of whether to feel defeated about this or to use it as an opportunity to take a new direction in life. If you have an overbearing partner who is occasionally violent, you have a choice about whether to stay or not. If your teenage child has addiction problems, you have a choice about whether to find out about help organizations and to investigate how family and friends might be inadvertently facilitating this. Nobody said these choices are easy, and they are indeed often complicated. There are many facets to the decision-making process and you may need to explore them, but you do have choices in most things (see Cognitive Thinking, page 66).

Find a Balance between Work and Home

A great myth of our time is that 'we can do it all'. We work hard, we play hard, we give 'quality time' to our children. But if you find that you are becoming exhausted by attempting to keep all these balls you are juggling in the air, it is probably time to make some choices. When working out your priorities and goals, you will inevitably come across conflicts between the needs of work and home, so it is as well to tackle this subject head on.

Failing to find an acceptable balance between work and home life is one of the most common causes of stress. We work long hours at the office, weekends can vanish in a mass of tasks, and taking time off when the kids are unwell becomes a major time-negotiation nightmare. Not surprisingly, this can lead to many stress-related health problems, including depression, anxiety and physical strains. The Japanese even have a word, *karoshi*, which means 'death by overwork'. *Karoshi* is listed on 10,000 death certificates each year in Japan (it is most often heart failure or suicide). These individuals clearly do not have the balance right between their work and home life.

Q: *I enjoy my job a lot but I feel guilty about spending time at work when it keeps me away from my family.*
A: If your vocation is your vacation (see Vocation, page 76) then you have got the best of all worlds because you really enjoy what you do. But even when this is the case, it is easy for work to creep into other areas and create an imbalance, leaving you feeling drained. It also does not take into account the needs of your partner and family, who might hope to spend more time with you. If you are married to your job, you probably need to discuss with your family how they feel about it.

Q: *Home life is lovely but it is inevitably a grind of 'things to do', whereas at work I get job satisfaction.*
A: Sometimes it is easier to value successes at work than those at home. This is, in part, because it is how we earn a living and also because there are recognized reward schemes (such as salary increase, being awarded contracts, promotion and customer/boss satisfaction). Successes at home are harder to measure, but recognizing and valuing them is an excellent step towards attaining a balance between home and work. Successes might include a loving relationship, enjoying your children, a vibrant home atmosphere or a few really good friends to count on – think of those successes that are relevant to you.

Top Tips for a Work–Home Balance

- If you find that you are always bringing work home, use some time-management techniques (see page 24). You may need to develop the ability to compartmentalize your various activities and get into the habit of creating cut-off times.

- Set yourself a fixed time beyond which you do not stay at work – and stick to it.

- Of course, this can all work the other way round. If your home and family or social life are more important to you, you might not be giving your best to your work life. You might be in temporary employment, drifting from job to job or just getting by in what you feel is an uninspiring job. This is just as unbalanced, and perhaps you might benefit from getting more excited about your job, no matter how short-term, and giving it all you've got while you are there. You will reap the reward from its becoming a more fulfilling experience.

- In the same way that you go off to an office or workplace to concentrate on your job, make specific commitments to concentrate on your partner, family or friends. Apart from their need to see you, this time is important for stress reduction and so should be a top priority.

Q: *I have nagging doubts about whether my kids need me to be at home more than I am. I get confused about how to juggle parenting and work. How can I establish my priorities?*

A: All working parents have to ask themselves one important question at some point or other: 'Will my job or my children come first most of the time?' The answer to this question helps to determine how you structure your life because it is really not possible to do it all. You have to ask yourself what you actually want and what is genuinely achievable. No one ever went to their grave saying, 'I wish I had worked harder'. It is more likely to be, 'I wish I spent more time with my loved ones and doing things that I enjoy'. It can be particularly difficult to juggle parental responsibilities with work life, because you feel such a huge commitment to both. Don't wait for a crisis to happen (illness, feelings of guilt, tiredness, difficulties in attending sports days or school plays). Evaluate what you need to do for your children and negotiate in advance with your employers about how you are going to handle this.

Exercise: Keep Work Worries in their Place

If work worries are keeping you awake at night, you definitely need to improve your compartmentalization skills. The best way is to use the techniques covered under Cognitive Thinking (see page 66).

For example, if you are worrying about getting a project in on time, you may be torturing yourself with automatic thoughts in which the problems seem worse than they are. To stop this from happening, write down these thoughts and then work out the 'antidotes' to each one, as suggested here:

Automatic thought: 'If I'm late with the report, it'll be a complete disaster.'
Diagnosis: This is an overgeneralization and it is unlikely to be a complete disaster, just a partial disaster!

Automatic thought: 'Everyone will be mad at me.'
Diagnosis: They probably value the work you've done and have been in similar situations themselves. If you forewarn them that it may be a little late, they can reorganize their timing accordingly.

Automatic thought: 'Why am I always late with everything?'
Diagnosis: This is another overgeneralization. You probably are not always late with everything – you very likely do plenty of other things on time. Seeing the situation in this more positive light means you now can work specifically on your time management.

Automatic thought: 'I'm running out of time.'
Diagnosis: You have two choices. You can do some extra work on a one-off basis to catch up, or you can delay the deadline. Talking to people might make it more workable than it seems at 1am.

Automatic thought: 'Help!'
Diagnosis: Panic is not constructive. Who are you asking to help you? Is this a suggestion you could take up and can you draft in someone to take some of the load?

If you have written all your automatic thoughts down as well as some more rational responses, you may now have a plan instead of an unstructured worry. Compartmentalize the worry and get on with your home life and your night's sleep.

Staying Flexible

Goal-setting is important, but to achieve your goals you must remain flexible. You will almost certainly need to re-evaluate your goals at regular intervals.

Q: *I've been accused of being inflexible but mostly it helps me stay focused on my plan. However, I have to admit I've missed out on some opportunities because I didn't change my plans, and sometimes I regret this.*
A: Even if you are currently happy with everything around you and do not feel the need for anything to change, it is still wise to adopt a flexible approach to life. Nothing stays the same – and if you can be adaptable, then the stresses and strains that life throws up will not seem like overwhelming crises. Get into the habit of looking to see how many paths you have open to you (it may take some practice to see these). A rigid approach will say, 'This is what I have to do', 'This is the only option' or 'This is just the way it is', whereas a flexible approach will say, 'These are the options I have' or 'I will seek options'. How many possibilities have you missed in the past because you were not allowing yourself to see alternative paths?

Q: *What's the point of staying flexible when you can't control everything that happens to you anyway?*

A: If you want to guarantee success in virtually every aspect of your life, the secret is to remain adaptable. In life you will encounter situations when you are not in control, but being flexible in the rules you use to govern your thinking, the meaning you attach to things and your approach to meeting challenges will see you through. You may be adaptable enough to deal with events around you, but how flexible are you towards yourself? Work out what your core beliefs are in life and challenge them, which will test their validity. Do they work *for* you, or do they work *against* you? You might be surprised by some of the negative core beliefs you have that are limiting your ability to be flexible. Core beliefs you will definitely want to work on and change (see Cognitive Thinking, page 66) might sound a little like some of the following:

- 'Life is difficult and requires hard work, and hard work is not meant to be fun.'
- 'I am not worthy of reward' (this could be in a particular situation rather than in general).
- 'I have to work harder than I already do but I still won't be worthy of reward.'
- 'I am unattractive and am therefore worth less than someone who is attractive.'
- 'There is something wrong with me.'
- 'Love is painful and I might get hurt.'
- 'The world is becoming a more precarious place all the time.'

Q: *I often end up doing something myself because I know I'll do it better than someone else and it's easier than explaining things.*

A: A rigid mindset is a guaranteed way to stay stuck in the same repetitive patterns in life. Flexibility means not being wedded to your own ways and thoughts to the exclusion of alternatives. If, for example, you find that you are incapable of cooking a meal with a friend because you can't bear the way she chops the carrots, then you need to loosen up.

Why Flexibility Is So Important

Stability in all areas of life is the key to a worry-free existence. We all have moments in our lives when suddenly everything is calm and balanced and we can heave a sigh of relief. However, the minute that one area of life becomes unbalanced, a flexible approach is what will restore stability. If you stay rigid, the situation will get more unbalanced and could eventually overwhelm you.

- Treat changes as challenges to overcome rather than as threats to your perceived order of things.

- Lack of flexibility breeds resentment and discontent. If, for example, you are moved sideways or are even demoted in your job, you have two choices. You can feel bad about it, complain, get depressed and feel that your world has been threatened.

Or you can take it as a wake-up call to change how you operate at work, use the opportunity to learn something in the new position or find something else more challenging to put your mind to.

- If you made a bad decision – say, you lost money on an investment – don't worry about what might have been. There is nothing you can do about something that has already happened. Being flexible will allow you to get on with the next option, which might work to your advantage.

- Visualizing the following image will help you understand the value of a flexible approach: *The rigid tree breaks in the wind, while the flexible one bends with the wind and springs back.*

Key Tool 1: Mind-Mapping

When sorting out your personal priorities, you may find it helpful to introduce yourself to Mind-Mapping. This is a fantastic tool for organizing your thoughts, planning and problem-solving. At its simplest, the mind-map replaces lists with a pictorial representation of the subject in hand and all its possible connections. Even if you believe you don't have a creative bone in your body, mind-mapping gives you access to your creative flow and intuition. It can also be a powerful way of improving memory, organizing projects and studying. Mind-mapping allows you to see the whole picture. Of course, the more effective you are at organizing your thoughts, the less stressed you'll be as your life gains order and your thoughts are permitted expression.

One of the things I like about mind-mapping is that understanding the basic principles is easy, and you can achieve quick rewards from your first attempts. However, like any discipline, the more you do it and the better you understand how it works, the more you get out of it. Some simple tips will open up all sorts of possibilities – and, because it is an expressive tool, you can use it in any way you wish and really personalize your approach.

When most of us want to remember or to plan something, we jot down a list. This is, of course, useful but it does not tap into the real power of memory. Lose that list and the chances are that you will not remember some of the items and would not be able to recreate it in the same way if you had another stab at it.

The problem with lists is that they are linear and do not encourage explorations of the associations and relationships between items on the list. The brain does not really work in straight lines, but in patterns of interconnectedness, which are best imagined as a web. The whole point about mind-mapping is that it is an approach that uses this interconnectedness. The process can even be thought of as an extended but highly focused doodle – which takes it out of the realm of a difficult technique to learn and into the realm of being quite good fun.

1 Take a clean sheet of paper. At the centre of every mind-map is a single thought
   or item. Write in your name or the word 'Me'. In this instance we will build a
   mind-map which allows you to access your extended network of people. Use this
   example to find help when setting up a small business, when planning a reunion
   party or when you just need help with a particular problem. Begin by creating a
   simple list – you might come up with between 20 and 100 people, depending on
   how extensive your address book is and how well connected you are.

2 Draw thick lines, radiating out from 'Me' at the centre, in such a way that you
   can write a single word on each one. These words might be: 'Family', 'Friends',
   'Neighbours', 'Local Services', 'Colleagues', 'Schools', 'Sports/Leisure Club' and
   so on. (You may well think of others more relevant to you.)

3 To each of these main branches you can now add sub-branches.

4 Notice that there are links between groups. You might want to highlight them
   with coloured arrows – this is not duplication but a true representation of the
   connected nature of our lives and our thought processes. These links are a help
   not a hindrance.

5 Remember that each one of these people has their own network, which means
   that your network can go even further than you first imagined. Persuade just a
   small percentage of these people (say a brother or sister, a couple of friends and
   a work colleague or two) to create their own network mind-maps of their
   contacts, and you will have a huge potential network, perhaps numbering
   hundreds of people.

You might wonder why you can't just do this as a list. But if you did, the chances are
that you would not remember half of your possible contacts. Adding to your list
would make it very messy with lots of writing in the margins. Your list would not
grow as effectively because your mind works in a pictographic way more suited to the
mind-map method.

Mind-maps work best when they are clear and well presented. One of the few
'rules' is to use only one word or thought on each line for clarity. You may even find
it easier to use an image – images can be much more powerful than words and
are excellent mnemonics for recalling things (particularly for exam revision). Your first
mind-map, such as notes taken at a lecture, might be messy, but there is nothing
to stop you from revising it and improving it, in order to make it a useful tool for
revision later.

Using colour adds to the clarity of your mind-map. On your 'Me' map, for
instance, you would use a different colour to draw the lines for each of the main

categories of people you know. This helps the eye, and therefore the mind, sort out the information more quickly when you need it. Another possibility is to use colour to represent the different 'levels' of people you know. So, for instance, you might use red for those in your immediate sphere, blue for those one step removed, and so on. Unless it is all very obvious to you, take a moment to add a small colour key in a corner of the page.

Now that you have had the chance to experiment with a simple mind-map, work on others. Trust your intuition and allow yourself to free-associate. Work as fast as you can, and without judgement or evaluation. You can review and amend it later if you need to.

Practise by doing a mind-map of your strengths and the support and blessings you have in your life. Focus on what is good in your world. Keep this mind-map and frame it, placing it where you can see it every day.

This is only the simplest explanation of how to mind-map, and I would urge you to explore the subject further as it is so simple and yet so powerful. You can use mind-mapping to sort out project outlines, as well as problems and challenges of all sorts, and you should find that it cuts across a lot of dithering. Mind-mapping is good for organizing time, for taking notes at lectures and meetings, and for helping sort out priorities and make decisions when you are faced with different options. At times when you are feeling low, it is useful for working out what it is that is contributing to depressing moods and what positive solutions might offer themselves up. It really gives a fast return for little effort, and it is fun to do as well.

Step 2

Practical Ways to Deal with Challenges

KEY MESSAGE:

Problems and Challenges

'Problems' just weigh a person down. A challenge is a problem that is expressed in a more positive framework. It is something to be dealt with and turned to your advantage. Working on the challenges in your life can be rewarding and move you forwards. Dealing with small challenges, and setting the scene for success, paves the way to tackling bigger challenges.

If you are going to create a life that is inspiring yet stress-free, you first need to work out whether you are in charge of your day-to-day life, or whether events and circumstances are driving you, sometimes in directions you are not keen on.

In this chapter we will concentrate on evaluating how in control you are. We will also look at the question of organizational skills and suggest lots of highly practical ideas for how to get more order into your life. Finally we will look at some of the personality issues that might hinder you and we'll give you strategies for overcoming them.

Communication Skills

You need to work on your communication skills if you are feeling misunderstood by others, finding yourself unable to say exactly what you really mean or struggling to get the best out of the people around you. This subject is dealt with further in Step 6, Better Relationships (see page 88).

Q: *I often feel guilty about talking about my needs and I don't like to be too demanding.*

A: Send out clear signals that can't be confused. Being confident about your needs may feel awkward. You might worry that you are being selfish or too assertive, a word that can have negative as well as positive connotations. If someone says that 'Jane is really assertive', they might simply mean that Jane knows exactly what she wants and how to get it, but many will hear this as 'Jane is difficult, unyielding and bossy'. Yet being assertive does not mean you do not take into account other people's feelings – rather, it means saying what you want as clearly as possible without aggression. Being assertive certainly does not imply that you have to step over other people to get what you want. You don't have to justify yourself, just state your needs.

Q: *When I try to deal with problems with my partner, it frequently just develops into a row. It is hard to be constructive in these circumstances as we just go off feeling bruised.*

A: One of the reasons conversations can escalate into disagreements is that one person feels as if they are being put under a spotlight and interrogated, which can lead to them clamming up. Peppering your conversation with such interrogative words as why, what, how, when and where may well make the person on the receiving end feel a little uncomfortable. Experiment with the following instead, and see the positive results you get. Wait until the other person has finished speaking (never interrupt). Then, instead of jumping in with an interrogative question or a comment or opinion, just say, 'And?' (or 'Because?' or 'And this means?'). By repeating these leading questions whenever it seems appropriate in the conversation, you will lead the other person to disclose more information and in a confident, comfortable manner. This is a basic approach used by therapists to encourage people to open up and come up with their own conclusions and answers. It is a simple, highly effective way of improving communication (and is also great for getting more information out of recalcitrant children).

Q: *I sometimes feel I change my behaviour to please whoever is around me instead of asserting my own personality. But I read somewhere that this is a way of getting what you want.*

A: Chameleon behaviour – changing your personality to please other people – is very draining and destroys self-esteem in the long run. However, mirroring – in which you reflect the other person to a degree and are in empathetic mode (see page 110) – is totally different and allows you to use empathy to tune in to other people and build a rapport with them. In one you are out of control and you cheat yourself; in the other you remain in control and true to yourself.

Q: *I often need 'courage from a bottle' when dealing with tricky issues involving those nearest to me.*

A: Don't try to blot out communication problems by drinking. Distancing yourself for a little while in order to get a perspective is fine, and taking time to find a suitable moment to talk is also fine, but don't miss the boat or numb your emotions with drink or other substances.

Q: *I have a dialogue that goes round in my head before I tackle tricky conversations.*
A: It is true that 'rehearsing' conversations can help to organize thoughts. However, be careful not to try to mind-read what their reactions are going to be or you may not do the conversation justice. Just get on with being inquisitive about their viewpoints, honest about yours, and not hurtful.

Exercise: Visualize Yourself Getting Along with People

If you have difficulty getting along with a colleague, friend or member of your family, work on a visualization exercise (see page 142) in the following way:

1 Spend a few minutes each day, in a quiet meditative state, imagining yourself with this person, and see yourself getting along with that person.

2 Visualize relating to each other using good communication, being honest and harmonious. Really imagine yourself in this situation.

3 Repeat the exercise at least a couple of times a day, and you will find that you slowly begin to improve the relationship.

4 Be aware that you cannot use this technique to control the behaviour of the other person, but are likely to move towards a better understanding by synchronization of thought patterns and body language.

Dealing with Communication Difficulties

- Clarify your understanding of the issues before you decide to make your statement. Don't be goaded into making decisions under pressure.

- Stand your ground for what you believe in while always listening to the other person.

- Look for alternative solutions.

- Remember that you have the right to say 'no' – and if you do so, say it with conviction.

- Give reasons and not excuses.

- Don't apologize or agonize over refusing.

- Don't get sidetracked.

Planning

Some individuals, particularly creative types, seem to thrive on a degree of disorganization, finding it stimulating, but most people find that being able to find that important phone number or file brings their stress levels down. Actually, many of us have split personalities when it comes to being organized. We may be fiercely efficient when at work, while our private lives flounder in a mound of clutter and a lack of time. In part, this might be a self-defence mechanism. Who wants to be a totally efficient automaton 24 hours a day, seven days a week? But it can go too far, and home disorganization, which contrasts so much with our professional lives, can impact on professional capabilities and lead to feelings of being out of control.

Q: *I'm always chasing my own tail so I don't feel I have time to 'get organized'. Anyway, I've got used to flying by the seat of my pants.*
A: If during the course of the day you don't even have time to make yourself a cup of coffee, you are in dire need of some planning. Time spent planning is never wasted and is actually a major time-saver. It takes only five to ten minutes daily. When you plan your day, make a point of also prioritizing. Use a star system or assign each task a number from 1 to 5 to indicate how vital it is to complete that day. Initially, you may spend some of the time clearing a backlog, but if you keep it up, before long you will be focusing on moving forwards. Being organized or disorganized is as much a matter of habit as anything else. If you get into the habit of always checking your diary daily, then you won't miss your dentist appointment for the third time in a row. If you spend just a few minutes sorting out your priorities for the day, first thing, then, for the most part, you can rule your day instead of letting it rule you.

Q: *I feel deflated at the end of the day as my to-do list gets longer not shorter and I still feel that I haven't accomplished anything important.*
A: When you have a list of ten things to do and realistically won't be able to do more than one 'big thing' in a day, choose that big thing carefully. The other nine will all need to be small. It is easier to concentrate on the 'big thing' if you either (1) get it out of the way first before distractions set in, or (2) clear the little things out of the way first to allow you to concentrate. If you don't know which method suits you best, experiment with both. One system may work better than the other for a particular task or day. However, there is always a danger with the second system that it will lead to procrastination. If you are prone to this, stick to the first system.

Q: *My partner is sometimes not particularly helpful with matters that I think are important and I find it annoying. He just doesn't seem to have the same priorities sometimes.*
A: There can be differences between your priorities and those of the people you live with. If you can't resolve these differences, learning to respect the differences may be the most peaceful way forwards.

Exercise: *Effective Planning*

If you have a large task ahead of you, you need to plan it out into smaller chunks and prioritize which are the most important.

1 Organize your thoughts, breaking the job down into manageable chunks.

2 Use subheadings to categorize the jobs, and put them into a date sequence – some things may need to run in tandem. For instance, if you have to do some research before writing to someone, list the research areas to check out.

3 If you need to delegate some of the tasks, write a list of who does what and what the completion times will have to be.

4 Write the jobs in your diary.

5 Set regular review times to check that you are on course. This way you can focus only on what needs to be done at that time, safe in the knowledge that the task won't run out of control. (It will also stop you from worrying in the middle of the night about the enormity of the job, if you are prone to this.)

Getting Up to Date and Staying that Way

A huge backlog of paperwork is death to any desire to get organized and prioritize, as it can engender feelings of hopelessness and lack of direction. If you have a few impossible-looking stacks before you, you could perhaps decide to set aside a full day to get through them and then vow not to let them build up again. Alternatively – and this is probably more realistic for most people – you can deal with them in half an hour or so as explained here. (This method can also be used when you return from a holiday to find a huge stack of post to deal with.)

• Place a wastepaper basket by your side, and arm yourself with some see-through plastic folders.

• Go through every item in the stacks of paper and throw out unnecessary items.

• As you work through the stack make separate piles of bills to pay, filing, things to read and letters needing replies.

• Put any bigger jobs that emerge in separate plastic folders, and write dates in your diary when you will tackle them individually.

• Pay the bills.

• Vow to yourself that you will deal with three or four of the remaining items each day (reply to a letter, file a couple of items, read something through) until, before long, you will have got through the whole lot – and the process will probably have been faster than you thought.

- Resolve to tackle your morning post systematically when it comes in each day so that it doesn't build up again.

- Bring deadlines forward by a couple of days. This is a bit like always keeping your watch five minutes fast to make sure you get to appointments on time. If there are any unexpected obstacles, you can still meet your deadlines.

- Keep your promises. If you say you'll do something by a given time, do so. On the other hand, think carefully before agreeing to do something you might regret later.

Time Management

Do you find that you struggle to juggle all your commitments? If you have decided that there aren't enough hours in the day, think again. There might be more time available to you than you realize. Sometimes it is easy to be busy just being busy. Rationalizing what you do could free up a lot of spare time – to enjoy yourself. Remember to be selective. Despite our plethora of labour-saving devices, we are busier than ever. Where once executives would have had secretaries, now they have laptops and e-mail and they do all their own correspondence. Because of the ease of photocopying and sending electronic info, we are bombarded with more and more copies, memos and circulars, most of which we have to read and file, not to mention having to respond to. This means that we need to be increasingly selective about how we spend our time and what we keep. Otherwise we run the risk of drowning in paper and never-ending tasks.

Q: *Where do I start?*
A: Make a point of taking five minutes at the start of each morning to plan your day, and also glance at how it impacts on the rest of the week. If you are overstretched, take a long, hard look at your daily schedule and decide if you are expecting too much of yourself. Make cuts if you need to.

Q: *I keep running out of time.*
A: Do a time audit. Keep a record for three or four days of how you spend your time, meticulously writing down everything you do. You may discover that you spend more time than you realize on irrelevant tasks. Spending 20 minutes filling in questionnaires in magazines, reading all the joke e-mails you have received or phoning to check the cinema listings at five different cinemas will result in you having to put undue pressure on yourself to complete more important tasks in less time. Or you may find that you are underestimating the time taken to complete the necessities of life, and so you feel pressurized. A time audit will help you see where your time is going and help you to prioritize tasks and allocate time sensibly. Delegate where appropriate. If you tend to

do everything yourself, investigate why. Use the techniques described in Cognitive Thinking (see page 66) to uncover more reasonable alternatives to statements like, 'I can't trust anyone else to do the job properly' or 'I don't like to be a burden'.

Q: *Is there a best time to focus attention on things I have to do?*
A: We are all subject to biorhythms (energy cycles when we are more, or less, productive) and you may be aware of these in yourself. In most people, brain power peaks before midday, so difficult jobs are best done between 8am and noon. Avoid difficult jobs in the evening. The exception to this seems to be some creative people who like to use the quiet night-time hours as thinking time. If you do work later in the day, avoid alcohol as it will deaden your ability to focus.

Time Management Tips

- If you find that you are repeatedly checking your e-mails, the chances are that this is distracting you from other activities. Make a point of reading your e-mails no more than three times a day, at preset times, such as first thing in the morning, after lunch and at clocking-off time. Avoid opening joke e-mails and other distracting material until you are ready – set aside time to unwind and then you can really enjoy them.

- Keep your paperwork in order and your files up to date. A small amount of time spent on getting organized will save huge amounts of time later when you are trying to find things in a hurry.

- Write down contact details on the inside of each folder, right at the beginning, to save you having to flick through reams of paper to find names and numbers.

- Regularly sweep through your computer files and delete or store on disk any you don't need. This will make it easier to access important files.

- If you have a large project to tackle, break it down into smaller chunks and put the resulting plan into your diary.

- If you allocate a set amount of time to a particular task and you can't afford for it to overrun, stick to this time allotment and don't be tempted to work late and eat into your down time. If you haven't finished, you will, of course, need to reorganize your priorities for the next day or the rest of the week, but at least you will be rested from a good night's sleep and will have topped up your energy levels, before you tackle it again.

- If you can't change it, don't sweat it. Once you have completed a task, you might reflect on it and want to make a change, and that is fine. But if, for whatever reason, you can't alter it, don't waste valuable time and energy worrying about it. Always remember to ask yourself the question, 'What is the worst that can happen if it is not perfect?' The majority of times the answer will be that it won't matter all that much.

- Don't waste valuable time thinking up excuses for why you haven't finished something. Come clean about it and get on with the task. Hiding behind excuses never works in the long term – it just creates stress for you and uncertainty for the person on the receiving end, while using up energy.

- Keeping in touch with friends is vital for a rounded and happy life. However, avoid chatting in the middle of your workday as this will inevitably throw your schedule out. Instead, set aside time to chat to people at a time when you can relax, give them your full attention and really focus on the conversation.

Overwhelmed?

One of the most stultifying feelings is that of being overwhelmed by the sheer volume of tasks you need to tackle. If you have a sinking feeling that you have just too much to do and can't cope, then you need to take some time to find the source of such overwhelming feelings. Once you know the underlying cause, you'll be able to change things around in a short time.

Exercise: Assessing the Problem

The first step is to work out whether your sense of being overwhelmed by things is actual (ie, practical problems) or perceived (your emotional reaction to them).

1 In a quiet place where you will not be interrupted, commit to paper all the things you are feeling overwhelmed by. Concentrate on detail and put everything down as you think of it. You can put it in some sort of order later.

2 Put a number from 1 to 10 next to each item to indicate how overwhelmed you feel by it, with 1 being the least and 10 the most.

3 Concentrate on the items you have rated 6 and above. Ask yourself whether they are principally *practical* things you have to do, perhaps involving scheduling problems (such as reports to finish or a difficulty in getting across town in time to pick up the children from school) or *emotional* issues (such as how you can communicate with a parent). Some may be both emotional and practical, such as an impending divorce.

4 Work out how you can resolve these challenges using the relevant sections of this book. Remember to set aside sufficient time to work through each item. You

may find it easier to tackle the practical issues first, using a logical, step-by-step approach. This can give you a much-needed sense of achievement. Or you may find that you need to address the emotional issues before you can even think about dealing with the practical ones. Either way you can make a plan.

Q: *In dealing with my feelings of being overwhelmed, I find the whole process a bit lonely, but I guess no one else is going to do it for me.*
A: Tell those who need to know that you are feeling overwhelmed and that you need to work it through. Your partner, boss and close friends may be supportive and may instinctively back off until you are feeling better about things; or they may be a part of the problem, in which case you need to explain to them how they can help.

Q: *I get really low when I feel overwhelmed.*
A: If you perceive that you just don't have the mental or physical stamina to address the items on your list, your feeling of being overwhelmed might be coming from a degree of depression. Turn to page 62 for information about this (but also read on in this section for more ideas).

Q: *I feel like an idiot for always getting myself into a situation where I have too much to do. I only have myself to blame, don't I?*
A: To reduce the possibility of feeling overwhelmed in the future, work out whether you habitually set yourself unrealistic targets with regard to practical tasks and goals, and your relationships with other people. Are you setting yourself up for disappointment and failure? Or are you able to say 'no', not just to other people but also to yourself? (You are probably your own hardest taskmaster.) Now also ask yourself whether the language (such as 'idiot' and 'blame') you are using against yourself (yes, against) is appropriate.

Practical Ways to Avoid Feeling Overwhelmed

- Feeling overwhelmed may come from stimulus fatigue. For instance, if you are the sort of person who has stacks of journals to read for work but never actually gets around to reading them, or whose heart sinks when accosted by a long list of new e-mails, you might need to do something about this. Become rigorous about binning junk mail, asking people who send round-robin e-mails not to send them to you and cancelling subscriptions to any magazines you don't read. You can also cancel your daily paper, lose the TV and turn off your mobile phone for a while. You'll be amazed by how little you really miss them and by how much this can simplify your life.

- Clear the decks. All the items on the list you created (see page 26) with a rating of 5 and below might not be the most important contributors to your sense of being overwhelmed, but they will certainly slow your progress. If you are able to set aside a couple of days (take time off work if necessary) to systematically work through them, using the principles set out on pages 19 and 32, you will feel better and be able to focus on the big issues. With many of these items you will just have to steam through them and not be a perfectionist about how you achieve them. If you have five thank-you letters to write, just pick up the phone and say thanks instead. If you are committed to doing some things but you need the spare time, and in any case you are not in the mood for them, cancel them – clearing time in your diary can be a huge help.

- Even if depression is a feature of your sense of being overwhelmed, you can still work through the practical, rather than emotional, aspects of the feeling. By doing small things to help, you can slowly gain a sense of control and begin to motivate yourself anew.

Multi-Tasking

If you find yourself nestling the phone between your shoulder and ear, hoping to have an in-depth conversation while you check your e-mails and simultaneously note down items for your shopping list, you might think you are an effective multi-tasker. Yet research tells us that in reality we do not complete jobs effectively and accurately if we aim to do too many things at the same time. Multi-tasking can also be pretty stressful. Give your full attention to a job and you will complete it more speedily and accurately, and feel less stressed and calmer at a stroke.

On the other hand, there are some activities that do lend themselves to multi-tasking. These are activities you can do when you don't have to concentrate fully on something else, such as watching TV.

Q: *Isn't my ability to multi-task an advantage?*
A: In a busy world, the ability to do several things at once might seem a benefit, but if you are hoping to think clearly about a given task then you are probably better off 'serial-tasking' – completing one task before you move on to the next. It might seem a little slow at first but the advantages are that you don't have to go over old ground correcting mistakes or get accused that you are not really concentrating on conversations. Most importantly, your stress levels are likely to be lower. A surprising amount of calm comes from focusing on one thing at a time.

Q: *Yes, but what about interruptions?*
A: You may need to train the people around you when you start serial-tasking. They may be used to interrupting you and getting an immediate reaction, and will have to learn to wait their turn.

Q: *Is multi-tasking always out of the question?*

A: Only when it gets in the way of doing important things well. It's another matter if you want to make best use of, for instance, travel time. Keep a notepad or book ready for those situations when you get extra time, such as the following:

- Read an enjoyable book or a newspaper to catch up with current affairs while standing in a bus queue.
- Jot down ideas for projects while on the bus or Tube (don't attempt anything more major or you could miss your stop).
- Write thank-you notes during a train journey.
- Give yourself a manicure or pedicure, or keep your wardrobe in order by sewing on buttons or mending drooping hems, while watching television.
- Enhance your healthy-eating plans by preparing vegetables to keep as crudités in the fridge or to add to a dish, chopping them while listening to a play on the radio or chatting to a friend who has dropped in for tea.
- Pick through a folder that needs weeding out or sort out your bag while watching the TV news.
- Listen to audio-books while travelling long distances in the car (your local library will have plenty to choose from). You could even learn another language by listening to tapes and practising in the car.
- Write shopping lists or a skeleton outline for a report while waiting in the doctor's or dentist's waiting room or in a car-park queue.
- Have cooking sessions with a friend and experiment with new healthy dishes to add to your repertoire. If you have children, you can do this with them as a playtime treat, which also gets their meal ready (eventually) and educates them about healthy eating, all in one go.

Diaries, Lists and Filing

We all have diaries, make lists and have filing systems, but if yours are not effective and do not work for you, then you might just as well not have them. Time spent systemizing these will be time well spent.

- You will probably have your favourite type of diary, but consider the following. The most efficient is probably one with a week at a glance on one page to list appointments and essential deadlines. The page facing is a blank page, for important reminders and to-do lists relating to that week. Get into the habit of crossing each item off as it is completed, so that you can easily see which items need to be carried over to the next week.

- Avoid cluttering up your life with loose bits of paper. If something is important to do, put it in your diary. Alternatively, have a spiral-bound notepad always to hand and keep a running log of ideas, lists and new phone numbers. Pull out the sheets as you deal with the tasks and they become redundant.

- Back up your computer disks. Back up your computer disks. Back up your computer disks. This cannot be emphasized enough.

- Keep just one diary for personal *and* work appointments, otherwise there is a risk that you will forget to look at one or double-book yourself.

- Keep an extra copy of all important documents, including your address book, in case of loss.

- Keep copies of your e-mail address book and mobile-phone telephone book, and update them regularly.

- Bulging folders of redundant papers clog up a filing system and make it unworkable. Clip your bank statements together by calendar year or by tax year. Weed out guarantees for long-discarded equipment, and bring your family's health records up to date with a master list of important info, such as vaccination history and medications, attached to all important documents. Have one large filing cabinet for historic papers that you can't throw out (such as old tax returns and important receipts) and one for bank statements and other current paraphernalia.

- If sorting out your filing system seems too horrendous to contemplate, just do one folder each day, three or four times a week, until you are through it. This can become quite a satisfying task to work on.

- If you are one of the growing army of freelance or self-employed people working from home, keep your work and personal files separate. Label a dozen clear wallets January to December (or April to March) and use these to store your receipts for each month. They can then easily be entered into a ledger or computer spreadsheet, or passed on to your accountant.

- Attractive filing boxes and diaries always help to make the job more pleasant.

- If you have trouble getting down to the nitty-gritty of organizing your paperwork, spend some time visualizing what you are going to do and how you will do it (how you will order it, what you will keep, what you will throw out). After this, doing the job itself is almost academic and it becomes easy to complete the task.

Delegating

Delegating is an essential planning skill, especially when you have a lot of responsibilities. Some people are terrific at delegating, while others will try to do everything themselves – drop the kids at school, finish a report, cook the evening meal – and end up feeling stressed that they have to do it all. Letting others take some of the burden is not a cop-out, it is a fact of life. Just make sure that both the task and the person are appropriate. There is no point in asking the wrong person to do a job – it will only lead to disappointment.

Q: *How can I avoid annoying people when I give them things to do?*
A: If you are constantly calling upon just a few people, remember that you might be pushing your luck – better to spread the load when you can. Make people feel good about accepting jobs or responsibilities. Avoid making confrontational comments like, 'It's your job to take the rubbish out'. Instead, say in a civil manner, 'I would really appreciate it if you could help me by taking the rubbish out'. Remember to say 'please' and 'thank you'. (This is very obvious, very basic advice but it is amazing how often we take other people for granted, especially those nearest to us.) If people feel appreciated they will always be glad to help. Trade small favours, write the occasional thank-you note and even give small gifts where appropriate.

Q: *I do everything myself because I'm a perfectionist.*
A: Remember that nobody is indispensable. If you believe that you and only you can do the job properly, then you are setting a trap for yourself. Clearly and successfully communicating the standards to which a job needs to be completed is the first step in making sure it reaches your ideal. It could be that your ideal is too stringent, so ask yourself, 'Does it really need to be so perfect?'

Q: *What about when people delegate to me?*
A: If you do agree to do something for someone else, do it wholeheartedly and without complaining. Don't expect anything in return. You will be surprised how good deeds have unexpected and wonderful pay-backs. Learn to say no when you need to. This is a great skill and will help you avoid overburdening yourself. It is possible to say no without giving offence. If you want to play for time, get in the habit of saying, 'I'll check my diary' or 'I'll check with my partner' and get back to them efficiently. Be honest but kind: 'I'd love to help out, but I am already over-committed'.

Q: *I am pretty good at delegating when I'm at work (probably because I know where I stand in the line of authority), but at home I get in a sulk because I seem to be doing everything for everyone else.*
A: If you want to delegate household jobs, this is perfectly reasonable. However, if one person goes out to work all day, while the other stays at home, the jobs should be allocated carefully so that neither person feels overwhelmed. Children certainly need to learn from an early age to be responsible for their part of the home. Get them into the habit of laying the table, picking up their toys and putting their dirty clothes in the basket –if you are firm and respectful, it won't be the struggle you might expect it to be.

Q: *I am hopeless at DIY but I hate nagging my partner, who is good at it. These small things really irk me.*
A: If you nag, the chances are that the job won't get done anyway – your partner may have a different set of priorities. Try starting to do the job yourself. You may surprise yourself and get a sense of achievement, or your partner might step in and complete it, with aplomb. Alternatively, save up all the jobs (keep a running list so you won't

forget them) and employ an odd-job person once every six months or so to spend a couple of hours fixing things and putting things up. It costs a bit of money but will save a lot of tension.

Less Is More

Clutter creates a sort of 'visual noise' that keeps the volume turned up all the time, and this can be pretty stressful. Yet it is easy to become surrounded by clutter without really noticing. It is hardly surprising that many of us do not manage to keep on top of this build-up in our lives, as we are deluged with junk mail, magazines and advertising tempting us to buy things. But clutter undoubtedly slows us down, making us less effective and less able to enjoy our free moments.

Don't buy into the idea that today's piece of junk is tomorrow's antique. If you are hanging on to things for the future in case they are one day of value, you might not be maximizing your mental energy today. Similarly, tackling the mountains of things that 'might one day be useful' – those gifts you never wanted, photos of people you have forgotten and household items you no longer need – will make you feel as if a weight has been lifted from your chest. You will dispense with the lethargy and aimlessness that chaos seems to engender.

You may have no idea how stressful your clutter is – until you get rid of it. If you are keeping the clutter under superficial control, you may not be thinking about it but it can still deplete you of energy. If, on the other hand, the clutter is controlling you (a sure sign of which is that hunt for an essential piece of paper among three teetering piles), then you will definitely be adding substantially to your stress load.

Clutter is all the things you no longer use: stacks of old magazines, clothes you might one day slim into, cups and saucepan lids without handles, or broken equipment. This also includes things you no longer love: the old tea set you inherited but don't really like, sale bargains that did not seem such a good idea when you got them home, small electrical appliances you never use, collections that were once a passion but that no longer enthral you (no, this does not mean your partner).

A Good Clear-Out

- Define what is junk. Broken objects that you can't or won't mend, items you hate to look at and clothes that don't fit all qualify as junk and need to be got rid of.

- Decide which items you really value and deal with them, either fixing the broken things or finding a good place for them, instead of being irritated by their placement each time you pass by.

- Get several strong boxes and give each a label: Junk for the Tip; Charity Shop; Repairs/Alterations; Things to Sort Out. Every time you come across an item that fits one of these descriptions, put it in the corresponding box. When the box is full, cart it off or sort it out as a priority. In your Things to Sort Out box you could also put items that you are in two minds about – then, if you miss them after a few months, reinstate them in your home. Keep the boxes on the go all the time, though hopefully after the first deluge there won't be quite so much to deal with.

Mail Order

Keeping your mail in order not only gets rid of an immediate source of clutter but also helps keep other areas of your life under control. Your electricity won't get cut off, your ancient aunt won't take umbrage at unanswered letters, and important letters won't get buried under the junk mail. Take ten minutes each morning (getting up a little earlier if you have to) to sort through your post and deal with it immediately.

- Separate out torn envelopes and immediately put them in the bin or in your recycling pile, keeping any large envelopes or jiffy bags that you might want to reuse.

- Bin junk mail. For an invitation, check in your diary and reply straightaway. For a letter that needs a reply, do it at once if possible, otherwise call, e-mail or write later the same day.

- Pay any bills immediately, making sure there's money in the bank before you post them (date the envelope if you aren't mailing it immediately). If you use phone or Internet banking, make a note of the dates when the bill should be paid, in whichever system you use as a memory aid (whether it's Post-It Notes on your computer, notes in your diary, or a computer program).

- Pencil in time in your diary for larger jobs such as filling in a tax return, which may take a whole day or more to work out.

Step 3

Making the Right Decisions for You

KEY MESSAGE:
You Already Have the Wisdom You Need

Within you are all the talents and energy you need in order to make the right decisions for yourself. If you don't know the answers, you have the skills to find the information you require to discover good solutions. You also have the flexibility to learn from previous experiences and apply that knowledge.

Decision-making is an inescapable fact of life. We are faced with choices on a daily basis, and thank goodness we are. Those who do not have choices, or who feel they do not, are most prone to the effects of stress. You need to hone your decision-making skills if you react to challenges with anxiety and usually struggle to come up with the best course of action to take. There are simple ways to speed up and ease the process, and, if applied consistently, they can lighten the load.

Searching for Solutions

The people who agonize most when trying to make decisions are those who see problems in every answer. Instead, the focus should be on seeing answers in every problem. Think in terms of 'challenges' rather than 'problems', and 'decision-making' rather than 'problem-solving'. Time spent worrying about things is time wasted, while time spent planning solutions is time well spent.

Q: *I worry about the implications of every aspect of something, which means I never make any big decisions.*
A: Life is full of 'ifs', 'ands' and 'buts' which complicate decision-making. The most difficult part is often the actual process of arriving at a decision. Once you have arrived at that point, it will usually seem quite easy. After you have made the decision, don't spend energy on worrying about what might have been.

Q: *I don't feel I have the confidence or skills to deal with problems.*
A: Get into the habit of changing your limiting attitude to yourself. Thoughts such as 'I am not good at this', 'I don't understand this' or 'I don't want this' are more crippling than you probably realize. They limit your potential and your enjoyment. As a specific exercise, spend the next week checking yourself whenever you are tempted to have a limiting thought. Have only empowering thoughts such as 'I can do this', 'I am able to find out the information needed' and 'I know what I want'. If a week seems too much, start with one day, and then do it for another day and so on.

Q: *I get worried that I am making the wrong decisions.*
A: One of the main reasons that decisions might be hard to reach is because of the chatterbox in your head saying, 'What if it goes wrong?' or 'What if I make a bad choice?' If you keep repeating these disempowering thoughts, ask yourself another question immediately: 'What is the worst thing that can happen if it goes wrong?' For 99 per cent of the time, you will realize that nothing too bad will happen. This can help to get the challenge into perspective.

Exercise: Problem-Solving

1 Arm yourself with the information you need. If you don't have this information, find it. If you don't know where to find it, do some research.

2 Spend no more than 10–20 per cent of your time examining the problem – or challenge – and 80–90 per cent of your time coming up with solutions.

3 Remain flexible, and if one avenue of exploration ends up being inappropriate, don't waste time worrying about this, but just get on with the next approach.

4 Remain true to your convictions. Whether you are taking big or little decisions, it's important to stay true to yourself.

5 If your decision proves to be less than perfect, don't get frustrated – learn from the experience.

6 Don't be afraid to ask for help (see Delegating, page 30).

Q: *I just wish life was straightforward. I feel crippled by decision-making so I end up doing virtually nothing, but I find this frustrating because I then don't feel in control.*
A: Problems (challenges) do not resolve themselves. Just thinking about them isn't enough – you have to take action, which means taking the first step, even if it is only a small one. The rest is easier.

Responding to Challenges

There are four main types of response when people are faced with a challenge. Understanding which category a response falls into can improve your own. The four categories are:

Fight response (external): You meet challenges head-on in a positive manner, often dealing with problems before they arise. You are assertive and positive in your approach. You may be a high achiever but find it hard to relax.

Fight response (internal): You appear calm and in control. You might have a fixed method of how to do things and so may not welcome change as it undermines your idea of how everything should be ordered. This lack of flexibility can be quite stressful.

Flight response: You pretend the problem doesn't exist, find it easy to give up and are happiest letting someone else handle it. This can make you feel you lack self-determination (see page 10).

Flow response: You accept problems without either fighting them or running away from them. However, you often find it difficult to make decisions, which can in itself be stressful.

Being Decisive

Learn to take responsibility for getting the wheels of change moving, so you can sort out challenges that need to be addressed. This does not mean that you can't bring in other people as resources, but that you recognize the buck stops with you.

Q: *I am realizing that one reason I don't make decisions is that I can't blame someone else if it doesn't work out.*
A: If you decide that a change needs to happen, it will be a temporary one unless you make yourself totally responsible for the change. For lasting results, you must accept the following sequence: It must change; *I* must change it; I *can* change it.

Q: *But surely this doesn't mean that I need to make all the decisions. I'm not experienced or knowledgeable enough to do so.*

A: Of course not. Often the best decision-making is the result of teamwork, or at least asking others for input. Use the wealth of experience and information around you. However, for some people this will serve to sway them in several different directions, depending on whom they are talking to at the time. Therefore, aim to stay centred and pull in all the information to help you come to a decision. When talking to people, ask relevant questions. Be clear about what you are seeking and spend some time jotting down notes before you start your survey. Throughout your conversations remain curious about how others picture the challenge, and adopt the elements you find useful. If necessary use a list of pros and cons (see next question) once you have talked to people – and then bite the bullet and make the decision. One decision may even be to leave things alone – on the basis that 'if it ain't broke, don't fix it'.

Q: *I get in a muddle and one minute convince myself that one course of action is right, but the next minute have persuaded myself that I should do something else. How do I achieve more consistency?*

A: Get into the habit of always writing down the pros and cons of a situation. If you keep these only in your head, they tend to swirl around in an unfocused way, but if you commit them to paper, a clear solution may emerge. Quite often one of the lists will be longer than the other and will automatically provide the answer. Mind-Mapping (see page 16) is an ideal technique for this (see also Cognitive Thinking, page 66). If your decision-making is clouded by emotional issues, then you need to take these into account (see Step 4 and Step 6).

Calm in the Face of Challenges

- Stay centred and calm throughout the process. Getting flustered or being anxious will not help to resolve the debate but will just take a toll on you as your stress levels rise. If you feel overwhelmed, do deep-breathing exercises and refocus your mind on looking for solutions.

- Work on positive affirmations (strong positive statements to yourself and about yourself), such as 'I am a resourceful person' and 'I have an innate creativity which helps me to find answers'.

- Tap into your instinctive creativity by closing your eyes and visualizing yourself standing in a circular forest glade, from which radiate a number of paths. Hanging from a tree at the entrance to each path is a notice with a solution on it. Walk down each of the paths in turn and see where they take you. In your visualization you always remain safe and can return to the glade. (For more about this technique, see Creative Visualization, page 142.)

Boosting Self-Esteem

Feeling good about who we are is the key to dealing with many aspects of stress, yet low self-esteem is widespread. Self-esteem is the subject of many books, and some people find that spending time assessing their self esteem is a great help towards understanding themselves both emotionally and behaviourally. Throughout this book, there is much discussion of why we often end up short-changing ourselves, as well as a variety of suggestions aimed at improving self-esteem. Knowing who you are is a fundamental aspect of stress-busting, and raising your awareness about how much you like yourself and why you are doing what you are doing will help you to work on your self-esteem. This section concentrates on offering quick-fix advice that can place you firmly on the road to improving your sense of worth.

Q: *I sometimes feel like I have a recording going round in my head running myself down, but I find it hard to stop.*
A: If you are in the habit of criticizing yourself, change this by learning to congratulate yourself instead. When you are telling yourself off ('I'm so hopeless', 'Why am I so thick?'), the easiest way to correct yourself is to imagine how it would sound to you if you heard someone else saying this about himself. You would probably think, 'He's being a bit hard on himself', and you might even say to that person, 'Of course you are not hopeless'. Do this every time you start to do yourself down.

Q: *I know I tend to talk myself down – any ideas on this?*
A: Don't highlight your perceived weaknesses to others, especially if they are likely to remind you of them later. It's OK to talk about your insecurities, but do so in a positive and practical way and not as a form of self-criticism.
  • Replace 'I know I shouldn't be eating this' with 'I'm enjoying this'.
  • Replace 'Don't mind me banging on about it/sorry if it's boring' with 'I feel strongly about it, so I tend to take every opportunity to do something about it'.
  • Replace 'I'm so disorganized that I'll probably drive you crazy' with 'My organizational skills could use a little work, but I do get things done'.
  • Replace 'OK, I'll go on the sailing course, though I may sink the boat' with 'Yes, I'd love to learn something new – it'll be an adventure'.

Q: *I can't afford to do anything fancy.*
A: Invest in yourself. Don't ask, 'Can I afford to?' Ask, 'Can I afford *not* to?' By investing in yourself you are signalling to yourself (and others) that you are worth it. At a basic level, this could mean a beauty treatment, perhaps, or signing up for something that interests you. You are also hopefully making a rational choice about how you spend your time. You might buy time by hiring some home help or pay for someone to promote your business. Investing intelligently will free up your other resources, such as time and mental stamina, to further your dreams.

Q: *I find it easy to deal with my problems... I just have a stiff drink and it all seems OK again.*
A: It is common to numb the pain of low self-esteem with drink or drugs. A similar reaction is to focus all available emotional energy on others (such as your children) or to throw yourself into non-stop activity. If you are doing any of these, stop, take a deep breath and start at the beginning of this section again.

Life Is a Series of Lessons and Opportunities

If you don't succeed at something, avoid berating yourself for what has or hasn't happened. Instead, do the following:

- Work out what you have learned from the experience, writing it down methodically.

- Apply what you have learned and change your tactics if necessary. Keep focusing on your aims.

- Do something about your body language. If you walk around looking defeated, what image will you project?

- Even if it hasn't worked out, it might be nothing to do with you and everything to do with timing. For example, you might call someone just at the point when their dog has died and their wife has left them. Does this mean your idea is not good?

- Avoid regrets and wishful thinking ('I wish I was able to...', or, 'Why did it have to happen to me?').

- Remember that countless successful people were turned down at some time or other (Fred Astaire and The Beatles, to name but two). You can gain self-esteem just from the process of trying something. Any success you gain is a bonus.

Criticism from Others

Other people can whittle away at your self-esteem if you let them. They might simply be people of a negative mindset ('I wouldn't do that because the chances of failure are high', 'Don't be surprised if you are disappointed', 'Do you really think that's possible?'). Or they could be predators disguised as friends (for example, your best friend commenting, 'I'm only saying it for your own good, of course, but don't you think you need to lose a few kilos?' or a friend who eggs you on to 'Go on, have a drink, just one, otherwise you won't enjoy yourself' when you are hoping to have a booze-free week). Or they might be bullies.

You can be firm in your convictions and not swayed by others if you work out in advance why you are doing something, what it means to you to succeed and why you believe it is the right course of action for you to follow. Then negative and tricky people can't trip you up so easily. Take pleasure in small victories and do not belittle, or allow others to belittle, their importance.

Q: *I've been told by others that I let my partner stamp on my personality too much, and I have to admit that I am beginning to think they are right.*
A: People with low self-esteem are often drawn like magnets to partners who will compound the problem. And sometimes people who start off with fairly good self-esteem will find that they are dragged down during the course of a relationship into low self-esteem. Getting back into a state of self-belief is made doubly difficult if someone is always pointing out your faults and making irrational accusations and demands. If you find yourself always subjugating your needs to those of your partner, remind yourself of your own desires and goals. Seek responses that give you respect, autonomy, freedom of thought, mental and physical health, safety, an emotionally stable home for your children. Give yourself small, manageable steps and goals along the way and you will get your self-esteem back in stronger and better shape than ever before.

Responses to Being Criticized

When you are faced with criticism – for example, from your boss – you are likely to have one of the following responses:

- The low self-esteem response ('I'm no good and always make a mess of things'). You then feel sad and anxious and you react by moping around and getting depressed.

- The denial response ('He's a pain and is always bugging me'). This makes you angry, frustrated and openly hostile, which then damages your relationship with your boss even further.

- The positive self-esteem response ('Here's a chance to learn something'). From a position of security you discuss the issues with your boss, define the problem/ challenge and find a solution. Your boss is suitably impressed.

Q: *I never seem to have the right words at the right moment and my reaction to criticism tends to be to go away and brood.*
A: If someone says something to you that stings and tugs at your self-esteem, don't just go home and dive into the ice cream tub (and then punish yourself further). Instead, work out, in your own time, your response and let your critic know in what way they were hurtful. If you are too shy to confront them, write a small note. Avoid recrimination but let them know how they can avoid hurting you in future (in other words, a positive outcome). In addition, work out why you have been upset by their words or actions and what you can learn from it. You might have interpreted an innocent comment as a poisonous one and seen it as confirmation of any self-loathing you already felt. Work

with cognitive thinking (see page 66) to find more appropriate ways of interpreting seemingly negative comments.

Q: *I'm feeling more vulnerable at the moment because a lot of things are going wrong. Am I overreacting?*
A: There are times when we all respond more acutely to hurts. If you're already feeling low, perhaps because a series of things have gone wrong recently, then a comment that would have been water off a duck's back at some other time, might really hurt. Use this knowledge to balance your reaction and accept that you need to get through the current phase intact. It will help to put the 'hurt' into perspective.

Realizing Ambitions

The words 'ambition' and 'ambitious' have mixed connotations. Ambition is sometimes frowned upon as being something that only highly driven people have, while for someone to be ambitious is viewed in a more positive light as being go-ahead and focused.

Having ambitions just means having dreams. And life would be pretty dull without a few dreams to pep it up. However, not realizing your ambitions might be a significant source of stress in your life. Seeing your ambitions through wise eyes allows them to be of more use to you and reduces their potential as sources of stress. A good reason for fulfilling your ambitions is that you don't want to be looking back over your life from your rocking chair in your dotage saying to yourself, 'If only I had…'

Q: *I really admire people who achieve their aims but I'm not sure I've got it in me.*
A: One way to help yourself achieve your goals is to study what successful people do. This approach is obvious in, for example, a budding tennis or chess player, who will endlessly study the techniques of the great players. But the strategy can be applied to any area of life. Watch what successful people do; use videos and biographies; see if you can interview them or even apprentice yourself to them if you are able. Analyse their behaviour and, putting your personal spin on it, emulate what they do to achieve similar results. The difference between winners and 'all the rest' is that winners *make* things happen while all the rest *let* things happen.

Q: *I can make all the lists and dream the dreams, but when it comes to it I just get scared.*
A: If your ambitions frighten even you, you can still attain them. We all operate within certain comfort zones. If your ambition seems hopelessly out of reach, resolve to make tiny almost imperceptible increments in your comfort zone until you feel able to go full-steam ahead to realize your dream. If your ambition is to write a novel (apparently we all have one in us) but you get dizzy at the idea of actually starting to write it, make small moves in that direction. Start by writing letters, essays and short stories. Join a writing group or class. Go on a weekend writing retreat. Put together an outline of

your book. Start to describe yourself to people you meet as a part-time writer. If getting published seems a huge hurdle, put some stories on a website. Invite editors to look at them. Start writing to agents and publishers with a synopsis and perhaps even a sample chapter. You wouldn't do this last step without having thought of what to write and actually embarked on it, but by taking these small steps to increase your comfort zone you will eventually get there. This is a strategy that applies to most big ambitions.

Uncertainties about Ambitions

- If your ambition means that you are permanently discontented with your current situation, this can be stressful for all concerned. View the present positively as a springboard for your future.

- Your ambitions are important – they allow you to fly. However, we are often promoted to the level of our incompetence. What this means is that we might be ambitious for a position that we are not really able to fulfil. When put into those situations, we struggle and our bosses are unhappy, leading to a lot of stress for all concerned. Without resorting to being pessimistic, take a long look at the opportunities you have been offered and evaluate whether you are really right for the job and whether the job is right for you.

- If one day you feel absolutely certain about your ambitions but the next day you are not so sure, do not allow yourself to be put off your dreams. It is part of the human condition to be troubled by frailties and doubts from time to time, but this does not devalue what we wish to aim for. Instead, take note of your uncertainties in a positive light and work out how you can appease them.

- If your personal ambitions involve other people, for example when you would like to be considered for a promotion at work, ask intelligently and in a non-threatening way. If you go in with all guns blazing demanding a promotion because, say, you have been at the company longer than others, you will probably be setting yourself up for rejection. If, on the other hand, you set out clearly your value to the company and the talents you can offer, then you will have a greater chance of success. In other words, build bridges and avoid closing doors.

Q: *I'm approaching my thirties and somehow I feel I've missed the boat – all my friends have done so much better than I have.*
A: At about this time confidence and positive expectations are often replaced by angst. The certainties of our twenties are suddenly transformed by doubts. This can be a time for feelings of low self-confidence often caused by the idea that you should have 'done better' by now. Do not measure your achievements against anybody else's or think that if you haven't done a thing by a certain age, then you never will. Remind yourself that many people do not achieve their aims until well into middle age, or even when they are

elderly. Make a point of listing all the things at which you feel you have succeeded in your life (even if you don't currently rate them highly) and use this as a starting point for rekindling your belief in your abilities.

Q: *It would be nice just to get on the property ladder.*
A: It is also true to say that many people in their thirties are now finding that they have to redefine their expectations of life. Soaring property prices may force them to live at home for longer, and delayed marriage and child-rearing can mean that youthful habits last longer. As a result, today many thirty-somethings do not have the financial responsibilities their parents had when they were the same age, but they do have more disposable income and are more inclined to borrow money for what they want or need. It may be difficult, but it is important that you find a balance between partying, working and taking care of yourself.

Q: *I'd like to change career but I don't know where to start.*
A: Some people find that changing careers can be a significant hurdle. All your training may have been in a particular direction, but you now feel that your career no longer suits you for a variety of possible reasons. Consider whether there is another kind of work that appeals to you, and set about researching training courses and companies concerned with that area. Find out as much as you can about a new career before cutting loose from your former job. Bear in mind that a complete change may not be what you want – instead it may be that you are simply tired of the rat race and wish to work only part-time or on a freelance basis. You probably need to discuss such changes with friends and family before taking action, setting up a business or broaching the subject with your boss.

Thinking of Others

- Be careful of your ambitions for your children as you may actually encourage the opposite. If you are tempted to 'hot-house' them in a particular direction, they may end up just rebelling, even at quite a young age. The stress imposed on them could be more than they can deal with. Instead, give your children as many opportunities as you are able to and they will reach a level of achievement that they are comfortable with.

- Don't forget other people in the rush to fulfil your ambitions. Take your partner or family into consideration and don't use colleagues as stepping stones. (There is a saying that the people you meet on the way up the career ladder you also meet on the way down – so keep them as potential allies.)

- Help your partner or child to achieve their ambitions by offering support and talking through the challenges with them.

The Challenges of Lethargy and Apathy

Feeling lethargic and apathetic can affect even the most positive of people and is a natural part of the waxing and waning of moods. However, if it is a regular occurrence, it may be a sign of depression or lack of motivation. It is common to experience weekend lethargy as a reaction to the structure of the working week. Apathy often plagues single people, who find that they mope around when on their own. Lying around staring at the ceiling and channel-hopping between equally dreary TV stations while subsisting on cheese sandwiches and instant coffee is bound to make you feel depressed, with time to think about all that is not right in your life.

Q: *I have a low boredom threshold and can't get myself enthused about doing more exciting things.*
A: Lethargy can be mistaken for boredom. If you find that you are bored by what you are doing, it is no surprise that you are unenthusiastic about life. Ask yourself why you are you bored. It may be because your job is too repetitive, you feel undervalued or your finances keep you from having interests. If any of this rings a bell, you will have to fall back on your resourcefulness and create an action plan (see Exercise below).

Q: *I work hard all week, so at weekends I tend to just crash, but I end up feeling unfulfilled – any suggestions?*
A: At weekends, you might feel that you just want to slump in front of the television to unwind. But those who remain moderately active tend to be less depressed, while those who crash on the sofa tend towards lethargy and depression. If you let the weekend creep up on you unplanned, it is more likely that you will fall into this trap. On Wednesday each week, plan at least a couple of things you can look forward to at the weekend. Any time of the week, if you feel 'flat' and uninspired, a short boost of activity can perk you up. Go for a swim or a walk, visit a friend, go to the cinema (to see something cheerful, not something depressing), visit an uplifting exhibition, treat yourself to tea in a nice place.

Exercise: Combat Apathy

There is a simple and effective way of lifting yourself out of an apathetic state, by creating a daily activity plan each day for a week. You then have a tool with which to focus yourself on satisfying and pleasurable activities.

1 Take a sheet of paper and draw a line down the middle to create two wide columns.

2 On the far left-hand side, write one-hour time slots, in a narrow column, from 7 or 8am to 11pm or midnight (whatever your normal day is). Date the sheet.

3 Now plan your activities for the day on an hourly basis. (They need not be elaborate – keep them realistic.) Write these in the left-hand column and head them 'Anticipated'. You may not carry out the whole of your daily plan, but by simply creating one you give yourself a structure to work towards.

4 Aim to make a balanced action plan that combines activity and rest, mental challenge and calm, work and play, achievement and indulgence. In the right-hand column you will write, at the end of the day, what activities you actually did, heading this 'Actual'. Write down everything you have done, even if it was just lying in bed.

5 Next to each actual activity add an 'A' for achievement and a 'P' for pleasure. 'A' represents activities that actually achieve something, such as taking a shower, preparing a meal, commuting to work or doing the laundry. 'P' denotes the pleasure you have received from doing something. It may be that you enjoy the activity or the satisfaction of having completed a necessary task. Rate each 'A' and 'P' from 1 to 10, according to how you feel. For example, a simple task such as brushing your teeth might warrant A3 P1. Cooking a meal might be A5 P2 or, if you enjoy it, A5 P7. If you are feeling depressed, even going to see a movie that you would normally enjoy might rate only P1. If you were dreading seeing someone or going somewhere but it turns out to be an unexpected pleasure, it might rate A3 P9.

6 Keep this chart going for a week. It will stop you from procrastinating, give you some structure in your day, make you think about what you *can* do and go a long way towards helping you understand what you *wish* to do. It is a first step towards self-reliance in the face of lethargy and apathy. You can now use this week's worth of information to help plan more enjoyable and satisfying activities in the future.

Q: *I find it hard to climb out of my drudge moods because I don't really have enough money to get out and about very much.*
A: If you are short of cash, work out what you can do that does not cost money. Here are some options to consider:
- Join a reading group and take books out from the library.
- Start jogging.
- Do crossword puzzles.
- Turn a hobby into a money-making scheme.
- Go to a museum or exhibition at times when they allow free entrance. If you need some ideas, get hold of a magazine from your library listing local activities – they are usually stuffed full with events.

Q: *I get overwhelmed by big tasks and end up doing nothing. Then I panic, which feels really bad. How can I motivate myself to get things done?*

A: If your apathy takes the form of procrastinating about a task (sometimes for weeks or even months), break it down into bite-sized chunks. If you need to write a letter, for instance, break the job down into Outline, Draft, Final Draft and Send. Grade the anticipated difficulty and satisfaction of each stage from 1 to 10. By writing this breakdown first, you will find it less daunting to start the job. At the end of each stage, grade the actual difficulty and satisfaction. You will probably find that you were anticipating more difficulty and less satisfaction than you actually felt in the end. This approach is highly effective for stopping yourself from putting off doing things.

Q: *When I'm feeling apathetic I am sure I make it worse by eating whole boxes of biscuits, which makes me feel even more negative.*

A: You need to eat healthily and regularly to keep your energy levels up. Blood-sugar balance is particularly important if you suffer from energy dips in the afternoon or if you just want to snooze on the couch after a couple of glasses of wine in the evening. See Healthy Eating, page 16, for more information about this. Brain-chemical balance is affected by food choices, and eating a little protein with each meal can help. Healthy snacks are also important, so focus on yogurt and fresh fruit, nuts and dried fruit, oatcakes and cottage cheese (all of which have a little protein in them).

Key Tool 2: Neuro-Linguistic Programming (NLP)

Neuro-Linguistic Programming (NLP) has enjoyed a huge surge of interest in the last few years, because it works so well. NLP is a highly flexible tool – a kind of instruction manual for the brain – that incorporates many approaches, including cognitive thinking and visualization (see pages 66 and 142). NLP is a fantastic yet simple way of reprogramming negative thoughts and habits into more positive ones. It is immensely powerful when used for goal-setting (see page 8).

NLP is often targeted at particular audiences, such as the business community. But it is also used by those interested in performing or public speaking and by health management and therapists. There are many books, courses, audio tapes and video tapes on the subject (for details, see page 202). Some of the principal tools used in NLP are summarized here.

Strategies for Success

We all have 'strategies for success'. Even the most apparently mundane activities that we do every day, such as travelling to work, explaining an idea to another person or handling a difficult phone call, can be done more successfully or less so. Understanding what your strategies are and transferring those skills to uncharted territory is one of the tools of NLP.

On the other hand, you may feel when you upset someone, miss a deadline or give up on a goal that you are lacking a strategy. Any one of these might have left you feeling deflated and frustrated. Yet, believe it or not, you did have strategies for handling those events as well – they just didn't work. What can you apply from the previous list of 'success stories' to those events where you wish to achieve a different outcome?

To change your strategies you need to understand your previous ones. Get into the best mental and emotional state. Visualize yourself succeeding and feel how happy you are as a result. Talk to yourself in a positive and encouraging inner voice. Take action. If you do not achieve your desired results, learn from the outcome. Repeat the cycle until you achieve your desire.

A strategy for success does not focus on the idea of failing or losing. There are only results that are measured against the desired outcome. If you achieve your desire, you achieve the result you wish.

Sensory Input

Some NLP approaches involve understanding your response to sensory input, and the responses of others around you with whom you wish to communicate successfully. This approach holds that because we often speak a different 'language', we frequently don't really understand each other; the resulting miscommunication leads to misunderstanding and diminishes the ability to achieve desired outcomes from conversations. Analyse your own language to find which technique you use most and whether it works for you.

Auditory: You take in information most readily from sound and respond well to audio tapes and soundtracks. You litter your language with expressions such as, 'Sounds good to me', 'I hear what you're saying' and 'When I understood the concept it's like a bang went off in my head'.

Visual: You are most likely to respond to pictographic and other visual stimuli. Your language tends to contain such expressions as 'I see what you mean', 'I couldn't see the wood for the trees' and 'A light went on in my head'.

Kinetic: You are more of a touchy-feely person and you enjoy experiencing things by participating physically. Your language contains many expressions such as 'I feel that the thing to do is…', 'I've got a gut feeling…' and 'I sense that what you are saying is…'

Analytical: As the name implies, you tend to weigh things up and analyse everything. You might say things like 'If I understand what you are saying…', 'On balance I think…' and 'In the final analysis…'

Time-Line Therapy

The principle of this NLP approach is to understand how you view your experiences in relation to your 'time line' and then to re-align them so that they work for you rather than against you. Your time line is an imagined line that mirrors your progress in a given area, such as your career. The line is best visualized as moving in front, behind or to the side of you. You might find that your career can radiate in various directions, it can spiral up above your head, it can involve large or small steps up or down, it can be scattered all over the place or it can even dig into you – it can be anything you imagine it to be.

An example of how we might make this image work is when we use an expression such as, 'I've put the situation behind me'. If you are fretting about, say, a broken relationship, and you are carrying the baggage of your feelings into your next relationship, it is obvious that it will affect you. By putting such feelings behind you, you will be able to free up emotions for a new relationship and progress unhindered. Applying the same principle to other areas of life is highly effective. When frustrated by lack of progress in your career, for instance, you may find that the image of your time line shows that you have put your career somewhere to the side of you, which is compelling you to shuffle sideways in your career, crab-like, instead of striding forwards.

Step 4

Being Happy Is Easier than You Think

> ### KEY MESSAGE:
> ## Happiness Begets Happiness
> Spreading a little happiness leads to more happiness all round. Say a kind word and it will be reflected.

Being happy can require a lot of practice! It involves focusing on the positive aspects of your life, which most people do not do enough. The most important aspect of this is to learn to feel positive about yourself. Love of self is the essential first step in improving your happiness quotient, and in being able to experience fulfilling relationships with other people. Yet most people need convincing that it's all right to love themselves, because they are confusing self-love with selfishness or arrogance.

We all want to be loved or at least liked – it is a fundamental need from childhood. Of course, it is not always possible to be liked by all the people all the time. Seeking popularity can wear you out in the long run as you try to please everyone. Because we are continually seeking approval, getting out of an addiction to people-pleasing habits can take time. Acknowledging that you can't always be popular is a sign of maturity. Ultimately it's your own approval of yourself, not someone else's, that matters, as you have to be able to live with the decisions you make on a daily basis.

In this chapter, in addition to reflecting on aspects of happiness, we will also look at states of mind like arguing, anxiety, depression and loneliness that can be a bar to happiness in everyday life. Dealing directly with any of these that affect your life should lift the clouds, leaving you feeling happy and positive.

Emotional Ups and Downs

If you are going through an unhappy phase of your life, it will pass. Remember to think of it as a transitional phase and not the milestone by which you will measure the future. People do adapt even to major problems such as serious illness or injury

Q: *I think I could be happy if only my partner was happy, too.*
A: Happiness is likely to follow when you lead a fulfilled life according to *your* standards and not the standards of others. Don't look to others for it – happiness will have more staying power if it has come from within you. The following exercise will help you with this.

Exercise: Learn to Love Yourself

1 Write down at least ten ways, and preferably more, that demonstrate you are capable of showing yourself love. This might involve changing how you talk to yourself, such as not apologizing for your failings, taking time out to give yourself treats, countering destructive comments from other people with life-enhancing thoughts, and saying 'no' when you want to.

2 Revisit this list regularly (daily if necessary) and add to it as ideas come to mind. Think about situations and how you would have handled them differently by being kinder to yourself.

3 Practising having a happy personality can pay dividends in so many areas of life. If you are cheerful and outgoing your marriage and relationships are more likely to last. You will have a stronger immune system and might even live longer. So it really does pay to find things to be happy about and grateful for. If you are uncertain about what these are, make a list or a mind-map (see page 16). No matter how small something is, put it in. Keep the list or mind-map to hand and build on it daily.

Q: *Do I need to understand my past feelings to deal with future happiness?*
A: Not always. Understanding your emotions can be a painful process, and most of us will do anything to avoid pain. Emotional stress may be caused by long-buried feelings about childhood, as well as ongoing anxieties about our personalities. People spend years burying their feelings, and the revelations that come from digging up old emotions can be difficult. While some people find it useful to examine past events or behaviour, it can lead others to live too much in the past, apportioning blame, which is not necessarily helpful. Often it is more important to get on with building an emotionally stable future.

Q: *Surely we can't expect to be 'happy' all the time. Life doesn't work that way.*
A: Realistically you can't live on the edge of joy all the time. Not only would it be a little manic, but there is a place for unhappiness, which is there to tell you that you need to change something about your life. Seen in this way, unhappiness becomes a positive tool for change.

Q: *What about when something serious happens in life?*
A: If you have been knocked sideways by some event, give yourself time to bounce back. Recognize that it is normal to grieve for a while but that there comes a time when looking back and having regrets will not serve you. You have to throw off the mantle of the past and look to your future happiness.

Q: *I often just put on a brave face, and I don't think anybody realizes I am not particularly happy, so isn't that OK for now?*
A: Being happy does not mean putting on a brave face. This will not change or solve anything. If you find that you are being brave on the outside and everyone thinks you are doing fine when you are actually unhappy inside, you need to find someone to whom you can talk and unburden yourself.

False Hopes

In chasing success it is easy to lose sight of what really might confer happiness, such as a good relationship with your partner and children or the time to pursue other interests.

Q: *It's said that money can't buy love or happiness, but don't tell me that I wouldn't be a lot happier if I won the lottery.*
A: Finances are not altogether irrelevant to happiness, at least in the society in which we live. Research shows that happiness is, to a degree, linked to income, but it is relative: you need to be relatively poor to start off with, for you to appreciate money and for it to make you happy. Few people in our society are really poor financially (most people have fridges, TVs, videos and other symbols of an affluent society). Feeling you are poor is not the same as being poor (not enough food on the table, not able to afford heating, finding it difficult to provide for your children). Go back to the exercise on page 50 and start counting your blessings.

Q: *I'm sure that I will be a lot happier when I succeed / lose weight / get rich/ finish my job / buy a new car.*
A: Don't put off happiness for something in the future. Anyway, 'success' – whatever your definition of this is – does not necessarily guarantee happiness. The need to constantly maintain that success (weight loss, paying for a car, etc) and the fear of losing it can dampen your enjoyment. Find what really makes you happy about your life right now, and then enjoy it to the full.

Q: *Work takes up a big chunk of life but I feel ill at ease. I'm in a muddle about how much I want to give of myself for work, and I think I could be happier with a different balance.*

A: Do you work to live, or live to work? Either way you might find a better way forward. If you work to live, what pleasure do you get out of your work? If you live to work, do you get enough balance in your life and appreciate other aspects? Both scenarios have their inherent stresses if you are not totally happy with them. (See page 12 for more on achieving a work/life balance.)

Arguing and Bickering

While arguments can act as a safety valve, if handled carelessly they can create an atmosphere that is counterproductive. There are different styles of arguing that develop between two people. Some will niggle and bicker all the time, while others build up resentments until they have major blow-outs that come infrequently but with huge ferocity. Understanding how you argue with someone you live with will help to minimize the impact of the arguments on daily life.

We rarely argue and bicker in quite the same way at our workplaces. Because we have a different, often hierarchical set-up at work, we tend to be more reserved about letting loose with our true thoughts. Frustrations at work are therefore usually dealt with in a different way (see Strategies in the Difficult Workplace, page 79).

Q: *When we don't agree with each other, which is often, we end up having a row, and it is happening too often.*

A: A disagreement is not the same thing as arguing unless you let it escalate. Disagreeing with someone is perfectly normal, but it is how you deal with those disagreements that makes the difference. Aim for a constructive outcome by listening to the other person, talking things through and making an action plan together – if necessary, by systematically writing down the pros and cons of the situation and of the various solutions. If the solution is a division of labour, refer to Delegating on page 30.

Q: *Our rows end up with both of us just talking louder and louder until one of us drowns out the other.*

A: Listen – really listen – to the other person. Not just to what they are saying, but also to how they are saying it. If your complaint is that they do not listen to you, the first step to remedy this is for *you* to listen to *them*. Avoid interrupting the other person or finishing their sentences for them. Let them have their say and then hopefully you can have yours. If they are still not really listening, maybe some work is needed on communication skills (see page 19).

Q: *My partner can't seem to stop fussing over all sorts of things, which drives me round the bend.*

A: Get things into perspective. Other people's habits and niggles are just that; they might wear you down, but they shouldn't. Adjust your thinking to 'This is irritating' rather than 'This is driving me crazy'. If you think it is driving you crazy, it will do precisely that and you will pay the price in terms of stress. Anyone who has had a major trauma such as illness or a car accident will inevitably say that it has taught them one thing – that the things we worry about on a daily basis are, in the general scheme of things, not worth the energy and adrenalin we put into them.

Controlling your Anger

Anger is such a powerful force that it needs to be contained and expressed in appropriate ways. If you allow it to persist, it will have a detrimental effect by keeping you in a state of physical readiness that is tiring and may fog your thought processes.

- If you find you are enraged by such everyday annoyances as a slow checkout counter at the supermarket, you may be living in a 'state of anger' which can have serious emotional and health consequences (see pages 121–125).

- Obviously, anger is sometimes perfectly appropriate and even valuable. There is no rule that says you have to feel sublimely calm if your child is picked on at school or you read about some terrible injustice in the world. It is this anger, and the accompanying adrenalin rush, that spurs many of us on to make changes in the world and to make it a better place.

- There is a theory that anger can be a positive force in healing. It is said that the enemy of recovery from a serious illness is apathy and a sense of inevitability. By getting angry, but not bitter, about the situation, in a constructive way ('I won't let this beat me'), you can muster your energy and force into healing. Of course, if you are feeling too exhausted to get angry this could be a moot point, but it might make you feel better if you are currently feeling rage at the situation you are in.

Q: *In the end one of us usually just walks out, with a last nasty dig before slamming the door.*
A: Beware of using arguments to undermine the other person's confidence – and don't let it happen to you. If you find you are getting nasty and going for the jugular, this is a bad habit. Remember to make arguing constructive. If one of your family spills something, avoid saying, 'You are stupid' or 'You are clumsy'. Take your comments out of the personal and offer solutions, such as saying, 'That was a clumsy thing to do – next time use a tray'.

Q: *I grew up in a household that argued a lot and it made me very sensitive to raised voices. My partner yells at me and the kids to let off steam. I would like to avoid a repeat of this affecting the kids.*

A: It is true that shouting doesn't really work and that children can become either desensitized to the message or anxious. Shouting can certainly make children feel vulnerable if the arguing is destructive. However, if they see that it is not destructive, that it is a way of resolving disagreements, that a constructive way forward comes out of it and that everyone kisses and makes up afterwards, then they can learn to argue, or more appropriately to have disagreements, in a constructive way. This is a skill they will take with them into adult life.

Tips to Reduce the Impact of Rows

- Minor frictions and tensions build up if not dealt with.

- A great sense of relief can be achieved just by admitting there is a problem.

- Avoid trying to mind-read. Just because he says, 'I don't want to go out tonight', he is not necessarily saying, 'I don't like you any more'. If she is saying, 'You are not pulling your weight around here', she is not really saying, 'You are always lazy'.

- If there is a pattern of bickering at home, aim to decipher it. Are you bickering with your children, parents, partner, flatmate? Identify the flashpoints, such as the washing up, muddy boots in the hall, bedtime routine or money. By understanding the patterns, you can do something about them.

- Laughter solves rows. Find a common line of humour without belittling the other person – make sure you are laughing *with* them rather than *at* them.

- Never go to bed, or say goodbye to someone for the day, with bad feelings. Make it a priority to make it up first, or at least make a 'date' to talk things through.

- Remember to say 'sorry' to kids after a row with them, as you would with an adult. Often adults will not think about doing this, but this is the training ground for adults of tomorrow. If they learn that saying sorry is OK, then they will be better for it.

- After you have had a row, do something thoughtful if you have not had time to make it up yet. A nice e-mail, a bunch of flowers or a cinema ticket is a good way to say, 'I care'.

Exercise: *Quick Ways to Change your Emotional State*

Daily struggles, petty problems, sensory overload, other people's moods, things to do – all these conspire to make even the most positive people feel deflated. Even if you are confronted with more challenging events, you can change your emotional state almost immediately in a few simple ways. Get into the habit of reading this list and putting it into practice on a regular basis. You are a resourceful person and these tools, when used regularly, will hone feelings of calm confidence.

1 Get into the habit of believing – really believing – that today is a once-in-a-lifetime opportunity. The present is all we have. As the saying goes, 'Yesterday is history, tomorrow is a mystery'. What are you going to do with the gift of today?

2 Pay yourself a compliment each day. And while you are at it, pay someone else a heartfelt and genuine compliment. Their pleasure will make you feel great.

3 Walk like a person who is happy and enthusiastic about life. If you throw your shoulders back, put a spring in your step, make eye contact rather than looking at the ground and greet people cheerfully, it is virtually impossible to feel down.

4 When faced with any challenge that tugs at your self-belief and you wonder, 'Could I?', 'Can I?', 'Should I?', empower yourself by asking, 'If I were not afraid, what would I do?' You have your answer.

5 Flirt. This does not have to be in an overtly sexual way. You can flirt with men and women of any age – it creates a buzzy feeling, in which humour is bubbling under the surface and there is a sense of fun and appreciation. You can flirt with people and you can flirt with life. You don't have to play the fool, just find what is good about a situation, appreciate it and communicate it to others.

Anxiety

The White Rabbit in *Alice in Wonderland*, repeatedly squinting at his watch and muttering to himself as he scurries along, epitomizes what many believe anxiety looks like. Sadly, such manifestations of anxiety do not always elicit a sympathetic reaction, as people are often told, 'Pull yourself together'. It is easy to say, 'Don't worry, be happy', but breaking the habit of worrying may need a bit more than this.

Anxiety is heightened worry. Research has shown that in people beset by anxiety there are chemical changes in the brain, which can lead to depression. There are times when it is appropriate to be worried or anxious, for instance when your child is playing near traffic. But if anxiety is breaking your spirit and ruining your enjoyment of life because you fret about things on a daily basis, then it is well worth addressing. Something needs to change, and you can change it.

Q: *I thought I could cope well enough with my anxiety but it seems to be dragging me down.*
A: You may feel that you are coping despite your anxiety, but 'coping' is not thriving, developing or enjoying life. Coping is simply getting by and making the best of a bad situation. Don't cope – deal with things. Relish the process of making things happen, and enjoy the here and now. Remind yourself of these positive thoughts regularly to help refocus your thinking.

Exercise: *What Is Making You Anxious?*

Anxious people are adept at 'What if…' thought patterns. They can't relax because they are always worrying about what might happen.

1 Counteract your anxieties about a situation by writing down your worries. Rate, on a scale of 1 to 10, just how anxious you feel about each.

2 Write down what your projected feelings are, such as 'I will probably forget everything I have learned', 'I will undoubtedly make a fool of myself', 'The traffic will make me late and everyone will be angry with me'. Rate these projected thoughts from 1 to 10 as well.

3 After the event, itemize how many of the things that you were worried about actually happened. Did they occur at all? If so, did they have as bad an outcome as you imagined? Were you able to deal with them? Did you come out of it relatively unscathed? What lessons can you apply to the next time you are in the same situation?

4 Get into the habit of doing this exercise every day if you find that you are feeling perpetually anxious.

Q: *I worry about my children but they are always telling me to back off and saying that I am only making things worse.*
A: Worry and anxiety felt for other people is common. It is different to deal with because the anxiety is one person removed. Parents will often feel anxious for their children (even grown-up children). A person might feel anxious for their partner until they arrive at their destination, or worry about a friend they have not heard from for a while. Go through the same exercise as above. Recognize the fact that because it is one person removed you can do nothing at the time about it – you can't sit the exam for your child and you can't take the plane for your loved one. It is also important to try to reduce this anxiety for others because there is every chance that your concern will be contagious, triggering off anxiety in them – a counter-productive chain reaction. You can turn such anxieties into positive actions: when, for instance, teenagers are hiking through a far-flung country, pack them a medical kit, take out insurance and remind them to e-mail home frequently.

Exercise: *Anxiety Control through Breathing*

Breathing exercises are a tried and tested way to moderate anxiety and tension. Do the following deep breathing exercise (unless you are hyperventilating or are about to have a panic attack – advice on dealing with these is on page 58):

1 Get your posture right, as it affects your diaphragm. Stand with your feet a shoulder-width apart. Relax your shoulders, so that there is no tension in your neck, your back is not rounded and your shoulders are not thrown back in a military stance.

2 Immediately after you exhale through your mouth, use your lower ribs to force the remaining air out of your lungs. (With normal breathing, we usually exhale only about a third of the air in our lungs.) By forcibly exhaling this, you create the space for a deep breath to follow.

3 Expanding your ribcage, breathe in a long, slow, deep breath (to a count of five) through your nose. Your shoulders need to stay still and not rise. (If they do rise, you are filling only the top of your lungs.) This may take practice.

4 Breathe out through your mouth.

5 Repeat the whole procedure five to ten times.

Q: *How can I deal with thoughts that suddenly race into my mind at inappropriate times?*
A: Thoughts come and go. You have the choice about whether to hang on to them or to let them go. If you dwell on a thought that is making you anxious, you will get all the associated physical symptoms, so work on letting the thought go. Replace it in your mind with the memory of a specific time when you were anxiety-free, peaceful and happy. You may find it easier to do this as a meditation exercise (see page 141). You can recapture feelings in a highly effective way by reconnecting to a time when you felt them in the past. If you felt like this once, you can feel like it again (see Creative Visualization, page 142).

Natural Anxiety Aids

There are many self-help techniques to reduce and control anxiety. Here is a selection of effective ones:

• Take a hike. Research has shown that brisk walking or moderate exercise of any sort reduces anxiety levels at least as well as tranquillizers.

• Try this powerful visualization. Stand outside with your eyes closed, and spend a few moments getting centred. (You obviously need to do this on a safe balcony or in a garden, a park or the countryside – a shopping district is not ideal!) See in your mind's eye, depending on the weather, the wind blowing your cares away, the sun evaporating them or the rain washing them away.

- Loosen up and make yourself free again. Find something to smile and laugh about each day, and practise, practise, practise. There are lots of things to make you smile – a child's antics, a shared joke, a hug, a lovely vista, a quirky cartoon, a funny film, a compliment (not brushed off), an old love letter.

- Try relaxation therapy, such as yoga, meditation or autogenic training (see page 136). These all have proven track records for eliminating anxiety.

- Spend time with small children you know – if you don't have any of your own, borrow nieces and nephews or friends' children – getting down on all fours and messing about. Lose yourself in play and see things the way they see them: children have an amazingly clear and uncomplicated view of life.

- Cut down on coffee. Habitual coffee-drinking is linked to anxiety disorders, and it actually increases stress-hormone levels over and above those that would normally be registered in anxious people. Substitute chicory, barley or dandelion coffee, which is caffeine-free and provides nourishment.

- Use aromatherapy to benefit from an anti-anxiety herb such as lavender. Add a few drops of essential oil to your bath or to an aromatherapy burner, or place a drop on each temple. Other anti-anxiety aromatherapy oils you could use are cedarwood, camomile, clary sage, frankincense, geranium, juniper, marjoram, rosewood, sandalwood and tangerine.

Panic Attacks

Panic attacks are a severe form of anxiety and can come on without any warning. Symptoms can include palpitations, a pounding heart, restricted breathing, the shakes, nausea, sweating, confused thinking and feelings of terror. When a panic attack first comes on, it can be so unsettling that you think you are about to die. Some people will try to hide the fact that they are having one because they are embarrassed. Panic attacks can worsen problems with self-esteem as they make you feel out of control. If they continue, they can seriously interfere with daily life. However, there is a lot you can do to get yourself through panic attacks and to eliminate them in the long run.

- Panic attacks can be a sign that the stress in your life is getting out of control. Use all the techniques in this book that seem relevant, but also seek counselling. Your doctor may be willing to prescribe counselling on the NHS.

- Cognitive thinking is particularly successful at treating those suffering from panic attacks, as it alters the way of handling a situation (see page 66).

- Initially, avoid situations that you know are most likely to bring on a panic attack. However, by taking this approach alone you run the risk of creating a full-blown phobia, so eventually you will need to address this with counselling.

- Relaxation classes can make all the difference to the frequency and severity of panic attacks as well as controlling them when they happen. Check out your local yoga, Pilates or autogenic training facilities.

- If you are over-breathing (hyperventilating), emergency measures include breathing into a paper bag for only a few minutes or, more discreetly, into your hands. It can also help to exercise the major muscle groups by, for instance, pacing up and down.

- In the longer term, practise steady breathing on a regular basis so that you know what it feels like. Slowly inhale though your nose, low down into your tummy (without lifting your chest), easily and regularly. Exhale. Avoid holding your breath or sighing. Do not do deep-breathing exercises if you are in danger of over-breathing.

- If you find that you get palpitations, your magnesium levels might be on the low side. Take 400mg of magnesium daily for two months and then cut back to 250mg with 250mg of calcium daily thereafter. Also take 100mg of CoQ10. See if this makes a difference after four months.

Guilt Complex

A strong guilt complex can interfere with your enjoyment of life. If you are not careful, you can find yourself feeling guilty for the whole human condition. Feeling responsible for everything, from leaving the milk out in the sun to guilt about a family bereavement, is a debilitating emotion that can deplete your energy and impair your health. Assessing whether it is appropriate to feel guilty about something is all about gaining perspective. The suggestions below will help you to deal with overwhelming feelings of guilt and to grade the degree of emotional responsibility that is appropriate to the 'crime'. Taking action and sorting out your guilty feelings will liberate you from this stultifying and useless emotion. (Are you already feeling guilty about feeling guilty?)

Q: *I always feel responsible if things don't go well.*
A: Misplaced guilt is a strong sign of poor self-esteem. Some people feel responsible for the happiness of everyone else and feel guilt for everything that goes wrong around them. If you are one of those people, then you are placing a massive burden of guilt on yourself, wearing yourself out trying to please others. This is a no-win situation. One of the best therapies for helping you see a situation differently is cognitive thinking (see page 66). For instance, you may think a fellow member of a committee is critical of everything you propose, which makes you feel as if all your ideas are rubbish, and so you volunteer guiltily for even more tasks. In that situation, you need to think of other possible reasons for the person's behaviour – they could be coming down with flu, they could simply have an aggressive tone, or they could be

critical of everyone, not just you. Thinking of alternative interpretations of an incident will help you realize that you are not 'bad' and that, in most circumstances, you are not responsible for other people.

Q: *When should I take the brunt?*
A: When you take responsibility for your actions, you will be responsible for the outcome. Then you will know if you really need to apologize for something or if you are expressing misplaced guilt.

Q: *I'm always apologizing for things – so much so that people around me pick me up on it.*
A: Have you noticed how there is an epidemic of apologizing? It has its place, but don't apologize for breathing. The habit of saying sorry for everything undermines self-esteem and soon enough you find yourself even saying sorry when someone else bumps into you. Children often think it is their fault that they are being bullied or abused. Employees might think it normal that they cover for their bosses' inadequacies, while an even more extreme example is victims of domestic violence, who blame themselves.

Q: *I worry when things aren't going well and other people aren't enjoying themselves.*
A: You are not responsible for other people's happiness – they are. While you may empathize with their situation, feeling guilty for what they are experiencing only undermines yourself. To take a simple example, you might have chosen the restaurant to go to, but your companion elected to go with you and presumably chose what to eat. If they did not enjoy the experience it is not your 'fault'. Instead of feeling guilty for choosing the restaurant in the first place, laugh about it together, learn from the experience (at least you won't be going back again) and move on.

The Guilt Cycle

The guilt cycle goes something like this: 'I feel guilty. Therefore I am worthy of condemnation. This must mean I have been bad. Since I am bad I deserve to suffer.'

- You are reasoning to yourself that since you feel bad you must be bad. With this cycle you end up punishing yourself in a number of ways. You work harder, you berate yourself, you overcompensate. If you choose to numb the guilt by overeating, drinking or worse, you may then use such reactions as further confirmation of what a bad person you are. Thus you feel more guilt and the whole cycle perpetuates itself.

- Break the cycle by finding more rational responses to your automatic thoughts. Take responsibility for your actions but refuse to take responsibility for those that are not attributable to you. This will require some practice. Take time out each day to give any processes and actions that are provoking guilt a cool appraisal. The more that you do this, the more objectivity you will achieve, enabling you to deal with any guilty feelings you have.

Q: *I know I should really buck up because life isn't too bad, but I still feel unhappy if things aren't going well.*
A: Inappropriate 'should' statements – such as 'I should be grateful for what I've got', 'I should want to be with my family', 'I should be happy I have a good job' – are a guaranteed way to make yourself feel guilty. 'Should' statements are the domain of the perfectionist, and very few people can live up to them. These statements also assume that one must always have a perfect response to a situation. Nobody can be grateful, happy and sociable all the time, and there is no reason to feel guilty when you aren't. This is an example of misplaced guilt and just serves to make you feel bad.

Q: *I'm worried about what influence my feelings of dread and guilt are likely to have on my children.*
A: As well as dealing with your own mantle of guilt, be wary of loading guilt onto others. In particular, you have influence over your children and their self-esteem. If you pile them up with guilt, you perpetuate the cycle. Focus on what their responsibilities are, and not on imagined links. Instead of saying, 'If you don't clear up your mess you will give me a headache', say, 'It is your responsibility to clear up your mess just as it is my responsibility to do the cooking – we each have our responsibilities'.

Q: *Are language and responsibility important?*
A: We need to be aware when we are reproducing unhealthy relationships from our past. We all carry aspects of both parent/child behaviours into adult life and some of us find it hard to shake them off. We might view ourselves as the child while seeing our partner/boss/flatmate as the parent, reproducing over and over again the same dynamic of guilt that we grew up with. Instead of saying, 'If you get us overdrawn again it is going to make me have a nervous breakdown', we should say, 'It is your responsibility to make sure you do not overspend so that the joint bank account does not get overdrawn and cost us a fortune in interest'.

Q: *What about when my partner refuses to take responsibility?*
A: The opposite of guilt is denial, which is a refusal to accept responsibility for a situation. Just to prove how convoluted and creative the human mind is, both denial and feelings of guilt can easily coexist. Where this has implications for the other person is when the denial takes the form of projecting the guilt or weakness onto them. Examples include if we nag someone to correct a fault that we need to address ourselves; and becoming a martyr to sorting out something in someone else's life when not sorting out the mess in our own.

Exercise: *More Quick Ways to Change your Emotional State*
The Exercise on pages 54–55 gave five ways to quickly change your emotional state, and here are five more.

1 Programme your brain to feel happiness. After reading Creative Visualization (see page 142), create a vivid and totally real picture of a time when you were happy, powerful, relaxed, confident, calm and balanced. Capture that feeling in every fibre of your body, every pore of your skin and every neuron of your brain. When you have achieved this, anchor it. You do this by making a small, discreet movement that you associate with the feeling. For instance, brush your finger against your palm or rub two fingers together. Having anchored the feeling, make a point of using this 'signal' a few times each day to recall the feeling. At first, it might be felt only weakly, but as you practise and get in touch with the feeling regularly, you will improve your ability to get there almost immediately, whatever else is going on around you.

2 Any time you make a self-deprecating remark, check yourself and counter it with a more realistic and preferably empowering statement. Do the same when other people talk down to you.

3 When you feel cowed by other people (either because they are overbearing or because you somehow feel inferior), remember they have to go to the loo as well! They are human too, with all the frailties that go with that condition.

4 Write out a mission statement for yourself. A mission statement focuses on the essence of who you are and what you want for yourself. Complete the following statements:
   • 'The person I choose to be from this moment on is someone who is …'
   • 'The qualities I am emphasizing and am enjoying in myself are …'
   • Now add, 'I absolutely commit myself to these qualities being the essence of who I am and am reinforcing them until they are deeply ingrained in my being.'
   • Sign and date your mission statement and look at it regularly.

5 Do something completely irrelevant to your everyday life. Decide that this is the day you are going to learn to juggle, balance a ball on your nose, rollerblade or skateboard in the park or knit a tea cosy – and then do so.

Depression

Depression is more than 'the blues'. We all feel low from time to time, which is normal. It is also obviously normal to feel depressed during times of difficulty such as bereavement. However, actual depression goes beyond this and can involve feelings of not being able to cope with everyday life. Depression and anxiety together make up about 80 per cent of GPs' mental-health workload. The two conditions overlap considerably and those who are depressed can also be anxious, while anxiety can also mask depression. Working though depression might seem, initially, like pushing a peanut up a hill with your nose, but if you persevere, a lot of good can come out of it. Not only can you ditch your depression but you may even develop a whole new take on life.

Q: How do I know if I am suffering from depression and it's not just a matter of needing to pull myself together?
A: The first step in dealing with depression is to recognize that you are affected by it, so that you can do something about it. Typical symptoms can include feelings of inadequacy, loss of self-confidence, loss of enjoyment of life, lack of motivation, avoiding people, withdrawing, agitation, change in appetite, changes in sleep patterns or loss of interest in sex. Early-morning waking is a feature of depression, though it can also involve excessive sleepiness. (Follow the advice under Sleep Quality, page 177.) Depression is often left undiagnosed because of not being seen as a 'real illness' and so help is not sought. There is a perception that one just has to carry on and muddle through. It is important to speak to your GP if you are depressed. Sometimes depression is diagnosed when the problem is really chronic fatigue or ME (myalgic encephalitis), both of which can include depression among the symptoms.

Q: I don't know why I feel depressed. I don't think I should, as life isn't too bad, but for some reason I just feel very low most of the time.
A: Life doesn't have to be obviously problematic for depression to strike. You may have a terrific job, a lovely family and a nice home, for example. But even with assets like these you might be finding it difficult to cope with pressures, perhaps feeling that you can't meet people's expectations and that the burden of responsibility is too great. It is common for those around a person who is afflicted with depression to be surprised when they find out about it. They may not see more than skin-deep, and the person may be doing a good job of hiding the depression while they are actually crumbling underneath the mask.

Q: I admitted to a couple of friends that I've been feeling depressed, and was amazed to learn that they have felt the same way in the past. Are my feelings quite widespread?
A: People can be thoughtless in their communication and make crushing remarks to others as a matter of course, without realizing the effect their words have. We particularly tend to do this to children for some reason ('Don't be stupid', 'Why are you so bad?'). Teasing at school, ribbing at work and cajoling by friends all can erode self-worth. Add to this some devastating events such as job loss or marriage breakdown and it is not surprising that most of us are affected by at least one bout of depression at some time or other. The point is to realize, if you are feeling depressed, that you are not a freak case and are not alone.

Q: *I feel as though I've been keeping my worries in, and I don't know if I can tell my family.*
A: Social support is important to help you through times of depression, so speak to your family, friends or a professional. Don't hope to wing it on your own. Let those closest to you know what you are going through and what they can do to help. Talking is vital – sometimes a friendly ear is enough for you to express your pain and fear. Crying can be a tremendous pressure release. If you need counselling, seek it; your GP should be able to offer help. For details of organizations that can help with depression, see page 202.

Q: *This voice inside me always criticizes everything I do, and it's really getting me down. What can I do about it?*
A: Cognitive thinking, which is the art of turning a negative thought into a more rational, useful or even positive one, is probably the best tool for correcting depressive thought patterns. Work through the exercise on page 67 and, if you find it helpful, investigate the further information, details of which are given on page 202.

Q: *I just don't seem to know where to start to unravel my problems and I'm feeling really rudderless.*
A: A sense of helplessness in the face of perceived problems is one of the most crushing and debilitating aspects of depression. To work on empowering yourself and giving yourself options and choices, see Boosting Self-Esteem, page 38.

Q: *I've heard that being more active would help lift my spirits, but I hate exercising and getting sweaty, so I'm sure it would have the opposite effect.*
A: Allowing yourself to sit and brood usually worsens how you feel. You might not feel like it but make an effort to get out and about. You don't have to work out in a gym – an activity as basic as a brisk walk will stimulate 'feel-good' chemicals in the brain that help to improve mood.

Q: *When I get depressed I eat really badly.*
A: It is common to anaesthetize feelings with fatty and sugary foods. You may not feel like eating anything but junk food, but this is a time to nurture yourself with healthy food that can help to balance brain chemistry. Concentrate on eating foods rich in zinc and the right type of unsaturated fatty acids, such as nuts and seeds (preferably unroasted); oily fish like mackerel, fresh tuna, sardines and salmon; a little lean red meat (game is particularly good); oysters and other shellfish; and beans and pulses. Also eat lots of fresh fruit, vegetables and salads.

Q: *I often boost my mood with a drink but then I get even moodier. Should I be drinking alcohol?*
A: Alcohol will worsen depression. It is a crutch and is not the relief you might think it is. Avoiding alcohol is important if you are depressed.

Q: *My GP has written a prescription for antidepressants but I don't want to take them as I'd feel a failure.*
A: Depression causes changes in brain chemistry, and righting these can be an important feature of treating people with depression. Medication, if it is deemed necessary, is not an admission of failure. A short course for a few months may help to overcome acute symptoms of depression, while working on the underlying problems in the longer term. However, there are possible side effects, which your doctor should discuss with you. For mild to moderate depression the herb St John's wort has been shown to be as effective as antidepressant medication but with fewer side effects.

Loneliness

Do you enjoy your own company? If so, you will rarely be lonely. Obviously we benefit from varied situations – time to be on our own, time spent one-to-one with a friend, time with a group of acquaintances. But if you operate comfortably only when you are with other people and you feed off their presence, you might find it difficult to be on your own. We can also be lonely even when surrounded by other people. Ultimately we have to be able to fall back on our own strengths. We have to *like* ourselves.

Q: *I spend a lot of time on my own and I get lonely.*
A: Keep at the front of your mind that 'alone does not equal lonely'. Use mindfulness (savouring the moment) to enjoy experiences you have on your own. You might also get pleasure from sharing these with other people, but don't feel they are less pleasurable for being experienced in solitude. Smelling a flower, seeing a child play, enjoying a film, eating a slice of chocolate cake are all enjoyable to experience without others. We do not necessarily need other people in order to experience joy.

Q: *I am struggling to get used to being on my own after a serious relationship has ended.*
A: If you have been in a long-term relationship that has recently ended, or the children have just left home, you may find yourself feeling lonely as your routine has changed. This void needs to be filled with activities. Make a list of the things you enjoy and start to build a structure to your life again. (If you are feeling apathetic, see page 44.) You might think that enjoying activities is not the true answer to loneliness and that they are temporary stop-gaps until you find the real answer to loneliness in the form of another person or people. But if you enjoy your life, others will be drawn to you.

Q: *When I am on my own I can't be bothered to do anything.*
A: Aren't you short-changing yourself? If you are with someone else you might create a fancy meal and pull out all the stops, but on your own you heat up a TV dinner. You are signalling to yourself that you are not worth the trouble and time, and that your time spent with other people has greater value. Even if you eat only a piece of cheese

and an apple, make it look nice on the plate as a small signal to yourself that you value your own company. If you do not make such small efforts you will create a self-fulfilling prophecy and, indeed, you will find it unpleasant to be on your own.

Exercise: *Make your Life Special*

1 As an experiment, next Friday evening plan to have a glass of wine with your meal, light a candle and set the table. Follow this with a scented bath and start reading a good book.

2 The next morning, after a leisurely breakfast take yourself off to the park for a walk or to feed the ducks and then visit an art gallery. Sit in a coffee shop and watch the world go by for half an hour.

3 When you get home, clean out a drawer you have been meaning to do for ages. Next, enjoy an attractively made sandwich with all the trimmings, and then continue reading your book. By now, you will be enjoying your own company.

Q: *I enjoy being on my own, but I still want to get out more.*
A: Having decided that you enjoy life and you like your own company, you now need to get out there to meet people. There is loads on offer if you look in your local paper or get involved in a charity, but you may need to organize something yourself. You could establish all sorts of clubs for activities that interest you, be it bridge, swimming, reading, theatre trips, music or walking. People will be glad that someone else wants to arrange things because often they are feeling the same way as you are.

Key Tool 3: Cognitive Thinking

Cognitive thinking is a powerful way of reorganizing your emotional responses, replacing destructive thought patterns with a more constructive and therefore more positive viewpoint. Retraining yourself out of a tendency towards negative reactions is an empowering experience.

Cognitive therapies were developed to treat depression and are based on the idea that our emotional responses depend, far more than we realize, on how we think. In a difficult 'emotional' situation we might cry, be angry or feel fear or sadness, depending upon what we are thinking. Becoming 'cognizant', or aware, of your thought patterns offers an alternative and, many would argue, faster route to well-being than other 'talking cures'. Many people find it easier to change their thinking than they do to change their emotional processes. As anyone who has been through any analytical therapy can testify, digging deep can often be a painful and difficult process which might even lead to taking a few emotional steps back before you take a step or two forwards.

The cognitive approach concerns itself with the immediate problem. Instead of being asked to delve into the past, clients are encouraged to look at how they perceive their truths and to discover where such thoughts do not serve them well. The value of exercises used by cognitive therapists is to get you to replace destructive, undermining, negative thoughts with practical alternatives – thought patterns that are more realistic and so have the power to give you back the ability to grow and to achieve your goals.

Depressed Thinking

The depressed person will see themselves, variously, as not having choices, being a failure or being inadequate and deprived of opportunities. However, from the outside looking in, this same person appears as a fine and capable human being. The depressed person's feelings about themselves probably don't tally with their actual achievements. This conception of depression as disturbed thinking recognizes that the individual's perception of themselves and their environment is the problem.

You don't have to be clinically depressed to think in this way. Most of us are familiar with such thinking to various degrees. We will often devalue our achievements, misinterpret other people's meaning and imagine negative outcomes that do not tally with the facts.

Cognitive therapy is extremely useful for handling stressful events. While you cannot always avoid experiencing crisis situations, you can change the way you think about and therefore react to these events. The cognitive process further affects the way you represent bad times to others, improving your ability to communicate your views without descending into bad feelings. One of the great advantages of cognitive therapy is that it has proved extremely successful as a self-help tool and is used by many counsellors and psychiatrists to treat a variety of crises. If you would like to investigate the subject further, see page 202.

Exercise: Rating How You Feel About Something

This exercise is so simple to do that it is easy to underestimate its power. It is also useful when you feel overwhelmed by worry.

1 Write down all your anxieties at that moment. (Just transferring your worries to paper has a powerful effect of de-cluttering your mind.)

2 Rate each worry on a scale of 1 to 10 and then you can tackle the most pressing concerns first.

3 If you habitually dread doing things, on the next few occasions rate your sense of dread before you do whatever it is. Then, after you've done it, re-evaluate your feelings, noting any sense of achievement or satisfaction you feel. By rating your feelings, and understanding them better, you can transform the imagined pain of doing something into the tangible pleasure of success, turning a negative experience into a positive one.

Cognitive Distortions

It was the Stoic philosophers of ancient Greece who stated, 'Men are disturbed not by things, but by the view which they take of them'. Learning how to monitor our thoughts and then to question our reactions forms a fundamental part of any cognitive therapy. To help you 'think about thinking', here is a list of the most common ways in which we distort our realities:

Jumping to conclusions: Assuming a reality that is not necessarily the case, such as 'Because she did not return my call today she is obviously not interested in what I have to say'.

Mind-reading: Imposing your belief system on what the other person might be thinking, as in 'My boss must think I am disorganized because I got in late today'.

Fortune-telling: Deciding in advance what the outcome of a situation will be, for example 'My parents will be angry with me if I don't do well in the exams'.

Personalization: Assuming responsibility for a negative event even when it is not the case, such as thinking, 'I must be a bad mother' when your child gets a black mark at school, rather than 'His behaviour was out of order and I can best help by getting him to understand why'.

Mental filter: Picking a single negative from a situation and dwelling on it, as in 'Because I forgot to tell them about my previous promotion I messed up the whole interview' instead of 'I forgot that detail but the rest went well and I can forward them a note with this information'.

'Should' statements: 'Shoulds', 'musts' and 'oughts' are used to whip up action. They feel like punishment and lead to guilt: 'I ought to phone my parents tonight' (when you are feeling tired) instead of 'I will phone them tomorrow when I am feeling fresh and able to have a more rewarding conversation'.

Emotional reasoning: Letting your emotions get the better of your thinking, for example, 'I feel terrible that he didn't particularly enjoy himself – I'm so selfish for having insisted we did what I wanted'.

Overgeneralization: Seeing one or a few instances as being typical, as in 'Why do I always mess things up?'

Labelling: Using a definitive term, like, 'I'm an idiot' or 'I'm a failure', instead of 'I made a mistake'.

All-or-nothing thinking: Assuming that anything less than perfect is not good enough, such as 'I messed up the first bit of the presentation so I am a complete and utter failure'.

Disqualifying positive data: Filtering out the good bits, for instance, 'If I am stuck with the kids it will be an exhausting experience' instead of 'I get tired towards the end of the day but before then we'll have plenty of good times together'.

Automatic Thoughts and Rational Responses

We usually have pre-programmed responses to situations, based on some of the information set out in the list of cognitive distortions, page 68. Chit-chat fills our heads with negative views of events. One way to imagine the destructive cycle this sets up is to 'hear' how it would sound if you heard someone, such as yourself, say it to another person or, even more powerfully, to a child. So if you are always saying, 'You idiot' to yourself, hear yourself saying it to a child, in the tone of voice you adopt to yourself, usually condescending and judgemental. Say it out loud. It is generally cringe-making, upsetting and demoralizing.

Working out rational responses requires first that you identify your automatic thoughts. Over a period of a couple of days write down, without fail, all your automatic thoughts – for example, 'I can't do that', 'He looks cheesed off with me', 'Why can't I get anything right?' and so on.

At a quiet time, link those thoughts to the list of cognitive distortions and identify what the typical patterns of your thoughts seem to be. Now write down, next to each automatic thought, what a more rational response might be. Instead of, 'My boss is looking miserable, which probably means he hates everything about the report', a more rational response might be: 'My boss is looking miserable – it could be that he had a bad morning getting to work, that he's had some bad news or possibly that he is concerned about the report'. If you feel that he is not happy with the report, then remind yourself that you can work on it. Approach your boss after you've thought the distortions through.

By regularly working through more rational responses, you eventually begin to change your way of thinking. You automatically check your destructive thought patterns and counter them with more positive thinking. To begin with, it may seem strange to counteract all your negative thoughts. But by replacing 'I'm so stupid' with 'I've made a mistake' you will gradually chip away at bad habits of thought.

An advanced level of the exercise is to add in a score from 1 to 10 to evaluate how much you believe the positive statements. At first you might only score a response of 1 or 2, but with practice and persistence your scoring will creep up nearer to the higher numbers. Keep up these sheets for as long as you can because you never stop learning.

It is also fascinating to take out the sheets a year later, when you are feeling more positive as a result of all the work you have been doing. Rereading your thoughts and comparing them with your views a year later is quite an education.

Food and Mood

If you tend to be moody, the food choices you are making could be having an effect. We all know that our moods affect the type and amount of food we eat. If you are even-tempered and happy, the chances are that you are choosing foods that nourish you and make you feel good. But if you are feeling the pressure mount, you may be indulging in 'comfort eating', or you might be the sort of person who loses their appetite until happier times. Food and mood also have another intimate relationship – the types of foods we eat and drink have an effect on balancing our moods and so they affect our emotional state and self-esteem. We crave certain foods for a variety of reasons:

- Foods affect the brain's serotonin levels, which are involved in moods. (Prozac and similar antidepressants work by changing serotonin levels in the brain.)
- Stimulants, in particular, but also carbohydrates such as bread and sugar, trigger a short-term release of stress hormones, which raise blood-sugar levels and make you feel better in the short term. In the long term, however, they can adversely affect energy levels.
- Compounds such as caffeine (and other methylxanthines) have a direct effect on brain chemistry, but the effect is short-lived and needs to be repeated soon afterwards.
- Some foods such as chocolate have compounds in them that trigger pleasure-giving brain hormones known as endorphins.
- Fat is recognized by the brain as necessary for energy stores in times of stress, but the desire to eat it does not switch off if stress levels do not come down.

The more stressed you feel, the more disordered your eating can become, and the more your moods will be adversely affected. On the other hand, if you motivate yourself to eat in a balanced way, it will help to even out your moods. (For basic guidelines see Healthy Eating, page 161.)

It is a general rule that the foods we are addicted to are those that we eat most frequently and find it hardest to go without. Such foods are also the ones most likely to affect both our moods and our general health adversely. To understand better which foods you are addicted to, keep a food diary for a week, writing down which foods you crave most and how eating them affects your mood.

Cut down on caffeine: We self-medicate with alcohol, coffee, strong tea (weak tea is fine), colas and sugar to make us feel good in the short term. It will come as no surprise then that when this wears off we want more. One or two coffees in the morning to help shake you awake ends up with you topping up with caffeine all day, which can cause tension and depression. Use your food diary to help you cut down on such stimulants. Start by restricting yourself to two coffees in the morning, and then reduce it to one. For information on making healthy substitutions for stimulants in your diet, see Disordered Eating (page 167) and Dealing with Addictions (page 183).

Understand your cravings: Analyse the feelings that your particular food or drink craving is associated with. These could run the gamut of comfort, mood calmer, self-loathing, creative energy, pleasure, dealing with fear and so on. Writing these sentiments down will help you gain objectivity about the feeling and therefore resist a compulsion to consume those foods.

Control carb intake: The most important area to focus on is how you eat carbohydrates, which affect the production of serotonin in the brain. Serotonin plays a large part in our mood swings and their relationship with the foods we eat – affecting how alert we feel, the urge to binge and the craving for stimulants. For instance, eating bread or pasta at midday could make you drowsy for the rest of the afternoon (if you are affected by carbohydrates in this way), and you might do better with a meal of chicken and vegetables. Save the pasta for the evening, when you don't mind feeling sleepy.

Preserve your equilibrium: Mid-afternoon tiredness and sugar cravings can be caused by a dip in levels of the hormone cortisol. Replacing an afternoon snack of cake or chocolate biscuits with a yogurt and piece of fruit, or nuts and dried fruit, or oatcakes with a little cottage cheese, will help to keep you on an even keel.

Damage Limitation

- If you are going to indulge in your particular mood-bending food or drink, at least be aware that it will rob you of essential nutrients – B vitamins, antioxidants (vitamins A, C, E), magnesium, chromium and calcium. Make sure that you take a daily multi-vitamin and mineral supplement to replace some of these. A bowl of cereal before you go out can help to slow down alcohol absorption and nourish you with some B vitamins.

- Drink long drinks made with juices if you can, such as a bloody Mary, a vodka and orange, or a white wine spritzer.

- Give yourself some alcohol-free days each week.

- If you need an excuse for avoiding alcohol when in a social situation, you could tell a little white lie – say you are doing a detox, are on antibiotics or are driving.

- If you just have to have that chocolate or sticky bun, eat a large piece of fruit first and then indulge if you still want to.

- If you take sugar in your drinks, reduce it slowly over time until you no longer need or even like it.

- The ritual of putting on the kettle and making a hot drink is often as important as actually drinking the coffee. Indulge in hot water with lemon, some grated ginger for zest and a little honey.

Step 5

Success Strategies that Work

Whatever it is that you are aiming to achieve – big or small, short-term or long-term – it is important to find strategies that will achieve them for you as painlessly as possible. You probably already have many of the necessary skills but, like most of us, need to organize them in the most beneficial way. We have covered several of those strategies already, such as setting priorities, making an action plan and staying flexible. In this chapter we will layer on further strategies to help you bring your goals into sharper focus. One way that you can make short work of this is to follow the lead of people you admire who have already achieved similar goals, which will help to shorten the odds and improve your own chances of success.

Start by defining what success means to you personally. Is it most important that you achieve professional acclaim? Is a happy personal life of paramount importance? Are you most successful in your mind if you can concentrate on your hobbies? One person's view of success is not necessarily what appeals to another person. Trying to fulfil someone else's idea of success is not going to achieve it for you personally.

Part of this chapter concentrates on financial and work-related issues. This is not because wealth is a definition of success (it is for some people, of course, but is not for everyone). It is because a major source of stress in many people's lives is connected with money management and jobs. Until they can sort out this element of their lives, they are unable to really relax, flourish and succeed (in whatever terms are most important to them). However, you could equally apply many of these strategies to planning other aspects of your life.

Inspiration and Motivation

Few things make a person more interesting, happy and forward-looking than if they are inspired by life. How do you find this inspiration? Get curious! If you ever wonder why something happens or what something is, find out – you never know where it will lead. Getting inspired about something is a terrific way to empower yourself and to start an upward spiral of satisfying emotions leading to a happier life. Just watch your problems fall by the wayside.

Get inspired by really focusing on something. If you have a lot of theoretical interests but never do anything about them, then you are fogging your potential with too many options and not enough action (see Overwhelmed? on page 26). Choose one activity that you really want to tackle, and make a plan, now, to do something about it. Enrol in classes, buy equipment or books, set aside time in your diary, talk to some experts, encourage a friend to come along for company – get inspired to take action.

Q: *Where do I start?*
A: Talk to people every day. Take an interest in others' lives and experiences. Instead of pigeonholing people, find out what has motivated them and what they have learned. Your grandparent, neighbour or friend of a-friend might have a whole dimension to them that you never thought to ask about beforehand. Be inspired by those who are around you or whom you admire from a distance. Understand how they view the world and what they find rewarding. This can give you ideas to mould for your own use. It will also set a wonderful example for your children, helping them to become resourceful and to follow their own inclinations. A child's enthusiasm can be an inspiration to you. (If you do feel inspired, however, avoid preaching to others. In any event, they will notice that you are happy, more fulfilled and active, and, if interested, they will seek out your views, but they do not need unasked-for information pushed at them. You will win more fans and converts this way.)

Q: *I tend towards being a pessimist but I'm thinking about changing that. What are the merits of optimism?*
A: An optimistic approach to life comes naturally to some people, while others may need to practise a little. Optimists usually expect the best from people and situations, view mistakes as learning experiences, safely release their frustrations and are likely to talk about the future with excitement. If you are still left feeling that optimists are a little irritating and unrealistic, take the middle course and head for realism. However, it is the optimists in this world who see obstacles as mere hurdles, view problems as

interesting challenges and achieve their aims most easily – in part by being flexible in their aims and avoiding rigid attitudes.

Q: *What if you are surrounded by pessimists? Doesn't that make it harder to stay optimistic?*
A: Take yourself out of situations where others squash inspiration and positive thinking with their negativity or, worse, with put-downs. By all means listen to good advice, but also learn to listen to your inner wisdom.

Q: *I worry about making a fool of myself and failing or being rejected.*
A: Take chances. This does not mean being reckless or dangerous, but it does mean expanding your boundaries. Unless you take a chance, you will never know if it was to be. Never let a fear of taking chances get in your way. Ask yourself, 'What is the worst thing that could happen if I do take the risk?' Even if the worst does happen, it is usually not that bad. Rejection can often have a dampening effect on inspiration, so work on seeing it as an opportunity to change your approach. Also, remember that one rejection does not mean that more will follow. You can enhance your motivation for something if you associate it with pleasure, rather than with pain. Visualize yourself succeeding at whatever it is you are motivating yourself to do, and get firmly in touch with the pleasure this engenders.

Q: *What about when I hit stumbling blocks?*
A: Stay on track. The beginnings of a new project can be extremely inspiring, but lack of consistency of action or stumbling blocks can soon erode this. Is your enthusiasm enough to carry you through? Where and how else can you renew your motivation? Take stock regularly to evaluate these feelings. Remember that things rarely go as smoothly as you expect and that every glitch offers learning possibilities provided you are open to them.

Q: *I know what I* don't *want but am not sure about what I do want.*
A: Being motivated by negatives never really works that well. Think about it. Wanting to leave a relationship because you don't find your mate attractive any more, you find your partner's habits irritating or you are no longer in love often means a long, drawn-out process until you finally can't stand it any longer. Similarly, being in a job you would like to leave because you don't like your colleagues, you are underused or the travel is too difficult is not likely to be the most forceful way of helping you make up your mind about what to do. By contrast, if you fall madly in love with someone or are inspired by a terrific job opportunity, you will be out of the unsatisfactory situation without a backwards glance. Whether it is right or appropriate to leave is a different question, and needs to be balanced against other issues, but what we are talking about here is inspiration and motivation. Finding a positive reason to make a change is a powerful motivator.

Routine, a Strategy for Success

Routine was, in our grandparents' day, something that was taken for granted. Sunday was a day of rest with the treat of a roast after church (or a Friday or Saturday for Muslims or Jews); Monday was washday; pay-day on Friday meant bills could be paid and food bought; and Saturday could mean a family outing. Our domestic lives are a lot less structured now, which allows for more flexibility but also more chaos. Sometimes just having a routine can release a person from having to make continual decisions about the next thing to do. If you think your life could benefit from a daily or weekly routine to reduce minor stresses, now is the time to apply yourself to it.

- Decide on your priorities. Some are so obvious that you do them automatically, such as brushing your teeth, showering and dressing before you leave home. We establish this type of priority without conscious thought. The trick is to identify areas of your life that you need to improve, in order to reduce stress, and push them higher up the priority list, from 'ought to do' to 'must do'. You can then introduce them into your daily or weekly routine – for instance, 'I must buy fresh fruit and vegetables twice a week', 'I must plan some time out', 'I must keep in touch with old friends'.

- A typical 'must do' list might allow, every day, half an hour first thing for your post, e-mails and minor errands, such as dropping off dry cleaning or buying stamps; half an hour for cooking and preparing healthy meals; and half an hour for yourself, so you can exercise, relax in a bath or just do your nails. Any less than this and you will be short-changing yourself, and your pile of mail, unhealthy eating and drooping hemlines will take their toll on how you feel about yourself.

- Avoid cramming too many things into your daily routine. Keep your 'must do' list simple and it will be more effective.

- Each day, allow enough time to get through your list.

- Don't have too many rules, and ensure that those rules you do have are well chosen and vital.

- By all means make a plan and form a routine, but if your routine is occasionally thrown out, don't let it distress you. Just restructure your routine.

- Within your newly organized routine, remember to plan for a day of rest. Regeneration is vital.

- Precious weekends are often wasted because of lack of planning. Keep a list of people you want to catch up with, a folder with film, theatre or art gallery reviews that have caught your eye, a list of places you would like to visit when you get the time. This way you will always be inspired and will be able to have weekend mini-holidays when you need to.

- Keep to a routine of eating meals as a family or with selected friends. If mealtimes are normally stressful, make them times for exploration and enquiry – discuss non-inflammatory subjects or play word games. A sit-down meal will allow your family to benefit from more togetherness and to eat more healthily than from meals eaten on the run.

Vocation

One of the stresses that can drag you downwards faster than anything is disliking or just tolerating your job. It might be that your occupation is a means to an end – earning enough money to live – but if you are unhappy in your job, both your work and your spirit will suffer. However, if you can follow a vocation – a passion, a calling, an occupation you really love – many common work-related problems, such as feeling put-upon or not wanting to give that extra ten per cent, cease to exist. If you get out of bed on Monday and think 'only five more days until the weekend', you could probably do with finding your vocation.

Of course, many people have never hankered after a particular vocation, and reading this section of the book is not necessarily essential for you to have a satisfying work life. However, if there is a vocation you have always felt drawn to but have not managed to achieve, you may find yourself getting frustrated in your work life. Some people just know from the beginning that they want to be nurses, vets, circus performers, artists or whatever. Even if you do have a vocation, there is a time in life to work on the treadmill (perhaps to earn a good salary) and a time to pursue your vocation (which you may be doing for the love of it).

Q: *How can I get an idea of what I want?*
A: We can't always do exactly as we want. Nevertheless, if your work can be as close to your ambitions as possible, you are more likely to be inspired by what you do. You might want to be a footballer but have two left feet, in which case maybe you could find job satisfaction by working at a sports-equipment company. If you are fascinated by the theatre, perhaps you could train for set design or costume-making. If you are a train enthusiast, you might wish to work in the railway system. If you enjoy talking to people, perhaps you could retrain as a counsellor. It is not ideal to be too analytical about choosing a vocation, as it tends to be more of an inspiration. However, if you are analytical by nature, you may find it helpful to mind-map your likes and dislikes, talents and skills, fantasies and limitations, to seek out your vocation. (See page 16 for how to use mind-mapping techniques.) Consulting a career counsellor might also be helpful.

Q: *I don't really have a strong ambition – does it matter?*
A: Not everyone has a burning desire for a particular vocation. However, don't assume that because you don't have one now, you will never have one. One day you might be

inspired to change the course of your life, and it is never too late to retrain. We are living longer, more active lives now, and instead of thinking of retirement you may well find a calling that takes you into a second career.

Q: *What are the practicalities I need to think about?*
A: Following your vocation might mean taking risks or a drop in income – are you ready for this? It also often involves retraining. In order to pursue this, you may have to plan quite a while ahead and restructure your life in the meantime. This may seem daunting at first, but if you have chosen well, the dream of doing something that inspires you can keep you motivated.

Success Brings New Challenges

We may dream of success in our chosen sphere, but when that success comes – what then? It can be every bit as difficult to deal with as failure. However, knowing about the possible challenges can help you to avoid this stress. The trickiest part is to retain a balance in your life. By keeping other aspects of your life in focus, such as family, friends, leisure activities and interests, and not sacrificing them to the god of success, you can maintain a balance and avoid feelings of disenchantment (see Finding a Balance between Work and Home, page 12). No matter how successful you become, don't forget those you love and people who helped you along the way. We are all a sum of the experiences and people we meet during our lives.

Q: *I've been offered a promotion that I've been coveting for a while but suddenly I am doubtful and am uncertain whether it is for me.*
A: Perhaps your inner voice is telling you something you need to listen to. Working your way up the company ladder can include unexpected hurdles. You may find that you are responsible for others, or it might be perceived that you can take an even greater workload than you were prepared for. Perhaps a job that you went into because you enjoy being 'hands on' has turned into a management job. Once you've got where you wanted, you may find that it is not all you dreamed it would be. Try to find out beforehand what is involved in a promotion and work out if you are happy with the terms.

Q: *I have my own one-man-band company but need to expand due to volume of business, and I have a certain amount of trepidation about this.*
A: Being self-employed does not necessarily make you immune to events similar to those described above. You might find that you have more demand than you can keep up with and are forced to decide whether to employ an assistant (with all the differences in working methods that this requires). You might find that demands are made on your time that are not actually cost-effective – a typical example is being asked to give talks or to do some fund-raising. It is surprising how such demands can

build up and require a lot of preparation. You may get something out of these activities, such as networking or feeling good about helping others, but if they become an unacceptable drain on your resources you'll need to learn to say no in a kind way.

Q: *I thought that once my business was successful I could go and play golf a couple of days a week – but it's not working out that way.*
A: When you've planned and worked hard to achieve your dreams, it can be a cruel blow to find that, far from just being able to relax and ride the tide of success, you have to work just as hard. For instance, success may bring all sorts of practical problems for the owner of a growing business, such as staffing levels, having to juggle stock levels (with large amounts of money tied up in the stock), dealing with multiple premises and being distanced from the customer. Often all the ideals that you started out with, such as offering a superb service or a good product at a good price, can fly out of the window when the company gets to an unwieldy size. Anticipating such problems in a reworked business plan is essential.

Q: *How do I deal with the fact that my business is expanding a bit too quickly?*
A: You would be wise to talk to your bank or financiers about contingency plans if you find that success brings a greater short-term financial drain. Avoid mortgaging your house against any financial drains that crop up with your business activities, even if you seem to be riding high at the moment. Sometimes people do this and win through, but many lose out. If you are seeking finance for a strong-enough reason, the banks will usually be interested. If they are not, then it's because they consider it too great a risk. Are you prepared to risk your home if this is their view?

Q: *We are going into a recession and I am very keen to continue to thrive in this environment, but it's additional stress and I know that, while some succeed, others will fail.*
A: Some people and businesses are successful even during economic downturns. Smaller companies often do better, if managed properly, than larger, more unwieldy ones. The smaller ones have a flexible approach and see it as an opportunity to excel over their competition, to expand and to acquire premises and expertise at lower prices. Recessions are opportunities to lighten up operating structure and negotiate harder. Keeping tight credit control at these times is vital.

Q: *I enjoy the rock-and-roll lifestyle attached to my work but my partner is worried that it could all get out of control.*
A: The culture in which we live suddenly throws some people, particularly film, rock and media stars, into the limelight. As a result, we have a chance to see in graphic detail some of the challenges that can arise from this overwhelming success. Often the way they deal with it is to use a large chunk of their new-found wealth to prop themselves up, and not infrequently we hear tales of descent into alcoholism or drug addiction. You have to be a strong person with a level head to deal with this sort of

fame, and many are simply not mature enough. If you have even a small percentage of this thrust upon you, take a deep breath and keep your wits about you. Understand that a rich alcoholic is just as miserable as a poor alcoholic, and decide early on in the game whether this is really what you want, or what you think you want.

Q: *I'd like to feel that what I am doing is worthwhile.*
A: If you have succeeded, you can be an inspiration to others. Take time to give something back to the system by speaking at a local school or helping out youngsters. If you are a high earner, you can support those who are less fortunate and who are unable to look after their own interests.

Q: *I ran a business that did well, but I have taken time off to raise a family and am nervous about getting back into the groove.*
A: If you have succeeded once, you know you can do it again when you need to. You only have to look at your previous success as an example.

Strategies in the Difficult Workplace

- Even if you are in a job you don't absolutely love at the moment, concentrate on the things you enjoy about it. Do you particularly get on with a few colleagues? Do you like the area your workplace is in and want to explore more thoroughly what it offers? Can you get your company and colleagues interested in other activities that inspire you, such as starting an amateur dramatics club, playing five-a-side football or supporting a particular charity?

- If you are in a job that you find unrewarding – you do not like your colleagues, the job is not satisfying, you are not appreciated and the money just is not worth it – you need to do something about it to put yourself back in control of the situation. Sit down now and plan your future by reading the section Setting Goals (page 8).

- Confronting a bullying boss takes guts but in the long run may be necessary if you are to retain self-esteem. Your boss may be the type who talks down to you in public, consistently expects you to sacrifice your personal life for your work life or undermines your work at every opportunity. If so, you need to start taking notes about the instances where you have found the behaviour unacceptable, so that you can think about the issues. Be clear that you are not going to put up with being treated in this way, and that, if you are to be criticized, it needs to be done in private and in a constructive manner. You may, of course, find that this backfires, so you'll plan for this eventuality. However, putting up with bad behaviour because of your fears (typically of losing your job) will, in the long run, exhaust you and cripple your self-esteem. You may need to look for another job.

- Some people within the work environment, who themselves have limited scope for manoeuvrability, inflict the same on subordinates or customers. These are the ones who suck air through their teeth and claim, 'It's more than my job is worth'. They become, in effect, mini-dictators presiding over their domain with all the ferocity they can muster. If you work for someone like this, it will be a debilitating situation and you will quickly lose all sense of self-determination if you allow it to continue.

Money Management

Whether we like it or not, money makes the world go round. Yet it is the source of misery for many people, often because they think they don't have enough of it, and just as often because they are simply disorganized about managing their money. In addition, we live in a society of buy-now-pay-later, and this, for some people, has caused their debts to spiral out of control. The situation is compounded by the fact that property prices have risen to a level that makes it hard to 'get on the ladder'. What's more, jobs-for-life are no longer a reality. If any of this affects you and you are stressed by the situation, some of the pointers in this section will help.

Exercise: *Be Clear about your Financial Priorities*

1 Do you tend to live for today? In other words, are you happy to spend what you earn and save little for the future?

2 Or do you mostly live for tomorrow as a conscientious saver and investor, forgoing costly fun and frolics now? For many of us these issues are age-related – we tend to live for today in our younger years, and for tomorrow as we age.

3 A conflict between these two approaches could give rise to considerable stress. One way of avoiding this is to realize what your habits are. There is no point in taking one approach while hankering after the other. By deciding which you are and embracing it, you are likely to be happier with your lot.

4 On the other hand, you could work towards achieving a middle ground between these two extremes and perhaps get the best of both worlds.

Q: *I always seem to be stretched financially, though admittedly I enjoy spending every weekend shopping.*
A: Don't confuse need with want. The more we have, the more we often think we need – a new sofa to go with the new curtains, for example. Yet if you take time to question your 'need' you may find that it's really a 'want'. Monitoring your material desires will save you money and avoid feelings of frustration. Be wary of advertising in particular.

As you know, they are continually devising sophisticated and ingenious new ways to make you crave things you never knew you wanted and to part you from your money. Rather than following trends, create your own style and supersede fashion in favour of lasting style and chic classics. We are lucky enough to live in a time where we have excellent design and production methods. This means that we can afford to take some time to research products we wish to buy rather than buying impulsively. Large white goods such as fridges and washing machines are often to be found more cheaply if you use consumer magazines and websites for information. Fashion and decorating magazines and books are great for ideas, inspiring you to be creative and get the 'look' for a lot less than your more hasty friends might pay. Make regular forays to browse for things you need in rural or out-of-the-way antiques shops, auction houses and markets, including car-boot sales. It takes time but can be fun, and there are some real bargains to be had. By turning the whole exercise into a hobby, you will lower the potential stress enormously.

Q: *My kids drive me round the bend wanting the latest labels, but I usually give in even though I can't really afford it.*
A: Teach your children about branding and advertising, and instil in them a confidence in their own taste. Try to convince them that it is more cool to have a unique style than just to follow the herd. (This is easier said than done, of course, since children and teenagers are incorrigible conformists.) When they pester you for yet another pair of expensive trainers, don't relent, otherwise they will learn that nagging will eventually make you give in.

Exercise: Basic Budgeting

1 If you have never worked out a budget, now is the time to do so. Working from your cheque stubs, bank statements and credit-card bills, write down what you spend on all the basics of life, such as rent or mortgage, utilities, insurance, food and travel to school or work.

2 Also work out what you spend, on average, on large but occasional purchases such as holidays and furnishings. For two weeks, meticulously make a note of every penny you spend – every round of drinks you buy, every newspaper and magazine you purchase, presents for other people, treats for yourself, meals out, clothes. At the end, you will have a good picture of your spending patterns.

3 Now work out your income. This will probably be simpler, especially if you have a single employer.

4 Now there is nothing else to do but marry the two up and find out why you are fortunate enough to be able to save, or why you are always in debt.

Bill-Paying

- Credit cards may be your flexible friends but if you lack self-control they are also a cause of many sleepless nights. These days we average, per credit-card owner, debts of £5,000 spread over store cards, credit cards and personal bank loans. If you are not able to control your spending on them or, more importantly, pay them all off each month, then cut them up. Store cards have notoriously high interest charges if you do not pay the bill off on time. One credit card, used only when you really need it, such as when making purchases over the phone or on the Internet, is enough for anybody.

- If you have a large credit-card debt, possibly spread over a range of cards, you may need to look into transferring all the debts to one source. Refinancing your debt at a lower rate of interest through a bank or other loan should work out cheaper than leaving interest charges to mount up on your cards. Make sure you work out realistically how much you can afford to pay back and over what period of time.

- In the old days, people would keep envelopes or jars in which they saved up money to pay utility bills or to use for big expenditures like holidays or furniture. There is something in this. While envelopes might be a little low-tech these days, you should at least work out how much you need to put aside, each month, into a savings account for regular expenditures.

- Check your bank statements regularly. Leaving them to sit unopened because you fear what is inside will not improve the situation. Ask for your bank statements to be sent to you every two weeks instead of monthly so that you are able to keep a tighter control over them. Or check your bank balance weekly on-line.

- It might be old-fashioned, but Shakespeare's admonition 'Neither a borrower, nor a lender be' is as sensible today as it was four centuries ago. The playwright obviously knew a thing or two about stress management.

Earning Power

If you value yourself, others will value you as well – yet people have all sorts of insecurities about their value in the market place, leading to uncertainty and sometimes resentment, which can be highly stressful.

Q: *I've done some market research and am considering pricing my services in the mid-range between the lowest and highest prices that I've found. Is this a good strategy?*
A: Those who consistently do well are those who are not afraid to ask for top prices and who give a good service. (You can't have the second without the first for very

long.) There is always a market for high quality. This is true even in an economic downturn, when it is the lower-quality goods and services that people dispense with. If you dare to charge more than others for your service, several things are likely to happen. Firstly, you will automatically be perceived to be better than the others. Secondly, people will be serious in their dealings with you. Thirdly, you will probably attract even more work or business.

Q: *I'm not sure I dare ask top dollar.*
A: Assuming that you are professional and provide a good service, you need never worry that you are 'ripping people off'. If the customer is not satisfied they simply won't come back. Never feel guilty or unworthy of your full earning potential. And if you earn more, you are then in a position to help others – either in your family or through charities.

Q: *How do I ask for an increase in salary?*
A: If you are looking for a pay rise, remember to ask for it intelligently – ask the right person in the right way (see Realizing Ambitions, page 41). Also avoid using disempowering terminology when you think about it. Avoid saying to yourself, 'I hope I will get a pay rise' – say instead, 'I know I will get a pay rise'. And if you are unsuccessful in your request? Don't think, 'What will I do now?' Just say to yourself, 'I'll handle it'.

Q: *I've seen a job advertised that is the same as my present job but offers a higher salary. Should I go for it?*
A: You can always change jobs to improve your income. But remember that salary is not the only thing your working life is about. You also need to evaluate how you feel about the location, your colleagues, your job satisfaction. Sometimes there is a hidden price to a job move and you have to ferret out what this might be in advance and then decide if you can accept it.

Investing and Saving

Don't be frightened of this area in the belief that you don't have a mind for it. With very little effort, you can learn enough about the basics of money management to make sensible decisions about your own savings and investments. Most of the national newspapers, particularly the weekend editions, have excellent money sections that simplify the whole issue. The newspapers also regularly feature different types of bank account, different spending profiles and investment plans, and they have informative questions-and-answers pages. Six months spent reading the money section of a selected paper can make a huge difference to your confidence and your understanding. Radio programmes and books are also good sources of simple, concise information about money management.

Exercise: What Are your Financial Aims?

1 Work out where you think you want to be, in financial terms, five, ten and twenty years from now.

2 What are your priorities? Do you need to get through higher education? Do you hope to buy a flat or house? Do you want to plan for your children's future? Do you want to ensure a secure retirement?

3 By working out what your needs will be, you can decide how to achieve these by saving and investing.

Q: *I want to save money for the future – is investing in the stock market a good way to do this?*
A: Investing is not the same as saving, and this is an important distinction. If you invest in, say, stocks and shares, or in a company-start-up scheme, you risk losing that money. If you put money into a savings account you do not risk losing it (except in very rare circumstances in which banks have folded and not been backed up by governments). Invest or save your money according to your needs and according to how much you could afford to lose if the worst came to the worst. However, remember that if you invest £500 in a stock which then rises to £5,000, but you leave it there and it eventually crashes to £250, you have lost £250 and not £4,750. If you never cashed it in, you never had it and it was just paper. This might help you to be more philosophical if you are ever in this situation.

Q: *How much should I save?*
A: As a general rule, it is a good plan to save at least ten per cent of your net income for future needs and contingencies. Planning for life's unexpected events is wise, because ill health, unanticipated additions to the family, responsibility for an ageing parent and other events can all stretch finances to the limit. Get professional advice, but be aware that financial advisers are often paid commission (though they are controlled by regulations). Truly independent advice is available only from advisers who are paid a fee or who earn a salary that is not linked to commission. The more you know, the more you will be able to use your educated judgement.

Spend, Spend, Spend

• Learn to walk away from potential purchases. Take a day to decide if you really want or need the item. Your desire will often wane but sometimes will be enhanced, and this will provide the answer about whether to buy it or not. On the other hand, if it has been sold when you go back, learn to be fatalistic about it:

it wasn't meant to be. And in truth, when you look back ten years from now, the chances are that you won't even remember it.

- Our desire to buy something is usually in inverse proportion to its availability. Sales people know this, which is why you will be pressed with 'It's the last one in the shop' and similar lines. Resist this and examine your feelings. In reality it is rarely the case that you will experience serious loss or deprivation if you do not get this item.

- Overspending is all about instant gratification in exactly the same way that eating a cream cake is. You want it, and you want it now. You are putting off the pain of worrying about the credit-card bill, in favour of avoiding the pain of not getting what you want this instant. It is only when the pain of the bills landing on the doormat gets too great that it affects the consciousness of the overspender at the cash till. Understanding this pain–gratification pattern can help to break the habit.

- It used to be that debts would arise because people got into difficulty over unexpected events such as illness or major property repairs. However, these days it is more likely that the cause is borrowing too much money. If you get into financial difficulty, the Citizen's Advice Bureau may be able to offer free advice to help you get on top of your finances.

- If you are in debt, don't take on further debt (especially to make payments on your existing debts). Make a list of all your debts: which are the most pressing? These are the ones where there are sanctions (such as repossession of a property or cutting-off of services) or legal penalties (such as council tax or child support). Negotiate repayments on your most important debts. You can refinance your non-urgent debts such as credit cards to spread out payments and rationalize the interest you are paying, but do not be tempted to increase your debt load.

Unemployed... or 'Resting'

Our reaction to unemployment has everything to do with how involved we were in the process of losing a job. If unemployment is a result of taking voluntary redundancy or 'constructive dismissal', retirement or a deliberate decision to take a sort of sabbatical, then the effect is not likely to be so intense. However, if unemployment comes out of the blue, as a result of illness, or from not getting a job in the first place when leaving education, then it can have quite an impact.

The main problems of unemployment are usually threefold: the financial impact, the effect on self-esteem and the lack of time-filling skills to benefit from the newly available stretches of time. One, or any combination of these, can be enough to bring on depression or other stress-related problems such as acute lethargy.

Many people are used to measuring their self-worth in terms of their productivity or their ability to meet sales targets or close deals. Transferring this need for productivity to other areas of life is the obvious way forwards. But if you are knocked back because you can't even get a job interview, then being productive with your time can be more difficult. Interestingly, many people get through recessions, which are times of highest unemployment, emotionally and financially intact even though they have been subjected to the same events and pressures as everyone else.

Q: *I've been made redundant and I'm pretty depressed about it.*
A: Aim to turn around your perception of unemployment. Instead of viewing it as the end of a road (which it isn't) or as a major step back (which it might be), look at it differently. Take the view that it is the beginning of another road, an opportunity to change direction, and that life is now full of exciting possibilities. (Even if you don't feel particularly excited at the moment, you can become so.) Increasing use of freelance workers has created a more insecure labour market. But looked at in a more positive light, this work fluidity also creates new opportunities for those who want them, and this may be something you can think about.

Q: *I'm feeling rudderless without my usual office routine.*
A: Take time out to make a daily and weekly plan. Structure your day and avoid floating aimlessly from activity to activity. Spend time researching options, networking and planning. However, do not be dismayed when things don't go according to plan – you need to remain flexible in your approach (see Staying Flexible, page 14).

Q: *My confidence has taken a bash now that I am redundant.*
A: Banish the word redundancy from your vocabulary. You are not a redundant person. There is a reason that actors use the word 'resting' when they are temporarily out of work. They may be working as waiters and may not see an acting job from one end of the year to the next, but they know they must stay positive. Acknowledge the power of language and describe yourself more positively: 'I'm looking for opportunities' rather than 'I'm out of work'.

Q: *Is there a silver lining to this particular cloud?*
A: There always is if you look for it. Focus your mind on the good things that are apparent in your life such as social support and love from your family. Enjoy the time you can devote to enhancing these important aspects of your life, such as spending more time with your children, grandchildren or nephews and nieces; nurturing your relationships with parents or siblings; or developing new friendships.

Q: *Now that I've lost my job, I feel washed up and gloomy about the future, and wonder if I'll ever get another job.*
A: How you view 'loss' is important. Immigrants to other countries will often leave behind everything – jobs, financial security, culture and sometimes even family. Yet some of our most successful people have been immigrants. Losing your job is, of course, serious but you can use it as the opportunity to make a new life.

Exercise: Building New Opportunities

1 When thinking about new options and opportunities, think laterally. List all your skills that are transferable – any expertise that you can transfer to new challenges in the job market. Could you become a self-employed consultant (see page 153)? Could you become a specialist in one area of your previous job (such as training people to do what you did previously)? Could you design websites linked to your speciality? Many people are even re-employed by their old companies on a freelance basis – it may be worth approaching them. Become a master (or mistress) of reinvention.

2 Put together a CV as soon as possible, or if you are selling your services design a marketing brochure.

3 As soon as you are able, sit down and draw up an emergency financial strategy – do not wait until you have worked through your notice period. Find out about available benefits and grants.

4 Speak positively about your activities to other people. Avoid complaining about being out of a job; instead, talk about opportunities and look for new ideas or new avenues to follow. People respond to positive people.

5 Now may be the time to learn a new skill, so take the opportunity to retrain if you would like to do so. Do you need computing skills, training skills, report-writing skills? Future employers will be impressed with your determination, and learning can reinvigorate you and trigger new ideas. Find out about courses run by the employment services, the local authority or local colleges – many practical schemes are available, such as how to do your own accounting, how to draw up a business plan and how to market yourself.

Step 6

Building Better Relationships

KEY MESSAGE:

We Do Not Exist as Islands

We need others in our lives. Nurturing relationships allow us to grow, thrive and blossom. Be generous with those around you and they will be generous with you.

Relationships can be a source of empowerment, comfort and joy when all is going well, but at times they can also be the cause of stress and conflict in our lives. Today, the wider family such as parents, grandparents or cousins, the people who often know you best, may live far away. Friends may be so busy with their own lives that they don't have time for you when you need them. Daily routines are dictated as much by our working lives as by the needs of our personal relationships, leaving us with a feeling that there is not enough time simply to enjoy each other's company. Finding ways to take time out to listen to others, spend time with them and enjoy spontaneous pleasures as they happen enhances and enriches our relationships.

The 21st-Century Family

Families are subject to changes and shifts in the way they relate. Just when you thought you knew everything there was to know about your family, they change. Remember that relationships are interesting precisely because they are complex. The saying 'You've learned to ride the bicycle, but the road changes every day' is very applicable to families – in other words, there is no instruction manual. The vagaries of family relationships are as different as the people involved in them. One of the greatest challenges lies in redefining roles within the family, and adapting to the changes caused by divorce and remarriage, which create new step-, half- and in-law families.

Q: *We've decided to get divorced and I want to protect the children from the worst of it. What is the best way forward?*
A: If you are divorcing and kids are involved, it is best if you and your ex can manage to get on with each other. If your self-esteem is good, you will not feel threatened by your ex finding a new partner, remarrying or having more children. You don't have to like any of these, but for your children's sake it is usually best to get on with all concerned. Of course, you can't be responsible for how your ex, or any new partner, might behave, but by being even-handed and non-judgemental, you may be an influence for more positive behaviour.

Q: *Sometimes my family drive me mad, but I suppose there is nothing I can do about it – should I just take it in my stride?*
A: Love them or hate them, your family are a part of you. Invest in your family whether nuclear (your immediate family), extended (your natural blood relatives across the generations and including cousins) or step- (brought together by marriage). These people form a valuable support system and are part of your identity. If you suppress your emotions in a relationship, it is more likely to suffer, but if you express your emotions in a relationship (this is not the same as criticizing – it is more about talking), it is more likely to thrive.

Q: *My family are antagonistic towards my new partner, which I find difficult as I am building a new life after splitting from my husband.*
A: After divorce or bereavement, you might have found happiness with a new partner, and yet your family seem determined to judge you and the relationship. There are no more harsh critics than your own children. Don't expect them to be happy for you. (They will see it in very personal terms – how it affects *them* – and they may still be mourning the passing of their parents' relationship.) You may need to steer them towards a confidante to whom they can talk and complain: someone who is neutral, such as a family friend or relative. Don't feel guilty if you find a new romance 'too quickly'. If your family and friends don't approve, deal with their complaints objectively. You can't please everyone so you might as well please yourself (as long as your children are not neglected emotionally because of it). Only time will tell whether they were right or not.

Q: *What is the bet way to start off with my partner's children when we all move in together?*
A: Taking on a new partner's children, either full-time or part-time, can be unfamiliar territory. While you can never be a replacement parent, you can be a 'significant other', and taking on the role of confidante is one way forward. Don't try to buy their

love, however – this will develop as a result of respect and kindness. It's important to establish ground rules early on – preferably with all the adults concerned, including the ex and new partners, agreeing on the same tactics. Otherwise, children will become adept at exploiting conflicts and playing everybody off against each other. Don't assume that step-children who are thrown together will get on – they may well be jealous of each other. This needs tact and careful handling. New half-siblings are also a milestone for older children, and their arrival needs to be handled intelligently. Involve older children in planning for the birth of a new sibling, generating excitement in the prospect. Do not make them feel in any way left out or usurped.

Q: *I am anxious about how to manage financially with a new baby on the way while I am still supporting my first family.*
A: Financial stress is a common occurrence when a partner is having to support two families. Sorting out your money in a fair and equitable way will remove the blind panic this situation can induce. Also don't forget you will need to make new wills. See page 203 for organizations that can help with a range of problems arising as a result of marital discord and broken or complex family arrangements.

A New Life Together

You've made that momentous decision to get married and set up home together, and making it work from the very beginning will involve give and take, as well as respect for the other person. But as you each get caught up in busy lives, rushing around and getting things done, it's all too easy to forget about stopping and thinking about the relationship. It is so easy to take a partner for granted, and then find that the relationship has been damaged. Cherishing those around us, listening to a partner's memories or saying, 'I love you…' are simple things we can all do, and maybe then we would enjoy our relationships more.

Exercise: Sorting out Premarital Specifics
At the stage in a relationship when you have decided to get married and are wearing rose-tinted spectacles, it is easy to gloss over possible sources of difficulty in the distant future, but it is as well to think about them as early as possible, before they become a source of dissent. You may think that this is very unromantic, or even a potential source of embarassment, but it never hurts to sort out an agreement about the details of an arrangement. It is common to have a loose understanding of what the other person wants, but to sit down and talk about the specifics and write them down is a useful approach. An agreement like this is valid even if you are getting married after having lived together for a while. It is amazing how the act of marriage changes people's assumptions about a relationship, which, if not voiced, can lead to misunderstandings. Here are some of the things you could cover:

1 Money – who pays for what, how finances are to be organized (joint, separate or household bank accounts?).

2 Work – who has what work ambitions and how much time you might actually be able to spend together.

3 Kids – who will look after them if you have them, how many you want (or if you want them at all), when you want them. (It is even a good idea to discover each other's attitude to child-rearing and issues like how you would handle a child with physical or mental challenges.)

4 Social life – how much or how little you both enjoy going out, how you feel about time out with others (such as the regular Saturday football match or visiting in-laws).

5 Cooking and cleaning – who does what and how (you may want to hire a cleaner but your partner may think it an extravagance).

6 Minor details – not so much leaving the lid off the toothpaste or the loo lid up, but any niggles you both need to air (nagging, interfering in-laws, etc).

7 Agree between yourselves to take time out to monitor the health of your relationship on a regular basis. Get into the habit of each of you saying what is on your mind and listen to each other.

Q: *We don't want to get married, though there is lots of pressure to do so from our parents.*
A: Very few people bat an eyelid these days about couples living together instead of marrying, or having children out of wedlock, but you may have parents who will disapprove. Explain your position to them calmly. You may not be able to win them round but do your best not to get impatient or cross – being of a different generation, they may see things differently. If you keep the channels of communication open, it is better for all concerned.

Q: *I am marrying someone from a different background to mine and both our families are unhappy about this. What can we do?*
A: Social and racial barriers are breaking down on all fronts, and we have become a real melting pot of cultures, ideas and influences. Nevertheless, interracial, cross-faith and cross-cultural relationships can create particular challenges. Crossing social classes can also present hurdles.
  • When you begin to think about long-term commitment, make sure that you both fully understand what you are entering into.

- Talk to others who have converted to your partner's faith, or not (depending on what you are planning).
- Be as open as you can with family and friends. They may have genuine concerns, or even hidden prejudices, that could take you by surprise and will need talking through.
- As time progresses some practical issues, such as different dietary requirements and dress and behaviour codes, may become more important, particularly if one partner becomes more embedded in their religion as the marriage progresses.
- Family gatherings may need special handling. Even if you are both content and at ease, members of extended families may not be welcoming. If you demonstrate that your relationship is an easy one and if you stand firm in your love and respect for each other, the family members are most likely to be won round. (Remember that you can't please all the people all the time.)
- Religious holidays can highlight some of the differences. One way to deal with this is to celebrate those of all relevant faiths and enjoy the diversity.

The solution to all of these is good communication. Build a firm foundation of respect and understanding through mutual consent to bridge any differences which have been inculcated since childhood. *Vive la différence!*

Keeping a Relationship Fresh

- Passion may have mellowed, but romance can be kept alive with just a little input. As music is the food of love, make a point of going to concerts (or operas or musicals) together. If this is not possible, spend the occasional evening together without the TV but with music you both enjoy and with the lights restfully dimmed while you just sit and chat.

- The seven-year itch is not uncommon (though it could be three or ten years, or any other duration for that matter). The solution to this is to retain some romance in the relationship. Take time out for each other, do nice things for one another, court each other, take surprise romantic weekend breaks together and listen to, respect and appreciate one another.

- Second marriages often break down because one person is not really over their first marriage or because of resentments that are still in place regarding the first marriage. Make sure you come to terms with the fact that your first marriage is over and that you have moved on.

- Working different shifts from your partner can easily lead to feelings of isolation, and it increases the likelihood of a split. Couples who cope well with this will make sure that the time they spend together is highly focused on their relationship, otherwise they will just drift apart, having different interests and social circles.

Keeping Money and Emotions Apart

It is as well to be aware that money plays a large part in relationships, particularly for cohabiting couples. Keep it separate from emotional issues and treat it simply as a form of currency. If you remain both impartial and open about money, it will help keep issues of conflict separate, which then improves your chances of having productive discussions.

Q: *We are about to start living together but have different attitudes towards money. What are the likely flashpoints?*
A: Money is one of the major causes of stress in relationships. We live in a materialistic world in which, it seems, people are valued according to how much they have. This idea affects personal relationships, and money, with its ability to provide us with the 'right' house or look, has become bound up with issues of trust, self-esteem and pride. People also find it hard to discuss money, which only serves to add to its importance as a complex emotional issue rather than merely being currency. Work out your financial arrangements before entering into a new phase of a relationship such as living together, marrying or setting up a business. Come to an agreement that ensures that bills and other costs will be shared fairly. This also goes for flat-shares with people you don't know well. Don't let previous assumptions about friendship or romance get in the way of a sensible discussion about money. If the other person is reluctant, or unwilling, to discuss these issues, treat this as an early-warning sign of potential problems. If you stand accused of being unromantic or untrusting, be aware that this is an inappropriately emotional response to a practical concern.

Q: *I am giving up work to bring up our children but I hate going cap in hand to my partner for money – it's probably because I feel it is his money.*
A: When one partner gives up work, leaving the other as the sole breadwinner, it can change the relationship. Unfortunately, money is often used as a source of power within relationships, and this causes a huge amount of dissent. Ask yourself whether by giving up your financial independence you are going to get into conflict over spending. Sit down and establish in advance what the issues are going to be – for instance, who pays the bills, who decides what the money needs to be spent on, how the money is to be divided, and so on. This can be a difficult process but may prevent arguments later on. Remember that even those in long-term relationships can be taken by surprise when the 'balance of power' shifts.

Q: *Should we join our finances together or keep them separate?*
A: Deciding whether you are going to have a joint bank account is a major decision when you set up home together. There is no right or wrong about this, it just depends on what you both feel most comfortable with. You may prefer one account for all activities, or you may prefer to each have your own account and any 'housekeeping' money to be transferred from one to the other. Another option is a joint account for household spending and separate accounts to retain autonomy for individual needs.

Common Money Problems in Relationships

- Not having enough money is, of course, a source of stress in relationships. If unemployment hits or if you are on a low income, this can be very distressing. Resolve to tackle it together as a unit rather than letting one person shoulder the whole responsibility. Avoid pointing the finger of blame for the lack of money and take steps to find solutions together.

- If your partner is prone to sudden spending sprees on extravagant items, then you need to establish parameters. Agree a set of rules concerning impetuous buys, such as consulting each other before buying anything over, say, £250. This strategy will help to minimize nasty surprises on the bank statement.

- Be absolutely open and clear when lending or borrowing money. Always treat these transactions as a business arrangement with a known repayment schedule, and put it in writing.

- Make a will. The number of people who die intestate is alarming. If you have children it is particularly vital to make a will to arrange guardianship. Remember that you will need to alter it following any change of circumstances, such as marriage, divorce or new children or step-children.

- Honesty is nearly always the best policy. Avoid hiding your spending or sneaking home with items that you know your partner won't approve of. It may feel like a harmless white lie, but it will put you on the slippery slope to dishonesty in the relationship.

Q: *I think my partner spoils the kids by buying them everything they want, and I don't agree with it.*
A: Teaching children about money is important. One day they will have to manage their own finances and earn their own money. If your partner spoils them with gifts all the time, try to come to an agreement so that you can present a united front. Discuss such issues as pocket money, gift buying, earning money from odd-jobs and saving money. Once you agree as a couple, you can then instil your values in your children. Children as young as five years are capable of understanding about putting a regular sum into a piggy bank.

Q: *We bicker a lot about big expenditure, such as a new car and holidays and always end up in a sulk. How can we avoid this?*
A: Who is in charge of choosing things in your household? Often one person will go to great lengths to do research on a particular item and go through the process of learning about and choosing something. The next thing that happens is that the partner comes along and criticizes the choice because they have not been through

the same process themselves. There may be accusations of extravagance, bad taste or even whether there was any need to buy the item at all, which can lead to a row. If this tends to happen to you, agree to discuss things at each stage, though this will mean poring over technical brochures or sales literature, and investing time in visiting showrooms. Alternatively, make one person in sole charge and then be prepared to accept their decision.

Celebration Times

When families are thrown together, ostensibly for joyous occasions, tensions and family dynamics can actually lead to quite a bit of stress. Suicides and divorce rates are known to rise at Christmas more than at any other time of year. Among the many reasons for this is the fact that families are no longer used to being in close proximity to each other and haven't acquired the skills to deal with the resentments and squabbles that are part of everyday life. Christmas, like many other celebrations, is also a time when we are supposed to be happy, an expectation that we may feel we cannot meet, which amplifies any feelings of depression. Yet another cause is the fact that Christmas is a time of financial stress.

Q: *My sister-in-law spends every Christmas with us, but she never lifts a finger, and I get more and more annoyed. I try not to let it show but it always spoils my Christmas.*
A: If you are the one who ends up doing all the catering at family gatherings and you feel resentful about it, you can change this. Let everyone know, beforehand, what their responsibilities will be. They could be asked to bring a pre-cooked dish, to wash up, do the shopping or clear away at certain times. And once they have started helping, they will probably become more aware of other jobs that need to be done and feel less awkward about offering help. This arrangement will be far better for everyone, because when you feel put-upon it does become noticeable, no matter how much you try to hide it, and that's no fun for anyone.

Q: *Whenever I am with my partner's family, especially when we get together at Christmas time, his mother starts organizing everything and telling me what to do, even in my own home.*
A: At family gatherings such as Christmas, birthdays and weddings, everyone usually has an opinion about how things should be run. Ideally, decide in advance who will be the 'queen bee' and who will be the 'worker bees' – this can be on a rota basis if you wish. However, it could just be that your partner's mother feels that you are not on top of things, so if you got more organized ahead of time, she might be content to remain in the background. If you know that she has a problem, however, it might be advisable to pre-empt a worsening of relations by helping her to express her feelings before the get-together.

Painless Present-Buying

Buying presents for someone should be a joy as you think about what that person would really like to receive. Ideally it is a time when you show thoughtfulness and understanding of the recipient. But in reality we trawl around shops with a blank mind, wondering what on earth we can buy, and end up buying in desperation something that costs more than we can afford. Here are some tips for pain-free present-buying:

- Keep a list in your diary or a notebook with the names of your nearest and dearest. If they happen to mention something they need or you have a brainwave or see something ideal in the shops, make a note next to their name. Then when birthdays or other celebration times come round, you have a ready-made list.

- Keep a drawer or cupboard of gifts. When you see something particularly nice or of good value, buy it and keep it in your stockpile. On birthdays and other occasions you can look through for something that person might like.

- If you have children, you will probably spend many weekends ferrying them to birthday parties, and because their friends are usually within the same age group, they tend to like more or less the same things. Buy presents for these, within your budget, in bulk and you won't have any last-minute panics.

- Christmas can be extraordinarily expensive, and yet most people can remember receiving only very few gifts that they really wanted. Therefore, why not draw up a present-exclusion-zone agreement? Buy presents just for children and ask everyone to bring only things that you can all enjoy together over the holiday period, such as a game, some chocolates, wine or a cake. This will save everyone a fortune and a considerable amount of present-buying stress, and you can focus on seasonal fun instead of sheer consumerism. Alternatively, make sure everyone has a stocking or pillowcase and put an upper limit of, say, £5 on gifts, which are then all thrown into the appropriate stocking for a light-hearted, not too serious present-opening time.

Friendship

You can have a bulging phone book, but how many really good friends do you have – ones you can truly rely on? Friends provide our social support system, and when you have good friends they can be an important part of balancing out the stresses in your life. If you invest too much importance in your social life, however, you could set yourself up for disappointment. Concentrate on quality rather than quantity.

Q: *My closest friend is asking more of me than I am willing to give at the moment. She has been going through a difficult time but I don't think she realizes that I have a life as well.*

A: With friends and with lovers, as in any other area of life, you usually need to strike a balance between give and take. Sometimes you may find yourself giving a little more and sometimes you are the taker. This is fine until it becomes unbalanced and you find yourself always giving or always taking, particular as the 'taker' in a relationship can get into the habit of taking and forget to do their share of giving. The major source of resentment in friendships is the feeling that you are doing all the giving – even if the other person does not see the relationship this way. You need to be careful to distinguish between real giving, and giving in the hope that you will be given to. Use your judgement to examine this negative feeling: it may be that you are giving too much instead of communicating your needs to your friend.

Q: *I feel like just turning heel and telling my friend to get lost but our friendship goes back a long way, so it would be a shame.*
A: Don't run away from the challenge of resolving conflicts with friends, as it will only deplete your vital energy and become a burden for you to carry around. Take a deep breath and work out how to build a bridge.

Staying in Touch

Show your appreciation of others. It is all too easy to take our nearest and dearest for granted, but small kindnesses will be repaid a hundredfold.

- Remember to say thank you, and to tell people how you appreciate them. Do small, nice things for people, especially those you are close to. Buy some flowers, leave a note saying that you miss them, run an errand for them, book tickets to a concert, or take them breakfast in bed.

- Keeping in touch is actually more difficult in today's busy world. You would think that with so many means of communication – mobile phones, e-mails, planes – that it would get easier, but it does not seem that way. Keep a stack of beautiful postcards so that you can quickly jot a friendly note on one and pop it in the post. It is so nice to receive something that is not a bill and that lets your friends know you are thinking of them – and it only takes a minute.

- Set aside 15 minutes to call friends and family. Concentrate on them during this time and free your mind of other tasks.

Q: *I don't feel that my friend and I have the same interests any more, and though I am still very fond of him I'm not sure I want to include him in my life so much.*
A: People change and this can test a friendship. You may think that everything is just so, and then your friend goes and finds religion, dates someone you don't especially like or gets a high-powered job which allows them less time for the friendship. Do you

ditch the friendship or do you move with it and still manage to appreciate each other with all the changes that have gone on? By embracing changes in relationships instead of resisting them, the friendships will generally become richer, more anchored and longer-lasting.

Q: *I expected my friend to pull her weight during a difficult time in my life but was disappointed, even though I helped her out previously.*
A: The real test of a friendship can be in extreme situations, for example when one of you is in trouble or has a problem. It's important not to expect too much of your friend. They will give what they are able, and if you expect too much you could be disappointed. On the other hand, don't be afraid to ask, as long as they are allowed to say no without recrimination. Avoid thinking, 'She owes me a favour'.

Q: *My social life is busy but not particularly rewarding.*
A: Your address book may be cluttered with 'friends' or acquaintances with whom you have little in common but whose friendship you keep hanging on to because you can't work out how to get out of it – and so you carry on sending those Christmas cards to each other year in and year out. Sometimes, however, you have to accept that the friendship has, in fact, petered out. You may need to de-clutter your address book, as you would your house or desk. Letting go of some 'friendships' will give you more time and energy to focus on people you really appreciate and enjoy. Be bold and rewrite your address book.

Generosity in Relationships

Despite the fact that it seems as if we live in a 'me' society based on consumerism and greed, there is a gratifying amount of fair-mindedness, and surprising numbers of people are willing to help others. Kindness and generosity spread good feelings around, helping to cancel out the negativity and stress of modern living.

We have different capacities to love and to receive love throughout our lives. A loving relationship is ideally one of give and take, but the balance might vary from one time to another because each person feels stronger at different times. Understanding this can reduce the amount of unhelpful conflict and unhappiness in a relationship.

Q: *We are not a very demonstrative family and the affection we all feel for each other tends to be unspoken.*
A: Remember to regularly tell those who are close to you that you love them, or if this is not easy for you, at least let them know you care. Your children will feel secure, your partner will reflect it, your friends will be warmed, your grandparents will feel appreciated and your parents will think it was all worth it after all! Nurture your love for another person by doing small and thoughtful things for them. Relationships are nourished with loving thoughts, nice little surprises and caring actions.

Q: *If I don't 'perform' in the way my family want me to, they turn their backs on me and give me the silent treatment. Because it makes me feel bad, I end up doing what they want even if my heart isn't in it.*

A: Many people give only conditional love, which is in effect saying, 'If you behave in a particular way, or give me something I want, then I will love you'. This is a travesty of love and is the height of manipulation. Above all, it is a form of emotional blackmail that damages the self-esteem of the person on the receiving end. If you are subjected to this by another person, you need to work out what you really want and learn to find your satisfaction from within yourself.

Q: *My friend has asked for a contribution to a project but he still hasn't paid back some money I lent him previously.*

A: Be cautious when lending money. It's best not to lend it unless you are prepared not to get it back again. Indeed, giving someone money is better than lending it, and then just hope that the boomerang effect (see below) will happen. If you do lend money, draw up a repayment-and-interest agreement so there are no misunderstandings later. (If your friend objects to this, you probably ought to consider just how good a friend they are and if you are really likely to see the money again. You have a right to be businesslike about your money, and emotional issues need not cloud the transaction.) Many a friendship is lost over money.

Q: *I have a friend who is always trying to drag me into his charity activities and I am avoiding him to get out of it.*

A: While the ability to give is to be admired, some people become professional givers and do so with the expectation that it somehow puts them in a position of power. They start organizing all around them, dragging people in (willing or not), bulldozing people's needs to fulfil their own and generally behaving as if their view is the only one to take on. You have the right to say 'no' even if it isn't easy.

The Art of Giving... and Receiving

Giving can involve many things – a helping hand, a kind word, time, expertise, money. What can you give, and to whom? There is a time to give and a time to receive. You may be feeling stressed at the moment and not able to give anything, which may make you feel bad, but eventually you will be able to give of yourself.

- When you give to others, make sure you do not expect anything in return. In the first place, it taints the act of giving. Also, if you expect something back, you might well be disappointed. And finally, if you don't expect anything, you will be pleasantly surprised.

- The boomerang effect of generosity is obvious to all who have experienced it. When you give (in the right spirit), you definitely receive – though it may not be in any way that you were expecting. It is quite surprising how opportunities open up, friendships are made, and emotional and financial riches are bestowed on those who give without looking for any return.

- If you are asked to give (of yourself, money, time, love), always take time to consider whether you are really willing to do so. When you give, you must give without any feeling of resentment.

- The problems of the world are too great for anyone to tackle on their own. Start in your own community. We can all make a difference – *you* can make a difference.

- Don't give from a sense of guilt ('I ought to', 'I should', 'It is expected of me') as this will only wear you down. Sort out your feelings of guilt first (see page 69).

- You may find it difficult to receive other people's generosity, whether in the form of compliments or of gifts. Instead of stammering that you are unworthy or that they are too generous, just thank them and enjoy it.

- Don't assume that a gift is covering up or assuaging guilt (say, a bunch of flowers when your partner is back late from the office). This suspicion will taint the relationship, giving off the subliminal message that you are untrusting. Even if it *is* motivated by guilt, sending out a message of undiluted appreciation will strengthen the relationship instead of weakening it.

- People may not always be willing to ask for help. Without imposing on them your belief about what they need, you might want to ask if they could do with some help. If you suggest something specific, they will probably find it easier to accept than a vague offer of help in general. For example, an elderly neighbour might welcome your picking up a little bit of shopping for them when you go to the supermarket, a friend might be grateful for a few hours of childminding or a colleague might find your professional experience useful.

Relationships at Work

Office relationships often are obscured by the duality of the situation. On one hand it is a professional relationship steeped in the necessities of working in the same place. On the other hand the amount of time spent with colleagues can sometimes be more than the time spent with friends or family, which means that familiarity and friendships develop. These different elements can be difficult to reconcile. While it is possible to be good friends with colleagues, this type of relationship needs to be distinguished from 'friendships' that are really just extensions of being thrown together by the work environment.

Q: *I've been told that I'm too pushy at work. Should I try to temper it? I'm hoping for a promotion.*

A: It's important to be confident in your requirements, particularly if you are up against a 'glass ceiling', an attitude of 'jobs for the boys/girls', a 'closed shop' or any other form of protectionism. However, you need to gauge the situation and determine whether you really are being a bit pushy – are you behaving differently at work to the way you would normally behave in everyday life? Notice what influence your behaviour has on your colleagues and environment. Is it just one colleague who thinks you are pushy, or could it be the general perception of you? Perhaps others feel threatened by your confidence.

Q: *My boss found that I wasn't happy about something because I confided in a colleague and they spilled the beans. My boss was not pleased.*
A: Don't complain to colleagues. If you have a grievance, deal with it in a professional way and take it to whoever will realistically be able to deal with it. Even if it doesn't actually improve the situation, at least taking positive action will make you feel you have done something positive about the situation.

Q: *The politics at work are getting to me. I try to ignore the situation, but there are a couple of people who seem to have an axe to grind and are always trying to line people up on either side of the divide they have created. How can I stay impartial?*
A: Whenever two or more people work together, there is the potential for office politics. Research shows that one of the major causes of stress is unhappiness at work, and this is often the result of office politics. Objectively, office politics are completely unnecessary, but they are frequently an integral feature of working life, involving gossip, petty resentments, favouritism and anxiety about promotions. The safest approach is to stay well out of it and avoid expressing an opinion, even if you sympathize with one side more than the other. Otherwise, you could be dragged down into the mire.

Q: *I feel that the office gossip gets out of hand sometimes but it is difficult to stay out of it without being marginalized.*
A: Don't gossip – ever. If you don't get drawn into chatting about other people, then you also can't get drawn into the office politics game. While exchanging information on work-related matters might be valid, gossip often involves individuals and is often damaging to that person. If colleagues who have less self-control get irritated by your lack of involvement in the office-politics game, don't give them the opportunity to believe that you are aloof. Stay friendly, open and honest – but still don't gossip.

Q: *My boss has just used my work as if it were his own. I am outraged but don't know what to do.*
A: If your boss is claiming success based on your work, this could be a major source of work-based stress for you. To a degree your boss has the right to do this because you are a part of the team. But if credit is never being given where it is due, you need to do

something about this or suffer the consequences in your self-esteem. Work out what your choices and options are and then make an action plan. If your boss is a bully, this might mean planning to leave.

Rules of Engagement for a Happy Office

- Take responsibility for all your actions. That way, when you refuse to accept responsibility for the failings of others they can't be irritated. If there is collective responsibility for team activities, you have to take your share of reward and blame – you can't pick and choose.

- Discrimination of any sort is never acceptable. Deal with it, but retain a sense of humour and fair play, or you lose out as well.

- Remain true to yourself. If you are honest, focused and kind to other people, you can set an example and lead from a position of strength without getting dragged down into the petty details of others' concerns.

- Nurture a more communal, caring environment in your office by focusing on constructive group activities, such as supporting a charity or setting up a book club. Communal activities can prevent the seeds of discontent from taking root.

Children

We have an idealized picture of childhood as being full of laughter and learning, but, sadly, anxieties, emotional problems and even depression often afflict children. In part, this awareness has come because we are better at recognizing when a child has been emotionally disturbed, but living in a fast-paced society, with changing family structures, also takes its toll. Whatever the problem is, remember that, first and foremost, a lot of love and understanding will go a long way to helping resolve most problems. Instead of dictating to the child what the solution is or being tempted to say to them, 'Don't be so silly', listen to their viewpoint, their anxiety, their voice. So often children just want to express their fears and be listened to.

Q: *What are the signs of stress in children?*
A: If children are not able to express their anxieties, they may signal stress in other ways. If you notice a change in behaviour at school, a change in appetite, aggressive behaviour, sleep problems, temper tantrums, bedwetting, inhibitions or some other unusual change, suspect an unvoiced anxiety.

Q: *My five-year-old child is still wetting his bed – shouldn't he have grown out of it by now?*

A: Bedwetting is one of the most common childhood stress signals. By the age of five, 85–90 per cent of children are 'dry', but bedwetting (nocturnal enuresis) can be the sign of something that the child is not able to express. It is not uncommon for it to come on when a new baby arrives in the family and is a form of regression. Bedwetting can cause the child distress and undermine their self-confidence. Make sure that you communicate nothing but understanding and reassurance. If you are cross or impatient, this can further erode self-esteem. Around 70 per cent of older children with bedwetting problems manage to be dry within 16 weeks with the use of an alarm (though some will relapse). For more information see page 202.

Q: *My child has a habit of not paying attention. Could there be a problem?*
A: Children have different attention spans depending on their natures and age. Children who have hearing problems (sometimes as the result of glue ear), those who are dyslexic or dyspraxic, or children at the very mild end of the autistic spectrum are sometimes misunderstood and believed to be inattentive or lazy. This is always something to watch out for, because the child won't be able to tell you, and teachers or other carers may miss it. Being misunderstood in this way can be very frustrating and demoralizing for the child.

Q: *I think my child is being bullied – what can I do?*
A: Bullying is something that most children come across at some time or other. If your child is being bullied, they may be reluctant to talk about it, but do your best to persuade them to. Otherwise, it can easily destroy your child's self-esteem and undermine their enjoyment of school, clubs or the local playground. If you suspect bullying, speak to the school at once, or to the parents of the bullies if you know them, lodging your concern. You may find that the parents of the bullies, or even the school or club leaders, are in denial about any trouble. Bullying can take a physical form with, say, a bloodied nose, or a psychological form with teasing and stealing of personal belongings. Make sure that your child always knows that they will be supported if they come to you, and reassure them that the situation will be dealt with. If necessary, enrol your child in clubs farther from home so that they do not need to come into contact with the bullies. (Bear in mind, however, that bullies exist everywhere, and you don't want your child to feel that escape is the only answer.) Team up with other parents if there is a general problem of bullying (avoiding a vigilante approach, however). Teach your child about victim body language and consider enrolling them in a martial arts class to build confidence. For more information, see page 203.

Q: *Do children get over bereavement or someone moving out of their life much quicker than adults do?*
A: A child may be showing signs of stress because of marriage break-up or the death of a family member. In dealing with their own problems, adults may forget that their child needs all the support they can get. A child's view of the situation may be

completely different from the parent's, and children may not voluntarily speak about what is bothering them. It may be tempting to draw a veil over the situation and not discuss the 'loss', but this is usually unwise and it is best to keep talking gently. It can be easier for another close relative or friend to get close to a child than it is for the parent. Don't worry, or feel excluded, if this is the case – it is simply that a child often finds it easier to unburden worries to a different ear and voice, away from the family home. Do ask for help from 'significant others' (grandparents, uncles, godparents) in your child's life, as this could be a way forwards.

Q: *I don't understand why my child is going quiet on me and I can't seem to get much out of her.*
A: Children can lose confidence if, for instance, they feel that they are not doing well at school or that a teacher does not like them, but they might not think they have the option of telling their parent. Try 'actively listening' to your child. Instead of asking, 'What's wrong?' as you distractedly make the tea, sit down and say something like 'You seem upset'. The child may walk off, refuse to answer or deny it but after a while will begin to feel they can confide in you and that you are truly listening.

Q: *How can I motivate my child to get involved in activities other than TV and computer games?*
A: Hobbies are a great way of encouraging all sorts of skills in children. Even if the hobby is something with no obvious educational merit, such as collecting cartoon cards, it still instils certain qualities such as organization, responsibility for keeping things, and knowing a subject well, which can foster a sense of pride. A hobby can also encourage the ability to research and plan and to be self-disciplined and patient. Helping your child to find a hobby they enjoy, or to look after a pet, can be a terrific way of supporting them. However, it is their hobby not yours, so don't take over. Remember to guide rather than instruct, to avoid making fun of it, to show an interest (even if you find it boring) and to be ready with praise. You may, however, need to set a time limit on the activity to stop it impacting on homework and sleep.

Q: *Is smacking my child all right?*
A: Discipline is always a contentious issue. Some people believe that smacking is fine while others abhor it. Occasionally, any child can drive a parent to the edge of being tempted to smack, but ideally it should be resisted. The main reason for this is that it shows the child that physical intervention is an acceptable way to get a result. (However, in families that very rarely resort to smacking, the event is likely to be such a trauma for all concerned that the child won't see it as a useful strategy anyway.) It's better to be firm about ground rules and to use deprivation (of treats, TV, computers, money, visits to friends, going out) as a punishment. To diffuse situations before they get to 'smacking point', try using 'time out', in which the child has to leave the room and go to a designated, and dull, place for an agreed length of time – such as sitting on the stairs for a count of 20.

Q: *I'm worried because my child has started hitting out when he gets upset.*
A: It is an uncomfortable fact that a number of children become violent, even towards their parents. Common contributing factors are an absent father, learning difficulties and witnessing violence regularly in the home. It can occur in families of all social classes. Giving in to violent children perpetuates the cycle, so you'll need to set clear boundaries. Limit access to TV, computer and video games, to which the child may be addicted. Be assertive (say, 'What needs to happen is…' rather than 'You shouldn't do…'). Punishment often leads to further rebellion, so it is better to get the child to think about what they are doing and the effects of their actions. Love them, value them, talk to them, praise them – every small positive victory is an opportunity to build their self-esteem. For information about professional help, see page 203.

Teenagers

The teenage years can be quite a challenge as so many major issues come bubbling to the surface, compounded by physical and hormonal changes. The first thing that any parent needs to do when there is a teenager around is to recall what they felt like in their own teen years. Remember that teenagers are trying to make sense of a plethora of major issues, including new responsibilities, independence, exams, finding employment, the temptation of alcohol and drugs, and their sexuality.

Q: *What is the best way for me to deal with my stroppy teenager?*
A: As the parent of a teenager, you need to accept that your child is now a young adult and should be treated accordingly. Talk to them calmly, seeking their opinion rather than laying down the law in a heavy-handed manner (though you have the right to be firm). Offer a friendly ear to discuss issues that are concerning them. The most useful approach you can take is to help them to build their self-confidence. Remember to pile on the compliments whenever you notice something praiseworthy, no matter how small.

Common Teenage Problems

- Deal with areas of conflict such as noise levels in the house, household duties and curfew times during school terms in a constructive manner, though you may also have to be prepared to negotiate on some issues.

- A major source of stress for teenagers is looming exams. Keep a sense of perspective if your teenager is going through exams, and if their results are not what you had hoped for, remember that they may well feel worse than you do and they do not need to have their self-confidence further undermined by criticism. Exams can always be resat. Offer constructive and practical help, but avoid nagging, which can be a touchpaper for another row.

- Distressed adolescents can grow up into distressed adults, so take note if your teenager is expressing angst. Any parent of a teenager knows that mood swings go with the territory – but be aware that mood swings are not simply physiological and might indicate an urgent need to talk. Although teens often find it difficult to ask for help, especially from their parents, they still need to talk through problems. Be prepared for subjects that you don't feel comfortable with, such as experimentation with drugs, eating disorders or uncertainties about sexuality. Or their concerns may be more mundane (but still important to them), perhaps involving acne, exams or the course of true love.

- Racism can become an issue at this time. As an emerging adult, your teenager has more autonomy, has to start to make appropriate decisions about how to handle racism and might make the wrong choices, such as getting into fights. Educating your child not to get wound up is probably the only practical thing to do. By getting upset they only give validity to the tormentors and damage themselves. Teach them to consider racist acts as beneath contempt.

Q: *I am suspicious that my teenager is developing an eating disorder. What should I look for?*

A: Eating disorders need special handling. Often, the last person to suspect that a child or teenager is anorexic or bulimic is the parent. A major feature of eating disorders is that the person is extremely clever about concealing the problem. The need to be in control is an overwhelming feature of these conditions, and certainly control over what others see of the problem is a large part of it. It is not quite clear why there has been such a huge increase in those with eating disorders. Fashion, confused health messages and stress are routinely blamed and probably all have a part to play. But certainly one can add to this a self-esteem problem, and any parent needs to be aware that constantly criticizing their child, particularly about their appearance, will not help. It is common for those with eating disorders to have unrealistically high expectations of themselves – only recognizing total success or total failure, with nothing in between. Not every teenager who follows a food fad, turns vegetarian or goes on a diet will become anorexic or bulimic, but be aware of the possibility. Also be aware that boys can be affected as well as girls. With anorexia there will be weight loss, or lack of weight gain at a time of expected growth. This is easily hidden with baggy clothing for quite a long time. Bulimics are expert at disguising the amount of food they eat and the purging (usually through vomiting, but often through the use of laxatives). You cannot deal with the problem of eating disorders on your own but need to seek expert help. See Disordered Eating (page 167) and the information on page 204.

Q: *And what about alcohol, smoking and drugs?*

A: Learning how to handle alcohol is a hard lesson, and more than a few teenagers wind up voiding the results of their experimentation on their parents' carpet. The temptation to smoke will be overwhelming for many, and solvent abuse is widespread. What can a parent do in the face of these? Being available at all times to discuss the issues surrounding these problems, without preaching, is vital. Some parents choose to themselves introduce their teenagers to alcohol and 'soft' drugs, such as cannabis, in the hope that it will take away the 'naughty' factor and make taking the substances less attractive. Certainly if you do not wish your teenager to smoke or drink heavily, then you must set an example and not do so yourself. There is every chance that a teenager will come into contact with drugs at some time or other. Drug abuse, as distinct from experimentation, undoubtedly can lead to addiction, crime, prostitution and the spread of diseases if the circumstances are right. Again the parent needs to be aware of the issues, and to a degree pre-empt the situation by educating their child on the issues. Do not alienate them if it turns out that they have tried drugs, but always keep the channels of communication open. Be aware that money is often diverted into buying drugs. If you are supporting your child financially and find that they are doing this, you may have some tough choices to make about withdrawing financial support (in the knowledge that they may go elsewhere). For more about this, see Dealing with Addictions, page 183. Solvent abuse is very damaging, so seek professional help. (For further information, see page 203.)

Q: *I am nervous that my teenager is a bit flippant about contraception and that pregnancy will result.*

A: Potential pregnancy is not the only problem — there is also the matter of sexually transmitted diseases. You should be aiming to talk freely and frankly about these important issues with your child, or if this is difficult, find sources of information that they will accept, such as leaflets, books, information films or counsellors. A teenage pregnancy is something that most parents dread. Educate your son or daughter on their responsibilities regarding relationships, sex, the girl's right to say no, contraception and unplanned pregnancies. If you avoid the subject or put off talking about it, it could become increasingly awkward for your to discuss, and you and your teenager may have to pay the price. If your daughter finds she is pregnant, you have to hope that she will confide in you as early as possible. In order for this to happen you need to ensure that you can have easy and relaxed conversations about a range of topics. Avoid being judgemental or dictatorial, as this will only put distance between you. A strategy for dealing with the pregnancy depends on your family viewpoint and, of course, her wishes. Dealing with issues such as your daughter wanting to keep the baby and you thinking it beter not to, will require soul-searching and the ability to cope with the practicalities. It is essential to keep communicating and to offer every support throughout the process of deciding what to do, as well as afterwards. You may also have to support her by talking to other family members and friends and to the father of the baby plus his family and friends.

Finding a Mate

The primal urge to pair up drives young and old alike to play the dating game. While many people are content to be single, the acres of print and the hours of prime-time TV devoted to the issue of finding a mate, not to mention the astounding rise of the dating-agency business, attest to the fact that many singles are looking for soulmates. If you find that either being single or looking for a mate is stressful, read on.

Q: *What is the most important factor in finding a soulmate?*
A: To find a companion with whom you can develop a satisfying relationship, you need to be happy in your own company in the first place. If you are interested in life and are someone who explores and develops your interests, you will automatically be a more interesting person and more attractive to other people. If you are in an emotional void that you just want to fill with the presence of another person, the search can be fruitless. Potential partners will often back off in the face of such neediness. Happiness through the presence of another person is valid, but it is not the be-all and end-all.

Q: *Why am I so unlucky in love?*
A: If you think you have been unlucky in love so far, this is a big message. You have not been unlucky – you need to change your strategy. If you feel that you have a history of attracting the wrong sort of person, or if you change, chameleon-like, with each new mate who comes along, then you need to do at least one thing different in the future to improve your chances of finding Mr or Ms Right. Go to different places. Network with different people. Develop your interests. Change your criteria of what type of person you are seeking.

Exercise: Recognizing a Potential Mate

You may be unsure of what are the most important qualities you are looking for in a potential mate. Follow this exercise to improve your chances of realizing that someone is the right person for you.

1 Ask yourself what you are seeking. If it is romance and commitment, then you are on the lookout for a mate. If it is companionship and someone to share a social life or holidays, do you think that it's actually more good friends that you need, rather than a mate?

2 Make a list of the important qualities, such as intellect, humour, danger, fun, stability, looks, kindness, responsibility. Do you want to go out with drop-dead gorgeous types who might have a cavalier attitude to life? Or would you prefer the plainer 'frog' down the road who might be responsible, stable, kind, loyal and the ideal mate once kissed? We often idealize our desires but feel we have to compromise in reality.

3 Once you write down what are truly the most important qualities, you may find that your ideals are different to what you have been attracted to or thought you were seeking. Knowing your most important expectations will help you to spot the right person when they come along.

Q: *The dating game seems to have changed and I'm worried that I don't know how to play the game any more.*

A: In the past, people did not need to travel very far to meet a mate and would often marry someone from their own locality. Marriages might have been arranged by the family or a matchmaker, which in a way made the choice easier (the smaller the choice, the easier the decision). But the fluid structure of our society today means that in the face of overwhelming choice and opportunity, many people flounder and there are no set expectations or rules any more. For this reason honesty is always the best policy. If you know what your expectations are, communicate them to the other person so that you can both know if you have common criteria. Romance is often a question of timing. You might be ready to fall in love, but is the object of your dreams also ready? Or vice versa, of course. Because your romantic hopes have come to nothing so far, do not get despondent and let it damage your self-esteem. The chances are that it was just not the right moment or the right person. On to the next one!

Q: *I am nervous about dating again and not even sure whether I will ever find someone else.*

A: If you have broken up with someone, don't convince yourself that this was your one shot at happiness, and that the chances of finding another love are remote. There are millions of people on this planet and there is always going to be someone else out there for you. It often pays to have some time on your own between relationships so that you can have a rest emotionally. Seen in this light, time spent on your own can be viewed as a positive benefit. If you have been in a relationship for a while and now find yourself 'on the market', the prospect of dating can seem quite daunting. When you are on a roll in the dating game, you take these things in your stride, but if you are out of practice, just the thought of dating can be enough to make you feel wobbly. Understand that this is the case for everyone in your situation. Also, remind yourself how much fun it is to meet new people who like you and how good it can make you feel.

Q: *Where do I start with finding someone?*

A: Go at it slowly, expanding your horizons. Get a new haircut to make you feel attractive and sexy, go through your wardrobe for new combinations of outfits – and enjoy yourself. Dress for yourself, and not for other people. If you are pleased with yourself, others will be, too. Dating agencies, singles clubs, singles holidays and lonely-hearts columns can work. Stick to some simple rules, however. Always meet in public places and keep safety to the forefront of your mind. Don't give out your last name or your address until you are certain that you are in company you want to continue to keep. You may not meet the person of your dreams, but you could well make some friends – treat it as fun and don't get too serious about whether this method of meeting people is going to work or not. Be cautious about parting with huge fees to introduction agencies before speaking to some people who have used the service and are happy with it.

Overcoming Shyness

Shyness can severely restrict your social life, but there are ways to overcome it. Initially, you can work on the effects of shyness, and as this gives you more self-confidence, you will hopefully find that your actual shyness slowly dissipates, at least to the point where it no longer interferes with your life.

• Be who you are. You will be appreciated for this.

• When you meet people, maintain eye contact with them. Avoid looking down at your feet or over their shoulder at other people.

• If you know you are going into a social situation where you will need to make conversation, but you regularly get tongue-tied, do a little planning ahead of time. Think up five topics that you can use as conversation-openers or to oil the wheels when the conversation dries up a little bit. You could pick headlines from the papers, something that highlights your interests or something about the event you are attending.

• We tend to change our body language when we want to get on with someone. Apart from flirting in a potentially romantic situation, we also mirror other people's stance, actions and movements. 'Mirroring' is not sycophancy but a natural way of building rapport with other people, as is dressing to fit in and speaking at a volume that matches our surroundings. We are attracted to people who fit in with our social grouping. Watch two people who really get on and you will find that they adopt the same poses, walk at the same pace and even cross their legs at the same time when sitting. By being aware of this, you can use this to help build up a rapport. We pick up small clues from each other without even realizing it. By subtly mirroring and matching another person's movements (in an understated way or it will just be artificial and irritating), you can leave someone with the impression that you are a really nice, empathetic person – because you move and act just like they do!

• Ask people about themselves when you meet them. This means that you do not have to think of something to say. It also means that the emphasis is placed on them talking instead of you, and just about everyone enjoys speaking about themselves. At the end of the conversation they will be struck by what an interesting person you are.

- You may think that you are the only person who is shy and that everyone else is confident, but this is most definitely not the case. Almost everyone confesses to feeling shy inside. Even the most accomplished stage performers can be excruciatingly shy, but they have learned to suppress it when they take on another character. You can adopt a similar strategy – by concentrating on the subject you're discussing or the people you are talking to, you may be able to forget about yourself and your shyness.

Jealousy and Neediness

The 'green-eyed monster' of jealousy is a destructive force, yet many people succumb to it at some time or other. Perhaps jealousy is a natural urge to protect what is ours from rivals and to acquire what we think we need for survival. But as with many natural survival instincts, it can be distorted by modern living and lead to expressions of neediness that only serve to alienate possible sources of help and comfort. In any event, these emotions are guaranteed to be a waste of energy, to lower self-esteem further and possibly to destroy relationships.

Q: *I suspect that my partner is cheating on me, so I've been checking up on him surreptitiously. I haven't found any proof yet, but I can't help being suspicious.*
A: If you are jealous without good reason, it is your behaviour that needs to change and not the behaviour of the person who is the target of your jealousy. (Their behaviour is a different issue.) Jealousy and neediness have broken up many a relationship without real cause. It can take the form of a self-fulfilling prophecy: 'I feel insecure and so I don't trust you, therefore you must be guilty of something, therefore our relationship is rubbish, and if our relationship is rubbish why are we together at all?' Even a saint would leave in the face of this. If something is bothering you, talk about it instead of resorting to supposition and spying. No amount of justification can get away from the fact that creeping around like this is demeaning and smacks of low self-esteem. But if your partner is cheating, you almost definitely do not need to go to these lengths. If they believe they can get away with it, the chances are that they will get careless in their subterfuge eventually and you will know anyway, without putting yourself through this behaviour. Then you have the difficult decision of what you are going to do about it.

Exercise: Understanding your Jealousy
Understanding your feelings is the first step towards controlling them. Analyse why you are jealous and what you are jealous about, using the questions on page 112. There are no right or wrong answers, but asking yourself the questions can help to sort out your own feelings about the relationship.

1 Are you protecting what you believe is rightfully yours? (Remember, we don't own other people.)

2 Do you have particular moral standards which, if transgressed, mean a certain course of action?

3 If you really love yourself, do you need to seek the love of other people, even your partner, to the exclusion of others?

Q: *My partner says I am crowding him and he needs some space.*
A: Neediness is oppressive and is not a way of showing you care. 'Why are you home late from work?' 'Why don't you want to spend more time with me at the weekends?' 'Why don't we do more together?' – these are questions that will exhaust both you and your partner. Improving your self-esteem (see page 38) will help you to feel happier in your own company and able to do things without needing your partner always by your side. Being content to pursue your own interests and develop your own friendships will lead to a mature and fulfilled relationship. This may take courage initially, especially if you have been in a cycle of neediness, but is vital to achieving balance in life. If you put your partner on a pedestal, then no activity will be enjoyable without them. It can be a tremendous burden for that person and also means you will not feel as satisfied as you could in that relationship. Having your own interests means you will have more to talk about and a richer relationship. Work on other interests at a pace that allows you to expand your comfort zones. Instead of dragging your partner on a shopping trip, go shopping on your own and have a coffee on your own. Eventually you may be happy to join a theatre group or a gym on your own. If your partner wants to come with you, it is done voluntarily and not because it is 'expected'.

Q: *My partner seems to think that the odd fling is OK as long as it doesn't become serious, but I don't feel the same way.*
A: Much jealousy can be avoided if you manage, early in a relationship, to set the ground rules for future behaviour. Do you mind, in theory, if your partner has affairs? What would you do about it? Do you think you could work through it, or that it would mean instant separation? Establish your views early on so that you have a framework to operate within, even if the reality is that your feelings change when you find yourself in such a situation. You might think this is unromantic, like a prenuptial agreement, but by talking openly about it you reduce the potential for ambiguities. Another strategy is to agree with your partner to have an annual review of where you are emotionally in the relationship.

Q: *I find that I am jealous of my friend's successes and secretly pleased when things don't go well, but I don't feel right about it.*

A: No matter how good a friend may be, if they succeed where you might have stumbled in the past you may feel a fleeting emotion of jealousy. Acknowledging this is not shameful. However, try to see your friends as allies rather than rivals. You will be a richer person emotionally if you can enjoy your friends' successes and triumphs unconditionally. Use the following affirmation to promote this feeling: 'I enjoy So-and-So's wins as if they were my own and support them unconditionally in their achievements. I can learn from So-and-So's successes.' Repeat this often (see Creative Visualization, page 142). If your jealousy is focused on other people having what you feel you do not, that is a train of thought that creates only negative feelings and leads to unhappiness, so it is best to forget it. Realistically, there is always going to be someone richer, thinner, cleverer than you. The most important competition is with yourself. You can't always be first or best, so aim to better your own score each time and you will always be ahead of the game. Life is truly not a competition. Enjoy other people's successes, be proud of your own and don't feel that others have set the pace and you need to keep up. Find your own level.

Achy-Breaky Heart

A broken heart may have no credence in medical circles, but most people will at some time or other use the expression to define how they are feeling. A broken heart is a kind of shorthand for a host of stressful feelings, including hurt, severing of a relationship (even if contact is still maintained), great disappointment and an emotional vacuum. Although a broken heart is most commonly associated with a broken romance, your heart could just as easily be broken by a parent or step-parent who leaves the home, a friend who betrays the friendship or any other significant person.

- There is a degree to which the afflicted person's self-esteem is bound up with the 'offending' person. The term 'broken heart' also implies a sense that there is unfinished business and maybe a hope that love can be rekindled. This makes it hard to draw a line under the relationship but that is precisely what has to happen.

- Often the end of a relationship just leaves a vacuum of activity that needs to be filled. You might be reminded of the person all the time and feel that this is yet more evidence of your broken heart. However, it might be that you simply don't know how to keep yourself occupied. Concentrate on other activities – you need to focus on getting busy again.

- The most important long-term resolution for a broken heart is to deal with your self-esteem and to work out why your self-worth is bound up with this other person and why rejection cuts so deep. This is no quick-fix solution but it is a more lasting one (see Boosting Self-Esteem, page 38).

- The most straightforward resolution for a broken heart is another relationship (but this is a bit of a cop-out as it doesn't address the underlying issues). Time does heal and there truly are plenty more 'fish in the sea' (see Finding a Mate, page 108). And the quicker you let go of your old attachment, the sooner you will find someone else in your life.

• Avoid bitterness resulting from a broken heart – it will only eat you up. Bitterness is like an uncontrollable emotional cancer. Feel sorrow or even anger for a while, but then determine to move on.

• Mending a broken heart is something most of us have to do at some time or other. Time is, indeed, a great healer, as is falling in love again. Until one of these two takes effect, you could experiment with some alternative therapies. At the top of the list are always the calming practices of yoga, t'ai chi and meditation. Herbalists recommend hawthorn to open up the heart, lemon balm for its calming influence and St John's wort to head off mild to moderate depression.

Divorce without Tears

Roughly half of all marriages end in divorce – it is a social epidemic of our times. Given this high statistical probability (though the positive slant is that half of all marriages last), what can you do to increase the likelihood of any divorce being 'happy'? The time leading up to the decision to divorce is often the most difficult. Lack of confidence, worries about what might happen afterwards and bitter arguments can stretch out the misery for ages. It is often during this time that the real damage is done because then the actual process of divorce can become a way for one or both partners to seek revenge. Once the decision has been arrived at, it can, quite simply, come as a relief.

Q: *We find it hard to have calm, non-emotional conversations and they usually disintegrate into rows.*
A: Before the relationship disintegrates, it might be helpful to seek couple or family counselling (see page 203). These counsellors are adept at helping partners to find the nub of the problem and to guide them to the other end of the tunnel unscathed. If alcohol or drugs are contributing to the break-up, seek out one of the relevant help organizations (see page 204). Money and custody arrangements are the biggest bones of contention in any divorce – it is worth seriously working at reaching an agreement because otherwise it is the lawyers who will benefit.

Q: *I feel totally distraught by the divorce and can't seem to snap out of it and get on with life.*
A: It takes time to get over a divorce – it can often be experienced in the same way as a bereavement. Allow yourself time to come to terms with the change. Do your best to avoid such destructive emotions as guilt, hate, bitterness, jealousy and blame. You may need to deal with depression (see page 62).

Q: *So how can I move forwards?*

A: Don't spend time worrying about what your ex is getting up to. Work on the need to move on. Introduce some joy into your life on a daily basis, no matter how small or tentative. Re-establish your sense of identity outside the marriage. Plan and set goals (see page 8) to avoid wallowing in the past. Forget what might have been and concentrate on what can be. There are a lot of practical issues you may have to deal with in the aftermath of a divorce which can take time to work through – many of them are covered in this book, including money management (see page 80) and loneliness (see page 65). You may also be facing being a single parent or dealing with being a remote parent. Stay hopeful for the future and learn from what went wrong in your previous relationship. Make lists of the lessons you've learned and what they mean to you.

Q: *The problem is that I am still attracted to my ex.*

A: A surprising number of couples who divorce end up getting back together again. The divorce may have been too hasty, they may have realized that the grass isn't actually greener or they may have found that it is easier to fall back into old patterns with someone who is used to them. It is also fairly common for divorcing partners to continue to sleep together through the divorce proceedings as they yo-yo between emotions and uncertainties. If you find yourself in any of these situations, make sure that you both consider the messages your children are receiving and that their needs are taken into account – you don't want to disappoint them.

Children and Divorce

Helping your children through a divorce is essential, and it is ideal if you and your ex can present a united front on at least this score. It may be difficult if the years leading up to the divorce have been turbulent, but it is well worth agreeing on a joint strategy for dealing with the children.

- Ideally, you both need to stay involved in your children's lives. Setting up a rota of care and participation in activities helps. If you can attend events such as school plays, concerts or parent-teacher meetings as a couple, your children will be much happier.

- Make sure that both you and your ex stick to the same rules about the children's routine, discipline and treats.

- Children will often feel confused, insecure and angry. Even if they feel relief that Mummy and Daddy are no longer arguing on a daily basis, it is still a time of huge change – one parent may move out and not see them as frequently or it may involve a change of home for them. Keep as many things as you can comforting and familiar. Children respond well to routine, so aim to keep these the same as far as you possibly can.

- However tempted you might feel, do not criticize or complain about your ex-partner to the children.

- If you have managed to keep the turmoil preceding the separation to a minimum and your children are not aware of the discord, it may come as a huge shock to them that the family is splitting up. You will both need to explain the situation to them as openly as possible, avoiding recrimination if at all possible and being patient about answering their questions.

- Children may not verbalize their confusion and frustration, reacting in other ways instead. They might become withdrawn or, at the other end of the scale, disruptive. See this for what it is, and give them every ounce of love you can. If they are, for instance, confused that they are not seeing the other parent for a while, but are not saying so, you could suggest to them that they telephone your ex-partner.

- Children often blame themselves for their parents' break-up: 'If I had been good this would not have happened' is a common reaction. If they find it hard to speak to you about such feelings, try to arrange for them to talk to a relative or family friend they feel comfortable speaking to.

- Let the school know what is going on so they can be supportive and watch out for changes in behaviour.

- Just because the parents are getting divorced doesn't mean that the children are divorcing half their family. Do everything you can to make sure they stay in contact with grandparents, cousins, aunts and uncles.

- Never involve the children in an emotional tug-of-war by asking them to take sides – you will live to regret it.

Low Libido

If the statistics are to be believed, we think about sex almost all of the time. Whether this is true or not, if you believe that your sex life is less than ideal you could well be building up feelings of anxiety about it. The contemporary obsession with sex, particularly in the media, can make it seem as if everybody is enjoying sex except you. Up to 40 per cent of women and 10–30 per cent of men are thought to have problems with loss of libido at some time or other. Obstacles to a satisfying love life can be many, including physical, psychological and social factors. It is important to understand that some people are less interested in sex than others. Knowing this can make you more relaxed about the subject and help stop you from putting pressure on yourself to 'perform'. There can be great differences in the sexual needs of the partners making up a couple, and this is best addressed by seeking psychosexual counselling. For help organizations and psychosexual counselling, see page 203.

Exercise: Find the Reasons for Low Libido

Some of the more obvious possible reasons for a low libido include the following:

1 Stress and low energy levels are often the root causes. If you have too much to do and are exhausted, it is not surprising if you are uninterested in sex. Decrease your commitments and make time for relaxation in your relationship.

2 Too much alcohol and some recreational drugs interfere with sexual desire. A period of time off the booze might make a huge difference. If this is difficult to achieve, you may have early problems with alcohol dependency.

3 Relationship problems can be at the root of libido loss. If you are always rowing, then you may not feel like having sex later. (Although some relationships resolve conflict with sex, this is not a long-term solution.) It is also common for withdrawal of sex to be used as a 'punishment' for relationship misdemeanours. You may need to seek relationship counselling (see page 203).

4 Menopause is a common cause of loss of libido as it can cause vaginal dryness and sometimes depression.

5 One of the recognized symptoms of depression is a loss of interest in sex. Although prescription antidepressants may help resolve the depression, they, in turn, can have a devastating effect on libido and sexual function.

6 Some types of contraceptive pill drain libido.

Increasing Sexual Desire

• Pay attention to your body's messages and you might find that there are times when you feel more like having sex. Note if there is a pattern to these times – for instance, a woman is most likely to be aroused around the time of ovulation.

• If we all treated each other as gods and goddesses in bed, we might feel sexier more of the time. You don't have to learn tantric sex: simply bringing some romance back into your lives can raise sexual interest. If you have children, get them to bed early so you and your partner can have a candlelit bath together. Even turning off the TV and eating a delicious meal by candlelight can create the right mood for sex.

• A successful technique for restoring sexual interest is for the couple to concentrate on touch and massage instead of penetrative sex. This takes away a lot of the 'pressure' of sex, helps to rebuild sexual drive and improves confidence and body image. You need, as a couple, to set aside time for this and initially concentrate on simple stroking and massage while avoiding the genital areas. You may start off with massaging the neck and upper torso only. This goes on for several sessions. With mutual consent (always important) you slowly build up the variety and type of touch, and the areas of touch. Eventually, if you both wish to, you can get to penetrative sex, though this is not essential.

- Sensuous exercise such as yoga, t'ai-chi, gymnastics or ballet can put you back in touch with your body, improve self-image and stimulate sexual feelings.

- Moderate exercise is linked to improved sex drive – if you increase your exercise out of bed, you will feel more like exercise in bed. Intense exercise is even more likely to have this effect, possibly by improving blood flow around the body.

- Diet is known to play a major role in hormonal balance, for example in menopausal symptoms, so there is every reason to suspect it is also important for libido. Of particular importance are phytoestrogens (found in foods such as soya, wholegrains, chickpeas and lentils), zinc (found in lean meat, nuts and seeds) and B-vitamins (found in wholegrains, liver and green leafy vegetables).

- Stress is a major inhibitor of sexual feelings. Also, when we are stressed it is common to crave fatty, stodgy foods or, at the other extreme, to stop eating regularly – both can impact on the libido.

- A bottle of wine shared between a couple can create a relaxed mood and lower inhibitions. In women, a moderate amount of alcohol can increase testosterone levels, making them feel sexier, but more than this has the opposite effect. Men, sadly, do not enjoy the same benefits of increased testosterone levels from alcohol, and we all know what too much alcohol can do. Too much alcohol also severely depletes B-vitamin levels (see page 197), which we need for energy and possibly libido (see above).

Male Impotence and Sexual Dysfunction

People often find it difficult to talk about their sexual problems, and the subject of impotence seems to be particularly taboo and awkward for people to express their feelings about. Male impotence is called erectile dysfunction (the inability to maintain an erection) and is different from infertility (the inability to produce viable sperm to make a baby). About half of all men will experience erectile dysfunction at some time or other, though only one in ten seeks professional help. Psychosexual counselling can help with impotence, premature ejaculation and retarded ejaculation (difficulty in achieving orgasm and ejaculation). In fact, couples often learn to live happily with male impotence, and sex can involve closeness and many types of physical contact that do not require the man to have an erection. There are various reasons for impotence, including the following:

Medical factors: One of the most common reasons for impotence in men aged 55 or over is prostate problems. Male impotence may also be linked to diabetes, hardening and furring of the arteries, prescription drugs, recreational drugs, leaky veins in the penis, hormone imbalance, previous surgery, spinal cord injury, epilepsy, Parkinson's disease and Alzheimer's disease. See your doctor to rule these out.

Performance anxiety: This can be a big issue for men and can worsen the erectile dysfunction. A flow of blood to the penis is required for erection, and tense groin muscles can impede this. Stroking, massage and caressing can often help to dispel anxiety and provide sufficient stimulation for erection (see pages 117–118).

Premature ejaculation: Another common form of male sexual dysfunction, this is defined as ejaculation that happens within a minute of, or before, penetration. Anxiety is a cause and may be linked to nervousness about being with a new partner. It can be helped by wearing a condom or using a local anaesthetic cream, either of which will reduce sensations. Tensing your buttock muscles while thrusting blocks nerve signals and may delay ejaculation. Another method is to squeeze the penis firmly for five seconds between the thumb and two fingers just below where the glans joins the shaft, and then wait for a minute before resuming sex. If you experience premature ejaculation, you may be able to have successful intercourse around an hour later.

Smoking and drugs: Cigarette smoking is linked to erectile dysfunction. Many drugs are also linked to impotence. Cannabis is initially a stimulant but high doses over time can lead to erectile dysfunction.

Female Sexual Dysfunction

Not only men have impotence problems. There is also female sexual dysfunction, which includes finding it difficult to be aroused, difficulty in reaching orgasm and pain during sex. There are a number of possible causes, including low sex drive or an unskilled lover.

A woman who encounters pain during sex needs to see her doctor in order to rule out endometriosis, pelvic infection and thrush. Other possible causes of pain could be poor lubrication (try one of the many types of lubricating gel available) or a psychological cause such as tension.

It can be difficult to find information about psychosexual problems, especially if you are shy and don't have a sympathetic GP, but see page 203 for organizations that can help.

Step 7

Go with the Flow

KEY MESSAGE:

You Are a Human Being not a Human Doing

Life really isn't all about meeting targets, deadlines and obligations. Many of us don't take the time to relax, nor are we spontaneous enough to use the opportunities that present themselves. Life is for living – it is not a dress rehearsal.

It has been said that in the 21st century we have changed species from Human Beings to Human Doings! We are all 'doing' things all the time, and often have to relearn how to relax, to smell the roses and to 'go with the flow'.

When you 'go with the flow', it doesn't necessarily mean that you are always laid back about everything. It simply suggests that you are mentally relaxed enough to take advantage of each opportunity that presents itself. You are able to unwind and to regenerate when you need to. You can live your dreams and you are able to enjoy your relationships, family and friends. It is a state of mind that allows you to be in control of the various areas of your life.

Finding Time to Live

Make time for the things that are genuinely important to you, whether you want to fulfil long-held ambitions or just stand and stare at something you find beautiful. No matter how busy you are, you will be able to find time for the things that really matter. It's all a question of priorities.

Q: *Is it always bad to procrastinate?*
A: There is a lot of sense in the well-worn advice to take a step back from whatever it is that has set you off, take a deep breath, and work out a rational way forwards.

There is a time to act, and a time to sleep on the situation. The next day you may feel completely different about it.

Q: *I find spontaneity a problem as I spend so much time planning.*
A: While organization will help your life, don't become a slave to it. If it is perfect weather, forget about the list you made for today – get out in the park or the countryside for the day. You can guarantee that if you postpone it until tomorrow it will rain. If you really want to take up an opportunity that presents itself, do it. Reorganize your schedule as best you can – the only thing you really can't do is to be irresponsible and completely let people down (though you might be able to defer).

Q: *Finding time to go to the gym or for long walks is a stretch for me as I'm always busy.*
A: You need to put pleasure higher up your priority list. Remember to fit in enjoyable, healthy activities like going to the gym or swimming baths. You may notice that dust on the mantelpiece but the chances are that others won't. If you spend all your time on such minutiae, and not on more important things like keeping fit or enjoying yourself, you need to prioritize (see Setting Goals, page 8).

Q: *I'd like to do other things that I enjoy but somehow life gets in the way.*
A: If you feel you are too busy meeting deadlines and you find it difficult to loosen up your attitude so that you can enjoy other pastimes, invest some time in visualization (see page 142). Imagine yourself actually booking that art class you were thinking about or going for early-morning walks. See what you would see, smell what you would smell, hear what you would hear. Get yourself into a state of enjoyment and relaxation and get inside the feelings of pursuing your chosen activity. You will then find it irresistible to follow your visualization with real activity.

Q: *I truly never seem to have the time to do what I want.*
A: Don't put off your ambitions. You don't want to get to the age of 80 saying to yourself, 'I wish I'd got round to climbing Mount Everest'. No ambition is too modest, and it can free you up creatively. If you want to learn square dancing or go to art classes, make time for it. Activities such as these will bring balance to your life, encourage you to re-focus and diminish daily stresses.

Anger Management

It can be hard to 'go with the flow' if you are plagued by bad moods and anger. As already mentioned on page 53, anger is actually one of the most destructive and least useful of all emotions and can be very inhibiting. The most idiotic saying ever has to be the comment, 'Don't get mad, get even'. Much better would be to say, 'Don't get mad, find a solution'.

Q: *I find it difficult to control my anger and I snap at the smallest thing. It particularly drives me insane when people say 'get a grip', though I suspect they are right.*
A: Maybe it would be better to express 'get a grip' as 'get it into perspective'. Inappropriate anger, such as losing your temper when the photocopier jams or the driver ahead goes at a crawl, will only wear you down. It is also a sure sign that you are not able to get things into perspective.

Exercise: Reducing your Anger

Each time you get angry about something (and this may be several times a day) try doing the following:

1 Make a note about what sets you off and what your thoughts are.

2 Grade how angry you are on a scale from 1 to 10.

3 Use the techniques covered in Cognitive Thinking (page 66) to find more appropriate responses.

4 Re-grade your anger after you have changed your statement. For instance, you might change, 'How dare he criticize me and get so personal' (graded 8) to 'He's allowed his views of me and I don't have to agree with them. I think I am an OK person, though I might take note of the last thing he said' (graded 2). Or you might change 'I hate being kept waiting, perhaps I've been stood up' (graded 7) to 'A chance for a break, and maybe she's caught in traffic. If I have been stood up, it's her loss, not mine. I'll give it 15 more minutes and then use the spare time to get some exercise walking home' (graded 1).

Q: *Is it all in my head?*
A: More or less. It is not events that make you angry but your responses to them. The meaning you attach to events dictates your emotional responses, and you can change your view of these events. You might get angry because you take something as a personal slight. Why do you care so much and does it really matter? You might feel helpless about something, but switch to a resourceful 'can-do' frame of mind, see what you can do to influence the situation and see how much better you feel. You can nearly always change your reaction. Change your thinking from 'You are making me angry' to 'I am making myself angry about something you are doing or saying'.

Q: *I can't shake off being angry about what happened to me and pointing the finger of blame – if it hadn't happened to me, I'm sure my life would have been a great deal better.*

A: Here is probably the most important tip in the whole book: if you have long-term anger, leave it behind. If you are angry with your parents for the way they brought you up, angry because something bad happened to you or your family, angry because of a divorce or financial problems, angry because of anything – it is time to let it go. You cannot grow, develop, learn or prosper emotionally if you hang on to old resentments. You cannot change the past at all. But you can change your future. If you are hanging on to your past, you will find it difficult to create your future; as a result, today, and each today that follows, will be less rewarding and happy.

Figure your Triggers

- If you know that a certain situation is likely to make you angry, you can do several things. You can avoid the situation, though this might not always be practical; you can change the way you think about it (see above); or you can stop it happening again by taking action.

- Change the way you feel about these things by changing the way you talk to yourself about them. Instead of saying, 'I am furious' or 'I am so angry I could scream', change this to 'I feel annoyed' or 'I am irritated'.

- If you are on the receiving end of criticism that makes you angry, this is an indication of lack of self-esteem. If your self-esteem were intact, you would feel confident about taking the criticism, evaluating it and even, if appropriate, using it to learn from.

- You might be setting goals that are unrealistic and then getting angry when they are not met. Reassess your goals.

Q: *If I feel strongly about something, losing my temper surely underscores how important it is.*
A: The person on the receiving end of your anger probably won't feel that they deserve it. Rage will just serve to polarize you both and make the other person defensive. You might get a short-term gain if they give in, but this will be followed by hostility and resentment, the disadvantages of which greatly outweigh the advantage of the short-term gain.

Q: *When I lose my temper I just pretend that nothing has happened after the event. I don't really see why I should apologize.*
A: If you lose your temper with someone else, it is important to later say 'sorry'. This is not always easy to do, but will heal both the situation and your own feelings. Say it unequivocally. You don't have to say 'sorry' for *what* you said, if you feel you were right, but you can apologize for the *way* it was said. You can say sorry for having a row instead of a discussion, or for any possible damage to the relationship.

Q: *The daily grind takes its toll on me and I've certainly noticed that few people look happy in queues or on the bus.*

A: Anger is one of the consequences of city life, in which proximity and impotence swiftly translate into rage (see also Urban Living, page 150). We are now seeing road rage, office rage and even, in the supermarket, trolley rage. We see the most placid people lashing out verbally at someone in a traffic jam. The biggest problem is when it escalates. Changing your reaction is the only thing you have control over. If you become uptight easily, get into the habit of preparing yourself in advance. In the car, have some good music at hand, and spend the time planning for something nice. In the checkout queue, spend your time people-watching and noticing what other people buy (always interesting) – anything rather than getting irritable and angry because the checkout person is a bit slow.

Relieve Transport Troubles

One day we might be able to dematerialize and then rematerialize at our destination. Until then, however, commuting and the stresses of travel form part of most people's lives. We live at increasingly close quarters, which is probably a major factor behind the phenomenon of 'road rage'. Forty-five per cent of people find the rush hour very stressful – yet commuters find themselves embroiled in it five times a week, 48 weeks a year. This has to be worth sorting out.

- So much depends on your attitude to the whole process of travelling. Stay relaxed and view the inevitability of a certain number of cancelled trains or roadworks as irritations rather than major catastrophes. Changing your perception of the problem is a good first step on the road to a calm travel experience. Remind yourself of any benefits of a delay, such as gaining more time to read your book or complete the work you are doing on a train or Tube journey.

- Minimize your anxiety about being late by letting the people at your destination know what's happening.

- If you experience constant delays that always make you late and stressed, then there is really no other solution than to get into the habit of allowing more time for your journey.

- Remember that it is better to arrive at your destination safely than not at all. Rushing raises levels of stress hormones, which can be dangerous.

- Talk to your boss about flexi-time or staggered working hours. Rethink your daily schedule. You may be able to share school runs, for example. Perhaps working at home for a couple of days each week is an option.

- Can you do without a car? If you live in a big city with a good transport system, this might be an option. It could even make sense financially. If you work out how much you spend on expenses like repairs, insurance, car tax, petrol and parking, you might be surprised at how much each trip is costing you in real terms. The savings would probably more than cover the cost of an occasional cab.

- Shopping by car can seem convenient but, again, if you add up the cost of time spent and petrol, there are many occasions when ordering from catalogues makes more sense. This is particularly the case if you live out of town.

- For longer trips, consider making travel a part of the experience instead of just a means to an end. In earlier days, travel was more leisurely, with whole continents traversed by train, and motoring a pleasurable pursuit. It is astounding how much less stressful leisurely travel is.

- Go green, and get fit – cycle instead of driving or taking the bus. (But be sure to wear a helmet.)

Q: *I get so disappointed by other people and it makes me fed up.*
A: Your expectations of others might be setting yourself up for anger. Do the following comments sound familiar? 'Other people should measure up to my standards', 'I should get promoted if I put in more overtime', 'Other people should act the way I do'. Who says any of these 'shoulds'? If you hear yourself saying the word 'should' frequently, then you have inappropriate expectations and it is you who will be disappointed. Once you stop this way of thinking, you may be surprised at how spontaneously nice and helpful some people are.

Q: *My partner has a habit of losing his temper and, to be honest, I am frightened and keep out of the way. The smallest thing triggers a rage.*
A: Some people are just bullies and use their anger as a weapon – they lose their temper at the smallest opportunity. Steer clear of these people. If you are in a relationship with someone like this, you may have some serious thinking to do.

Staying in Control

- Anger distorts logical thought processes. If you are going to get mad, make sure it is with the right person. If you are taking your anger out on someone, such as a clerk, who hasn't the power to resolve the problem, this is not logical.

- If you are talking to an apparently unhelpful complaints department or service engineer, it will do no good to rant – they get difficult customers all the time. Be firm but polite and pleasant. Always take a name and reference number so they know you can get back to them, and tell them when you will call back. If they know you are going to follow it up and be a pest, your file will go to the top of the pile – guaranteed.

- Losing your temper really doesn't solve problems. Promise yourself that from now on you will take a constructive approach to dealing with 'challenges'. Practise safe stress. If you are feeling like you just have to let rip, use the tried-and-tested method of beating up or screaming into a pillow.

- You have two choices – you can spread happiness or unhappiness. We have all experienced anger as a chain reaction. Someone loses their cool with you, so you go home and take it out on someone else, resulting in misery all round. A smile and a friendly word will do the opposite and create a chain reaction of joy.

- Children are experts at making parents lose their tempers. But remember that if they see you lose your temper regularly, they will have your example before them. If they then lose their temper with their schoolmates or teachers or family, they are following your lead. It is common for parents to yell at their kids, 'Don't you dare speak to me like that' or 'How dare you hit little Johnny?' But often the children have only been copying what they are seeing.

Exercise: *Defusing Other People's Anger*

Dealing with anger in other people is an art. Here are some possible ways of handling it:

1 Defusing the situation with humour is a valuable tool, but, as mentioned on page 54, you must be careful to laugh *with* the other person and not *at* them.

2 Talk calmly and slowly to stop the disagreement escalating.

3 Empathize with the other person's feelings before stating your point of view. 'I understand that this situation has made you angry. My take on the situation is…' By using empathy you can take some of the heat out of the confrontation. Notice the lack of the word 'but' in between the two sentences. The minute you insert the word 'but', you have changed the whole meaning. Rather than signalling your understanding, you are actually rubbishing the whole of the previous sentiment in favour of your point of view in the second statement. Say the sentence both ways out loud and see the difference this small word makes.

4 If you refuse to respond, this can make some people get even more hot-tempered (this is inappropriate, but a reality). It's better to say that you want time to think about their viewpoint, then walk away and come back to the situation when everything has settled down a bit.

5 Your response to other viewpoints may not be helping. Your anger might just be an automatically triggered, conditioned response when you are faced with disagreement. Disagreement is merely a divergence of opinion, so do you really need to make the other person see your point of view? Ask yourself why. There

may be a good reason (in which case, act on it) but if it really doesn't matter, why wind yourself up?

6 Some people argue 'below the belt', in which anything you say will be turned against you, and old grievances often dragged up. To avoid this, it can work well to put your point of view in a note or letter. Because it is in black and white, the meaning can't be twisted. However, take great care about what you write!

Fear and Phobias

So many people walk around being fearful for much of their life. They spend a lot of their time thinking, 'What if it all goes wrong?' Fear is one of the most stultifying emotions. It stops us dead in our tracks and prevents us from progressing or panics us into avoidance. In evolutionary terms these are perfectly valid reactions, as fear is an appropriate response to real danger, and retreating is a sensible way of dealing with threats. But when the fear is of commonplace activities or objects, then it is misplaced and will disempower you faster than anything else can.

Q: *When I am scared of something impending, I find I am gripped by a feeling in the pit of my stomach that stops me doing anything positive. How can I get round this?*
A: First of all, understand what it is exactly that you are fearful of. For instance, if your fear is of speaking in public, break down your concerns until you get to the root cause of your reaction and confront it. Your fear could be of looking out at the sea of faces, making a fool of yourself, forgetting the points you want to make, being unable to answer certain questions or being a boring speaker.

Fear of Failure and Success

- Fear of failure is particularly paralysing. Thinking, 'If I fail at this I am no good, which means I will fail at everything' is, of course, a huge over-generalization to make, yet many people think in precisely this way. It is impossible to fail at everything and we all (including the most successful people) have our share of successes and defeats.

- Often the major stumbling block to realizing our ambitions is actually a fear of success: 'If I succeed, I won't be able to sustain it and then the truth will be out when I am recognized for the failure I really am' or 'If I succeed, I will have so much more to lose that it's better not to succeed in the first place'. If this sounds like you, work on positive affirmations (strong positive statements about yourself – see page 143) such as, 'Success breeds success'.

Q: *I have a driving test coming up soon and am petrified by the prospect. I don't think I can go ahead with it.*
A: Defuse the feeling of fear by altering your description of the driving test or other event you are frightened of. Instead of saying, 'I am petrified by…' or 'I get rigid with fear when I…', say to yourself, 'I am concerned about…' or 'I am worried about…' We programme our minds with the words we use, and if we repeat the disempowering ones often enough they have a suitably negative effect, whereas if we employ the modified versions they lessen the fear. Therefore, if you use empowering terminology, you are on the way to working through your fears. You might say, 'I enjoy the challenge' or 'This is a growing experience for me'.

Expanding your Boundaries

Just because this is a short tip, don't underestimate how successful it is at dealing with anxieties, fears and even phobias.

- What is required is consistency of approach in working on whatever your issues are on a daily basis. Taking small, measured steps towards expanding your operating boundaries is a tried-and-tested means of dealing with many fears and phobias.

- For example, if you are frightened of spiders, you might initially look at a drawing of a spider, then a photograph, than a video clip, then a full TV programme, then a small real spider in a glass jar, then a larger one in a glass jar, and then a few spiders in a glass jar. Finally, you could look at a loose spider from the far end of the room, then from a little closer and so on.

Q: *I'm terrified of driving on motorways, but I know it's completely irrational, so I try to pretend I don't mind it. Unfortunately, I still break out in a sweat when I approach one and will drive miles out of my way to avoid it.*
A: You may have a stoical approach to dealing with your fears, telling yourself, 'Just get on with it no matter what the cost to myself', and in this way you suppress your fear. But in the meantime you may live with constant anxiety and dread. It is better to ultimately confront your fears (though obviously not with anything dangerous).

Q: *I feel overwhelmed by the enormity of tackling some things and am worried about what will happen if they don't work out. I feel that this holds me back quite a lot and makes me too tentative.*
A: Probably the most important and empowering question you can ask yourself in any given situation is, 'What would I do if I were not afraid?' The answers may surprise you. To make your dreams more tangible, break them down into smaller chunks. Your fears and inhibitions are probably compounded by the fact that you are focusing on the end result alone, which is daunting for you.

Help for Fears and Phobias

- Phobias are irrational and involve all sorts of knee-jerk reactions. The adrenalin begins to flow, your hands become clammy and you just want to run away. They are sometimes linked to compulsive behaviour ('If I flick the light switch on and off ten times, going into the room won't be dangerous'). Most simple phobias in children, involving reacting to a single thing, tend to disappear without treatment. However, phobias which persist, which come on in adulthood or which are compound or social phobias usually need treatment through counselling. (For help groups, see page 203.)

- Cognitive thinking (see page 66) allows the fearful or phobic person to see what is actually going on rather than what they perceive is happening. For instance, if you are excruciatingly shy and are phobic about going into a room full of people, you might believe that you are sweating profusely and flushing. However, if you are shown a video of yourself in a social situation, you will probably observe that, in fact, you are not sweating or behaving oddly in any way. Seeing it for yourself rather than taking someone else's word for it can have a strong impact.

- There are several holistic remedies that seem to help many people. Bach Flower Rescue Remedy for fears and phobias can help. Calming aromatherapy oils that can help in the face of fear include camomile, cypress, frankincense, geranium, lavender, marjoram, sandalwood and tangerine.

Mood Swings

Mood swings can be an effect of stress and anxiety. The feeling that you cannot seem to control your moods – one minute you're happy, and the next you are going off the deep end at someone – can further deepen that stress and anxiety. There are a number of steps you can take to regain a sense of balance.

Other common causes of mood swings are hormone imbalances (for instance in pre-menstrual women and in teenagers around the time of puberty) and low-blood sugar due to irregular or unhealthy eating.

Q: *I get cross and I don't know why. To be honest, I feel quite confused a lot of the time.*

A: Mood swings can be an indication that you do not know your own mind and that you need to sort out what the problem is. Work on setting your priorities (see Setting Goals, page 8) so that you are more comfortable about the demands that are being made on you or that you are making on yourself. You might be reacting in a seemingly irrational way because you are resentful of how you are having to spend your time. If you are not brave enough to state this to others, or to yourself, your resentment could be coming out as moodiness. Once you isolate the problem, you will be well on the way to stabilizing your moodiness.

Q: *I know that people around me give me a wide berth when I am in one of my moods, and if I am honest It often suits me.*
A: Beware of using moodiness as a tool, such as a way to avoid unpleasant tasks: 'I am in a mood so don't even think of asking me to…' If this becomes a habit, it will cause long-term communication problems and may become an unwelcome facet of your personality. If there are things you do not wish to do, it is better to get into the habit of saying, 'I don't want to… because…' or simply 'I am busy right now'. Clear communication will cut across the frustrations caused by mere moodiness.

Q: *Isn't it normal to be moody premenstrually?*
A: Not really – there are many cultures in which the diets and physical activity levels are different to ours and the women don't experience the same degree of premenstrual problems. If you find that mood swings come with alarming regularity when you are premenstrual, then they are linked to your monthly hormonal cycles. Regular exercise will release a steady stream of the brain chemicals known as endorphins, which calm moods and help to balance female hormones. Managing blood-sugar levels is of paramount importance for balanced moods (see below for specific advice), and healthy fats build healthy hormones. Evening primrose oil is particularly helpful, as are those found in fish oils. Caffeine is linked to premenstrual problems. Supplements such as the herb agnus castus and the nutrients vitamin B6, calcium and magnesium are renowned for restoring calm feelings premenstrually.

Q: *I know I enjoy my booze too much and I drink loads of coffee but they do steady my nerves, so are they OK?*
A: Dependency on any substance can worsen mood swings. If you drink alcohol regularly, take drugs or consume large amounts of caffeine, this may affect your moods adversely. Reduce your intake of these stimulants gradually.

Q: *My diet is quite erratic, so could this be the reason for my mood swings?*
A: The brain needs a steady supply of glucose and nutrients, and if it does not get these it responds with unpredictable behaviour. Your mood swings could easily be linked to an irregular diet that is producing unfavourable blood-sugar control. Eating a wholefood diet and reducing dependency on sugary foods, stimulants such as coffee, colas and alcohol, as well as refined carbohydrates such as white bread and rice, can have a dramatically positive effect on mood swings (see Food and Mood, page 70). Important nutrients for brain health and balancing moods come from a healthy diet, but you may want to boost them with supplements. The most useful are the B-complex vitamins (50mg daily), the minerals selenium (200mcg daily), zinc (25mg daily) and magnesium (250mg daily), and the EPA fatty acids found in fish oils (take sufficient supplements to achieve 1–1.5g of EPA daily).

Step 8

Unwinding

We live such busy lives, on so many levels, that many of us need to relearn the art of unwinding. The ability to be 'still' is something that we have to make a concerted effort to bring into our lives. The previous chapter, Step 7, dealt with behavioural aspects of learning to take time out, while this chapter seeks to help you find inner calm by offering practical techniques you can use.

Learning to Relax

If you find it difficult to relax, it can pervade every area of life. When you are keyed up and always on the go, you may find that even during your down time, you are living on adrenalin. You may believe that you are not happy unless you are doing something, you may feel guilty about resting and you may even be a bit manic on holidays. Perhaps you feel your restlessness is a creative force for good, and many people will undoubtedly envy your apparent energy levels – but are you paying too high a price in terms of your health and relationships?

Q: *I sort of define myself as an adrenalin junkie and I think I do best when working at full pelt. But lately I find I am making more mistakes and am feeling pretty tired. Should I take the hint?*
A: The first thing to understand is that we all need to unwind to regenerate, remain healthy and think clearly. One day your tendency to overdo it will, almost certainly,

catch up with you. If you are wearing yourself out, take heed and actively learn to relax so that you can slow down from time to time. If you are twitchy and find it difficult to rest, follow the tips in the Exercise below.

Q: *I find it hard to relax – there is so much to do that my mind is buzzing all the time and I end up working till I am too tired to carry on. How can I break this cycle?*

A: You need to give yourself 'permission' to get off the merry-go-round and stop for a while. Focus on the fact that if you don't get some down time when you need it, you will become less and less efficient, which serves no one in the long run. You deserve regular time off. If you saw someone else working so hard, you would be the first to say, 'Take a break', so why don't you say it to yourself? Pick a cut-off time and then simply down tools. You need to create a new set of habits where you value your time off as much as your time working. If your brain is always buzzing with the next job to do, you might not be able to focus on what you are doing at the moment. This can lead to errors and an inability to enjoy the moment. People around you might be irritated because you are not really participating in your time with them.

Exercise: Make Yourself Slow Down

Work through this list over the next few weeks and see what a difference it makes to your ability to relax and unwind.

1 Work consciously at slowing down your speech, which will slow down your breathing and heart rate and allow you to think more clearly.

2 Do at least one thing each day at a snail's pace and really savour the experience. In doing this, you will learn to focus and appreciate things more. See the information about mindfulness on page 142.

3 You might be doing a lot, but are you enjoying what you do? Ask yourself this question at regular intervals. It is often easy to be busy for the sake of it. Cut out activities that do not gratify you.

4 Categorically avoid doing more than one thing at a time.

5 Ask others who are close to you to tell you every time they see you fidgeting, pacing the room or allowing your eyes to wander off to the next thing you are thinking of. Awareness will help you to relax more easily.

6 Make a strict cut-off time beyond which you will not do anything more active than taking a warm bath or reading a book. Restlessness is a habit that needs to be broken and by making firm rules you can reset your habits.

7 Your restlessness may be linked to anxiety (see page 55) or guilt (page 69). You might be overcompensating for low self-esteem (page 38) by doing more than others around you. This never quite works because if you don't deal with the underlying self-esteem problem, no amount of activity will satisfy you.

8 Visualize letting go of your stressful thoughts as 'dumping the junk'. Think of yourself standing on a cliff with a warm breeze blowing away all the unwanted thoughts that are cluttering up your brain (see Creative Visualization, page 142).

Exercise: Five-Minute Stretches

A five-minute stretching routine can make you feel more energized and calm. Do the following for 45 seconds each, with 15 seconds in between to change position.

1 Standing up, stretch your arms over your head one after the other, feeling the stretch up the side of your ribs.

2 Still standing, roll your head slowly around to create a semicircle and stretch your neck muscles, then repeat in the other direction. Do two more times.

3 Holding on to the back of a chair with one hand, use your other hand to catch the foot that is on the same side as your free hand and slowly pull it up behind you, feeling the stretch in the front of your thigh. Switch to the other leg.

4 On all fours, stretch your back like a cat then cave in the other way.

5 Lying down on your back, with your arms in a T-shape, pull your knees up to your waist and lower them to the floor on one side, then slowly switch to the other side.

Ways to Wind Down

- To switch mood and get comfortable, change your clothes when you come home.

- Music and lighting will change the mood immediately. Depending on the atmosphere you are aiming for, put on something upbeat, mellow or calming and adjust your lighting (get some dimmer switches fixed if you need to). Within moments of arriving home you can adjust your mood instantly.

- Candlelight creates an even more calming and mood-altering atmosphere and is flattering as well.

- A five-minute shower to freshen up always helps to reset mood.

- Open a window and take five deep, oxygen-filled breaths to re-energize yourself.

- The herb eyebright is soothing for tired eyes. Mix one teaspoon with one cup of boiling water. Let it steep and cool, strain it, then dip cotton pads into the solution and place them over your eyes. While relaxing in a chair for five minutes with the eyepads on, soak your feet in a tub of hot water with one cup of Epsom salts added.

- Colour yourself blue. While you are relaxing with your eyepads and footbath, visualize yourself bathed in light from the calming blue, mauve or green spectrums or healing white.

- You can buy amazingly effective gel-filled eye masks which feel cool against the skin and are very good at making you feel alert and refreshed after five minutes' use.

Q: *The office I work in is a madhouse. Most of the time I find it inspiring, but sometimes I just want to lock myself in the loo as it is the only quiet space I can find. I feel pretty drained as a result. Surely it can't be healthy.*

A: As the pressure mounts in the office, dissociating yourself from it for even a short while helps to preserve your sanity and keep you focused and energetic. People are not automatons and if you don't 'take five' from time to time, you run the risk of depleting your spirits and affecting your health. Take time out every hour or so to run through a five-minute de-stress routine and make yourself feel better. You probably do this to a degree anyway – many people hang around the water fountain or coffee-machine, or take a trip to the loo, for just this reason. But your de-stressing can be more creative and productive. Take a brisk walk around the block – this will get you out and calm you down. While in the office, take five to ten deep breaths every hour: this is invigorating and calming and reduces lethargy. For more suggestions see the Exercise below.

Exercise: De-Stress your Office Environment

1 Staring at a computer screen encourages eye strain and may trigger tiredness and headaches in susceptible people. Take regular breaks by adjusting your eyes and looking into the distance. Use soothing eye drops.

2 Sorting out your desk drawer may not be your idea of fun, but a fairly mindless task like this helps to de-stress while also clearing clutter.

3 Do a five-minute stretch routine somewhere quiet (such as the staff room or the stock room).

4 Open e-mails from friends, and read personal text messages only when you decide to have your five-minute wind-down – a good laugh is always de-stressing.

5 If someone is making your blood pressure rise, you can transform your stress
   response instantly. Imagine that person doing something stupid or looking silly,
   say wearing a clown's nose or speaking as if they had taken a breath of helium
   (all high and squeaky). Such amusing images will instantly cool you down. You
   can even use this technique to calm you down ahead of time – if, for instance,
   you know you have to call a client you dread speaking to.

6 Talk to your bosses about introducing a 'red-cap' system. If anyone is feeling
   over-pressurized by too many interruptions, they can create a mini-sanctuary by
   donning a red peaked cap for up to 20 minutes. During this time no calls are put
   through, nobody speaks to that person (even to offer a coffee) and they have
   total peace to do what they wish.

Maintaining a Balance in Your Life

It is hard to unwind at the best of times, but you could be making it doubly difficult for
yourself if you are trying to be in several places at the same time. Follow these tips to put
the balance back in your life:

- Don't volunteer if you don't have to when you are already overstretched. Some
  people are always the first to put their hands up and give of their time, but it is
  often at the expense of their home life. If you want to volunteer, don't do it
  impulsively but after taking time to consider all of the issues, and do it on your
  own terms.
- If you are using the workplace to escape from problems at home, this needs to be
  addressed. For example, if you argue a lot at home, or you find that you can't get
  any down time because you are always having to do things for others at home,
  these are specific problems that need sorting out. Just spending time at the office
  doesn't solve the problem and by ignoring it you may precipitate a crisis. Look
  through Step 1 (pages 7–18) and Step 5 (pages 72–87) again.
- Realistically there is a limit to how much you can burn the candle at both ends.
  Keep your fun and frolics to evenings when you don't have to be at work the
  following day – you'll enjoy your nights out even more.
- Don't feel guilty about how you achieve a balance between work and home.
  Silence the little chatterbox in your head that makes you feel inadequate about
  what you are not doing. Focus on what you are doing and feel good about it.
- Take time to smell the roses – whether at work or at home.
- Do something positive to unwind and, if you are able, get away. Changing the
  scenery is one of the best ways to alter your behaviour patterns, which is why
  holidays are so valuable. If you can't get away, switch to an activity that has
  positive associations for you, such as walking in a calming place or playing football.
  If this isn't possible either, at least spend some time relaxing and visualizing a
  calming place.

Q: *Even if I wake up in a good mood, I get pretty stressed by the news and all the bad things going on in the world. Am I oversensitive?*

A: No, you are not oversensitive. In fact, being in touch with your feelings on these matters is a good thing. One of the biggest problems we face is becoming desensitized when overexposed to bad news – it detracts from our humanity. But it is easy to feel overwhelmed during bad-news days. Add to this the fact that we are in information overload all the time anyway and you can see how stressful it is. We are bombarded by information, advertising, telephone salesmen, junk mail, spam e-mails and news alerts that it is hard to relax. As an experiment try taking an information holiday. Unplug your phone at home, switch off your mobile, avoid the TV, leave your e-mails unchecked, cancel the newspapers and don't watch the news. Do this for two days, and then, if you dare, for a week. Stress often melts away and you can then focus on the important task of unwinding and reading a good book or watching a comedy movie.

Q: *I need my little 'fixes' to keep me going, but as I am not addicted can I presume that I am coping all right?*

A: Drugs such as amphetamines (speed), appetite suppressants and cocaine have the effect of increasing restlessness. You may think that you are doing fine and appearing normal while able to cope with more things, but in the end drugs do not solve the problem of having too much to do or overcoming obstacles in your life. (For more information on addictions see page 183.) You can also become hyperactive from having too many sugary foods in your diet or by ingesting too much caffeine from coffee or colas. Reducing your intake of these will combat that buzzy, distracted feeling. Drink calming herbal teas such as camomile, vervain or lemon balm instead.

Q: *Is there such a thing as adult ADHD? I think my partner is affected.*

A: Yes, about 40 per cent of ADHD children go on to be ADHD adults. A high percentage of children and adults who are hyperactive and who are diagnosed with ADD (attention deficit disorder) or ADHD (attention deficit and hyperactivity disorder) can be very successfully treated with diet and nutritional intervention. There may be many factors contributing to ADD/ADHD but the triggers are often dietary and involve low levels of essential fatty acids (EFAs) found in fish oils. Taking a high dosage of EPA (eicosapentaenoic acid, one of the omega-3 fatty acids), say 2g a day over at least three months, may have a calming effect. EPA is found in fish oil supplements. Caffeine, sugar, food colourings and other additives, and food sensitivities are also strongly implicated. It is best to get specialist advice to ensure a balanced diet and safe use of any supplements. For more information see page 203.

Exercise: Autogenic Training

Autogenic training is a powerful aid to relaxation. It has a proven track record in reducing depression, anxiety and stress-related conditions such as irritable bowel syndrome and psoriasis. You have to make time to do the basic ten-minute exercise three times a day for the first three or four weeks. (The best times might be on first waking, just before sleeping and at some other convenient time during the day.) After this you can cut back to once or twice daily. The basic exercise is deceptively simple, though you might find it better to sign up for a course of training in the self-discipline, to explore its uses and to deal with the 'discharge of stress' that can happen (sometimes making you feel worse for a short while before you feel better). The basic exercise is as follows:

1 Lie on your back (in bed if you wish) and get comfortable. Close your eyes. Take a deep, slow breath and pause for just a moment. Exhale fully. Throughout the session continue to breathe slowly, naturally and easily.

2 Feel your body sinking into the bed or floor. Repeat each sentence that you are going to say three times (this is important). As you repeat the sentences, feel and acknowledge the corresponding feelings in your limbs and other areas. These are the phrases that are each repeated three times: 'My left arm is heavy.' 'My right arm is heavy.' 'Both arms are heavy.' 'My left leg is heavy.' 'My right leg is heavy.' 'Both legs are heavy.' 'All my limbs are heavy.' 'My left arm is warm.' 'My right arm is warm.' 'Both arms are warm.' 'My left leg is warm.' 'My right leg is warm.' 'Both legs are warm.' 'All my limbs are warm and heavy.' 'My breathing is calm and easy.' 'My heartbeat is calm and easy.' 'My solar plexus is warm.' (Your solar plexus is the area just behind your navel). 'My forehead is cool and clear.' 'I am at peace.'

3 Now you are ready for the return, bringing you back to normal consciousness. Quickly clench both fists. Take a deep breath. Stretch both arms upwards. Breathe out slowly. Return your arms to your sides, with unclenched fists. Open your eyes. Lie for a moment taking in your surroundings and just 'being'.

Building Exercise into Your Life

Exercise is one of the most important ways we have of de-stressing our lives. It actually clears excess stress hormones out of the body and triggers the release of feel-good brain chemicals called endorphins. This is why a brisk walk will make you feel so much better after an argument or after a tough day. These endorphins allow us literally to self-medicate against feeling tired, stressed and depressed. Exercise has also been shown to improve immune resistance and reduce susceptibility to stress-related diseases.

Q: *I know I need to get more exercise, but I just can't find the time to go to the gym and I don't feel motivated to get out when the weather is bad. How can I avoid being a slug at home?*
A: You can probably choose from health clubs, swimming pools, tennis courts and running tracks near your home or workplace. But for people who are not exercising

regularly, home is the easiest place to start. Staying motivated is the key to being consistent with an exercise regime, and we all know people with unused exercise bikes stashed in their lofts. It helps if the exercise does not cost the earth, does not involve a commute and is something you enjoy.

Making Time to Exercise

The biggest hindrance to exercising is making the time in a busy schedule. It always seems that there is something more important to do. If you really want to commit to reducing the stress in your life by increasing your fitness, you need to make a plan of when you are going to exercise. One or two of the following are likely to work for you:

- Get your exercise out of the way first thing so that for the rest of the day you can forget about it.

- Use your commute for exercise: factor-in walking or cycling some of the way to work. Remember to wear a pair of comfortable trainers or weatherproof footwear, Manhattan-style (where a brisk walk to work is a tradition).

- If unwinding is your problem, make a point of exercising at the end of your working day, but not if you are going to cop out when the time you were intending to exercise finally rolls round. Late afternoon to early evening (4–6pm) is around the time that our muscles reach their performance peak.

- If watching the telly while you exercise means you will stick to your regime, check the TV schedule the night before to pick out an interesting half-hour programme during which you can strut your stuff.

- If you think you will work out three times a week, the chances are that it will end up being once or twice, so to achieve three to four times a week, plan to work out five or six times a week.

- Alter your plans for winter and summer. Different seasons usually mean different exercise routines. It is a shame to run on a treadmill in a gym when you can get outdoors on a magnificent spring day, and it is less likely that you will venture out when the gloom descends in winter.

Exercising for Free

The beauty of exercising from home is that it is free and is immediately available.

- If you enjoy your chosen form of exercise, you are more likely to persevere. Most of us like music, and moving to music works on many levels. Not only do you improve your metabolism and get your heart rate up, but you also improve coordination. All you need is a tape- or CD-deck and some suitable music. Close the door, hang up a do-not-disturb sign and go for it.

- All the expensive home-gym equipment in the world is unlikely to beat a workout on an inexpensive mini-trampoline or rebounder for stamina, combined with some well-planned yoga poses and stretches for suppleness. Resistance-training improves strength and muscle tone and can be achieved using large, exercise-quality elastic bands, plus a couple of large food tins as weights.

- Skipping is great aerobic exercise and you can take a skipping rope anywhere.

- There is nothing like a good, fast, half-hour walk to clear the cobwebs and get your heart rate up a bit. Or if walking is too staid for you, how about rollerblading?

- Invest in some exercise DVDs. They work – but only if you use them. Switch them around and use three or four different ones during the week to stop yourself getting bored with them.

Relaxing Holidays

We all need down time to unwind and de-stress, and in theory we take holidays for just this reason. However, there are many reasons why holidays are sometimes less relaxing than expected. The destination may not be as idyllic as you imagined, your child may get sick, you may lose your luggage, or your expectations of the holiday may have been unrealistically high. So if you have ever come back more exhausted and frazzled than when you set off, it's time to think through your holiday planning.

Q: *In theory I like to go on holiday but I often come back more tired than when I went. Family bickering plays its part. Should I just not bother with holidays?*
A: Vacationing with children can be a source of mixed feelings. You probably love being with your children and watching them enjoy themselves, but you may also need some time out for yourself. Most children love camping and caravanning, but on this type of holiday you are unlikely to get much peace yourself, unless you take it in turns with another adult to skip away for a couple of hours. Find a company that specializes in family holidays, where there are activities, or even clubs, for children. Some holidays offer baby-minding services – even villa-rental agents usually know of at least one reliable babysitter. Taking a young friend along as company for your child could be another solution (but choose the friend carefully). Teenagers present particular challenges as they often want to break away from parents and do their own thing. While it is important to allow them some freedom, you need to establish rules before you go, particularly with regard to safety.

Q: *Our friends have asked us to share a villa with them on holiday, but I'm worried that it might spoil a good friendship.*
A: Pick the friends you go away with carefully. Don't say yes just because you don't know how to say no. Do you know them well enough to be confident that the close

proximity and forced togetherness won't make you all irritated by each other? Do they have the same interests and expectations as you? Are their needs similar (children of the same age, for instance)? Are their drinking (or non-drinking) habits akin to yours? Do they feel the same way about sightseeing vs sunbathing, eating out and what to spend money on? Sorting out these aspects in advance can prevent strained relationships and broken friendships. Also check on the accommodation, so that there are no hard feelings about who has the best bedroom, or embarrassment over sharing a bathroom or listening to someone's loud snoring.

Top Stress-Free Travel Tips

- Reduce holiday strains by minimizing things that could go wrong. Make sure you have photocopies of your passports, airline tickets and insurance documents. Divide cash and credit cards between you and your partner for safety. This way, if you do lose something, you can avoid the additional tension of finger-pointing and blame.

- If possible, schedule your weekend break or holiday for a time when everyone else is not going away, too. Travel can be the worst part of a holiday, so don't spend it stuck in interminable traffic jams or queuing in a packed airport.

- On self-catering holidays make sure that you agree a division of labour beforehand. No one likes to feel that they are doing the lion's share of boring domestic chores, and this can be a principal cause of seething resentments.

- A high percentage of people use their holidays to plan the rest of their lives. If you are spending all the time thinking about your career, this may not be restful. Set aside time before you go to deal with these issues, so you can really rest on holiday.

- If your idea of the perfect holiday is to get the adrenalin going with lots of high-energy activities, that is fine as long as you don't also feel worn out when you get back. If you don't engage in such activities regularly, you could injure yourself. Prepare as necessary and make sure you pace yourself. Think about taking a more restful holiday next time.

- Frequently people will suffer from the post-holiday blues on their return. There is an emotional cost to a holiday that is to do with once more having to face the realities of daily life, such as the sharp contrast between the bright sunshine abroad and the gloomy weather at home.

- To reduce the risk of picking up a tummy bug on holiday in an exotic location, take acidophilus and bifidobacteria, and also ideally FOS (fructo-oligosaccharides), for at least two weeks before going. Some products combine all three in one.

- Other natural essentials for the traveller are ginger capsules (or crystallized ginger) for travel sickness, neem or citronella as insect repellent, grapefruit seed extract as an all-purpose antibacterial agent and tea tree oil for cuts or burns.

Meditation

Meditation has a proven track record for helping to reverse the physical and psychological changes brought about by stress. Blood pressure, breathing rate, heart rate, metabolism and muscle tensions are lowered, calmed or relaxed, while brainwaves slip into calming levels. All sorts of conditions can be helped by meditation, including irritable bowel syndrome, chronic pain, anxiety, panic attacks and chronic fatigue.

Q: *I've often thought about trying meditation, but I'm not interested in alternative lifestyles or philosophies.*
A: Many people have been put off meditation because of common misconceptions. Mistakenly seen by some people as a 'tune in and turn on', 'hippy' philosophy from the sixties, meditation is not about switching your mind off in order to achieve some kind of enlightenment. In reality it is simply a heightened, more focused form of what we naturally do to unwind. Think of it as achieving a high level of awareness. If possible, go on a meditation course. However, if you are not interested in Buddhism or transcendental meditation, finding one may be difficult (see page 203).

Exercise: How to Meditate

1 The easiest form of meditation is to sit in a comfortable position in a quiet room, close your eyes, focus on your breathing and become aware of your in and out breaths. Do this for 10–20 minutes daily.

2 As an alternative, choose a soothing word or sound that is meaningful to you. This is called a mantra and is used to focus your attention so that your mind can return if you are distracted. The best-known mantra is the Sanskrit term 'Om' (meaning 'I am all of that which is divine'), pronounced a-a-o-o-u-u-m-m. However, you can choose any sound, word or phrase that you find calming. Focus your attention on your mantra as you repeat it in a low, rhythmic voice, for 10–20 minutes a day.

3 Thoughts coming into your mind are a part of meditation. But instead of allowing them to interfere with the process and struggling to blank your mind, recognize them as simply being 'thoughts', distance yourself from them and retake control. For instance, if you begin to think that you can't cope with something, meditation teaches you to observe yourself thinking this, so that you are not directly affected by the fear of lack of coping skills.

4 You can also use other focuses for your attention, such as a candle flame, a positive statement, a feeling (of kindness, warmth or loving, for instance), a visualization or a rhythmic physical movement, as in t'ai chi or yoga.

5 A form of meditation called 'mindfulness' is particularly good for relieving stress. To prime your ability to focus, devote an hour a day for a couple of months to sitting quietly while concentrating on breathing and meditating. Mindfulness then involves focusing on all actions as specific experiences. So, for instance, if you are about to eat a tomato, look closely at it, noting its texture and colour and how you feel about eating it. As you bite into it, be aware of the interplay of tastes and sensations. Chew and swallow it slowly, all the time being aware of the experience. You can practise mindfulness for, say, 30 minutes daily as an exercise, but it will have a longer-lasting effect than this and has the habit of insinuating itself into people's lives, making them calmer and more focused.

Key Tool 4: Creative Visualization

Visualization is a way to focus your imagination in order to create what you want in your life. It can also be directed towards healing and resolving anxieties and phobias. You will find that visualization is a skill that you are already using in your everyday life, though in an unconscious way. For instance, if you have an appointment with the bank manager tomorrow and you are a little anxious about this meeting, the chances are that you are playing out the situation in your mind and rehearsing the possible conversation. If you are to play tennis, you might be seeing yourself, in your mind's eye, serving the ball superbly. If you are unwell, you might be imagining being fit. What you need to learn now is to channel your visualization to a higher level, so that it becomes a tool to use whenever you wish. Imagine that bank manager handing over the overdraft you want, see the ace you'll serve and visualize a healthy, pink-cheeked you striding through the countryside. Initially, it is probably easiest to practise creative visualization when relaxed or meditating. Here are some pointers:

- Do not worry if you are unable to see a 'picture' when you practise visualization. Some people see clear images, others have feelings, perceive a general ambience or replay conversations or sounds in their mind.
- A simple beginner visualization exercise involves closing your eyes while in a relaxed position, at a comfortable temperature. Imagine a time when you were happy, say on holiday on a warm beach. Feel the warmth of the sunshine, hear the sounds of the waves lapping on the shore and gain that sense of calm and contentment that you felt. It is as simple as that. You can imagine any happy time, such as cradling a baby, eating a delicious meal, walking hand in hand with someone you love or giving or receiving a massage.
- Passive visualization means allowing thoughts and feelings to come to you as and when they appear. Active visualization involves consciously choosing what you want to imagine. Guided visualization is when another person takes you step-by-step through a description, such as 'You are on a beach in warm, sunny weather, listening to the sound of the waves, feeling relaxed'. The person would then possibly guide you through relaxing the different muscle groups in your

body, and finally seeing yourself in a given situation with a beneficial affirmation (see step 4 below), or perhaps tapping into your self-healing capabilities.

- You can use any visualization you find helpful while meditating (see page 144).
- If you reach a block in your visualization, this may point to a fear, probably subconscious, that is stopping you from progressing. It can usually be worked through once you are aware of it.

Exercise: Four Steps to Creative Visualization

These are the four steps to creative visualization:

1 Set your goal. Choose goals that are easy to believe in and that are small steps, usually along the way to greater goals.

2 Create a clear idea or picture of what it is that you want. Think of it in a positive form and in the present tense. Do not think of it as an abstract form at some time in the future, or in a negative form.

3 Focus on your visualization frequently, not only at dedicated times but also at other times, whenever you are able, throughout the day.

4 Give your visualization vibrancy and energy. Make strong positive statements to yourself and about yourself. These are called affirmations.

Using Creative Visualization

Here are some practical applications for your creative visualization exercises:

- Imagine yourself applying to do a course you have always wanted to do. How does it feel? What do you have to do to apply? What is it like to start learning something new, which interests you?

- Imagine yourself in a situation where you are doing something you do not enjoy. Notice what happens to your body – do you tense up anywhere? Does your pulse race? Hold onto the thought while consciously relaxing those parts of the body. Visualize the unpleasant experience waning in importance. See yourself coming through it intact and happy.

- Stand 'at ease' with your legs a shoulder-width apart, your arms hanging loosely by your body and your neck muscles relaxed. Feel balanced, and imagine a nourishing white light all around you, feeding your energy centre in your solar plexus (behind your navel), as you grow tall and strong and confident.

- Imagine yourself playing a sport you enjoy. Visualize yourself actively participating and enjoying what you are doing. Imagine yourself performing better than ever before. If swimming, imagine rhythmic strokes that carry you faster, while each arm extension takes you further. If doing gymnastics or dance, imagine yourself extending your limbs further and finding strength in your solar plexus. If playing football, imagine being more nimble, running faster and scoring more goals. You will find that your confidence grows and your performance improves.

- Visualize yourself going to a gathering and meeting new people. Imagine yourself energized and interested in the other people. See yourself finding the other people a pleasure to meet and find out what is best about them. Imagine it being an enriching experience and that you can learn something positive from every person you meet.

- Create a positive visualization that helps you to 'bounce' bad events off you. See yourself as surrounded by a shimmering white light hovering just outside your body, from top to toe. This light fills you with warmth and energy, giving you the strength to deal with whatever comes your way. It also creates a protective shield around you, off which bad events, bad feelings and unpleasant comments just bounce back out into space. They can't touch you.

Step 9

Creating a Home that Inspires

KEY MESSAGE:

Your Home Is a Place to Nurture your Dreams
Turning your home into a pleasing and safe emotional haven will enhance your life.

Home is where the heart is – ideally. If, however, your heart sinks as you walk in the door because it is not the cocooning nest you think it ought to be, or if you find yourself going out more than you want to, then it is time to do something about it.

The daily routine of your home life and the people who live with you all affect your stress levels. If everything is running smoothly, then it frees up mental and physical energy for other, more pressing aspects of your life – like enjoying yourself. Conversely, even minor mishaps at home, such as a child's messy room or a lost bill, can build up stress, which then impacts on work life, relationships and even health.

This is a book about stress-busting and not about interior design. However, it makes a huge difference to daily stress levels when home is a place you want to be – hence this focus on how to organize your home.

Personal Space within the Home

Everyone needs their own space – a sanctuary to retreat to and a place where worries about work and life outside the home can be left behind. Achieving this can help to eliminate a lot of life's petty stresses.

Q: *Our flat is small and I sometimes feel that I have nowhere to go if I need a little peace. How can I make my own space?*

A: Not only do *you* need your own space, but so do others in your household, including your children. Respect other people's space and they are more likely to respect yours. If you want 'time out', let people know – don't make it a guessing game for them. By not clearly communicating when you need 'own time', you will end up feeling resentful that your time is being called upon when you are not really willing to give it. If necessary, ask your partner to take the children out to the park so you can get half an hour of peace.

Top Tips for Making your Own Haven

- An ideal place to create your own sanctuary is the bathroom. You can probably lock the door, light some candles, turn on some nice music and wallow in the bath for quite a long time before anyone has the nerve to disturb you.

- Losing yourself in an activity is another way of creating a mental sanctuary. Anything that requires concentration will do, such as crossword puzzles, jigsaw puzzles, embroidery or model-making.

- If it is difficult to create your own sanctuary at home because of the daily hubbub of life or because there's not enough space, find space elsewhere. Take regular trips to the library to read, sit in a hotel lobby and watch the world go by, take a stroll in a park, have your regular table in a cafe to scan the daily papers.

- Art classes are an ideal sanctuary because you can, in effect, leave the left side of your brain (the more analytical, judgemental half) outside, and take the right side of your brain (the more creative side) in with you. It doesn't matter if you think you are artistic or not, just give it a go – you might be surprised.

Q: *I look though all the decorating magazines and fantasize about a calm space to return to at the end of the day. But in reality I don't seem to be able to get the hang of sorting things out. What is stopping me?*

A: How do you view your home? Is it a nest to which you return at the end of the day with a sense of relief? Is it a place where you enjoy receiving your friends and visitors? Is it a place that enhances your life? Or is it just a place into which you decant the various elements of your life in the hope that it will all somehow sort itself out? If your home does not enhance your life, you could be amazed at the positive effects of being in surroundings you enjoy. Start small so that you won't feel too overwhelmed by the task. For example, if you can't envisage doing a whole room, at least create a corner of enjoyment. It could involve draping a sofa with an attractive throw, placing a table next to it with a good light or some candles, a small bowl of water with a few flower heads floating in it, and a good book or glossy magazine. This can be enough to create your first retreat, and your enjoyment of this space will radiate outwards to other areas of your home.

Q: *We live in permanent disarray and I seem always to be picking up other people's detritus. I get to the point where it is easier to turn a blind eye and just live with not being able to find anything. It all seems too much to deal with, but should I tackle it head on?*

A: Have you noticed how other people's mess can be more stressful than your own, especially if you have to live or work around it? If your partner/flatmate/co-worker is guilty of leaving too many belongings around for a sane life, you may have to have a gentle word. Explain how it is affecting you and why it is difficult for you to live or work with. Offer constructive solutions such as your helping out, setting aside an hour a week to work on it, buying boxes or allocating a couple of drawers and labelling them accordingly. It might be that other people are simply unaware of how awkward you find it, but you also have to be ready for their criteria to be different to yours. Do your best not to be critical or judgemental, but constructive. Outline the benefits to them (such as ease of finding things and more efficient time management).

Q: *Adults might see my point of view, but I doubt if it will make any difference to my children.*

A: If you can't persuade your children to clear up their rooms, don't let that be another source of stress. Make three important rules they must adhere to:
- They always keep their door shut so you don't have to look at their mess.
- They are responsible for picking up dirty clothes and bed linen and putting them out for the laundry on a given day of the week.
- They don't come complaining to you when they can't find something.

If they break these rules, the penalty is that they have to clear up their rooms.

Neat Surroundings

To maintain an atmosphere of calm in your environment, it helps if the places where you spend your time – home, office, car – are organized, neat and uncluttered.

- Aim, at the end of the day, always to leave your desk tidy. While you may not be able to get through all the work, organize projects by subject matter and leave them neatly stacked for the next day.

- Photos, cuttings and mementoes are a constant source of clutter. If you know in your heart that you are never going to get round to pasting them all in albums, do the following: invest in lots of foolscap wallet-style folders with fold-over flaps. Mark the first one with today's date using a thick marker pen. Place in it all your precious mementoes. Decide then and there which things you wish to keep, and get rid of the less-than-wonderful children's drawings and repetitive photos. Into the wallet put in, as they crop up, all photos, precious letters from friends, school reports and children's artwork. When it is full up, secure it with a large elastic band and put the finish date on it. Now start the next folder and proceed in the same way. You will probably end up with two or three folders per year, which you can stash in a large box out of sight.

- Look around you and notice the clutter-magnets in your home. Areas where clutter tends to build up include window ledges, countertops and open shelves, behind wardrobe doors, by exit doors. Being aware of this will help you to stop things being dumped there in the first place.

- If you are lucky enough to be the owner of an attic, spare room, dry cellar or shed, don't make the cardinal mistake of chucking in everything and hoping for the best. Invest time in adding shelving – warehouse style – and stack everything you need but don't use very often (such as toolboxes, ladders, ski equipment, suitcases).

- When using storage bags, choose clear ones you can see through, or make sure you label them really well. Arrange the bags so that you can see the items you need at a glance.

- Poorly chosen colour and lighting can make uncontrolled clutter look even worse. Clashing colours or designs and harsh lighting (say from a single overhead bulb or strip lighting) do nothing but emphasize chaos. Calm shades such as neutrals or the blue palette, or well-coordinated bright colours, can enhance the sense of order. You only have to pick up a Sunday newspaper supplement and look at the home-decorating spreads to see how colour can work to bring things together in the home. Too many busy patterns on curtains, upholstery, wallpaper or carpets can also prevent a room from looking calm.

Q: *My partner and I have decided to live together. I love her kids and am excited about becoming their new dad but have to admit to some trepidation about the fact that I've never actually lived with children before. How can I keep a lid on the inevitable mess?*

A: Nothing transforms a home faster than children. Depending on your viewpoint, they fill a home with laughter, movement and colour or with noise, mess and disorganization – and more often than not it is both of these scenarios at the same time. Children are only children for a very short time and it is essential to appreciate them. You can never go back in time to recapture these precious moments. But children can also be mini-dictators if we let them. Remember that it is their home as well – not your home in which they are guests (unless of course they are visiting you for a while). Teaching them to respect their own and other people's homes comes from your example. Respect children and they will respect you.

Top Tips for Kids in the Home

- Discuss situations with them and explain your viewpoint. Ask them why they are insisting on something – if you hear them out, at least they will view you as being fair. If you decide to decline, explain why, such as lack of money, value for money, or health and safety reasons. Work out the flashpoints – typically homework, bedtime, mealtimes, supermarket check-outs.

- Establish rules that you agree on together (this is dependent on age but can start quite young – say two years old). Prioritize safety and respect for others, and allow flexibility for special occasions – let them eat their party-bag sweets! Once the rules are established, you have a reference point. But remember that the rules govern you, as well as the children, and so you also must stick to them.

- Re-evaluate these rules from time to time. Rules might be something like these: Bedtime will be at 7:30pm sharp, but 8.00pm at weekends, and a parent will always read a story. A piece of fruit (or a fruit- or vegetable-based dish) will be eaten with each meal, followed by a small treat if at least half the main meal has been eaten.

- Children respond much better to rewards than to threats. (Rewards are not the same as bribes.) This does not take away the value of well-placed punishments, such as withdrawing a visit to a friend's house, but always to be threatening ends up sounding hollow and demotivating. Use a star system to reward good deeds – with a mini-prize (such as a comic, some home-made cookies or some sunflower seeds to plant in a pot) after ten stars and a maxi-prize (say, a trip to the cinema) after 30 stars.

- Remember that you are the adult and you have the right to say no – firmly and without shouting. When you say no, make sure you mean it and then do not waver. Once children learn that 'no' means 'no', and not 'maybe' or 'yes, if you bug me enough', they will realize that 'pester power' has limited effect.

- Avoid giving children the answers to questions all the time. Teach them resourcefulness and help them develop the ability to find answers. You can do this by asking the questions back to them (with little hints) so that they can find the conclusions, and by showing them how to find the answers for themselves in reference books or on the Internet. If they are young, you may need to find the answer together. This simple habit instils in children the life-long ability to be curious about life and to find solutions.

Urban Living

You might not wish to change your fast-paced, cool, urban life, but if you want to stay sane you might like to think about some of the effects it can have. Urban living has a huge impact on relationships of all kinds, and understanding some of the pressures it creates can help to relieve them.

We are assaulted on so many fronts in urban centres – traffic, radios, people, roadworks, visual intrusions such as billboards – that most of us aren't even aware of it anymore. We deal with this onslaught by a process called sensory adaptation, filtering out all that is not immediately necessary and, in essence, becoming numb to the stimuli. But even if we are not conscious of them on a minute-by-minute basis, our senses are still overloaded and this takes its toll. By taking ourselves 'out' of the situation on a regular basis, using relaxation, visualization, meditation or other means (even a warm, scented, candlelit bath), we can rejuvenate ourselves and heal the damage of this sensory overload.

The sheer volume of people in urban centres means that we behave in particular ways towards our fellow urban dwellers. We don't look people in the eye (it is too challenging and invasive), and we rarely even acknowledge their presence. We deal with small courtesies, such as holding the door open, with curt acknowledgement in case it is seen as an entry point for communication. In fact, we create invisible barriers around ourselves. This lack of human contact is actually quite stressful because it emphasizes our aloneness and distances us from other people's feelings.

You can spread a small, but significant amount of bonhomie by smiling at people and making eye contact with them (no, they won't put you away, nor will this be an invitation to every madman – you can still use your judgement). But what you will find is that people smile back at you (mostly) and this will immediately put you in a better mood. Once you have got into the habit of smiling at people, you can take a further risk and say good morning to five people on your way to work each day.

One of the ways of dealing with the artificiality that urban anonymity engenders is to treat your immediate environment as a village. Get to know your neighbours, your neighbourhood shops and local services. If you regularly go into the same shop, acknowledge any familiar faces and you will gradually build a sense of belonging in your community. You can't grow and learn and prosper if you shut out humanity. What's more, by getting to know your neighbours, not only will you be able to call on them in emergencies, but you will be able to pre-empt any local problems with friendly discussions rather than with antagonism.

Whereas once upon a time families lived within a short distance of each other, urban living often means that there are large distances between generations or between cousins. If you live in a city and want to maintain strong family bonds, you need to work at it a bit harder, and this requires energy and dedication. But the payoff is that when times are tough you can often fall back on your family, and they will probably understand you as no one else can.

If you are new to the city, you might find that it can be a lonely place. There are a lot of opportunities to meet people but nobody is going to bring them to you on a platter

– you will need to go out and find them. Frequenting the same places so that people get to know you, joining clubs and classes and just getting out and about will be the first steps towards achieving this.

Maintaining personal space in an urban setting is an important issue. On an empty Tube, people will sit as far apart as possible and then new arrivals will slowly fill in the seats between in a pattern until there is no choice but to sit next to someone. Yet during the rush hour we all snuggle up to our neighbours' armpits out of necessity – while rarely making eye contact.

Exercise: Understanding Attitudes to Personal Space

You can do an exercise with some colleagues to test the different attitudes we have to personal space. You need five or six people of both sexes to make this workable.

1 Pair up, and one person in each pair stands still while the other places him or herself about two metres away.

2 The latter person starts to move very slowly towards the first person.

3 At any time the person who is standing still can say 'Stop' and the other person must do so. The idea of the exercise is to find the point at which you feel uncomfortable because that person has got too close and is entering your 'space'.

4 Now change partners and repeat with a different person, observing whether the distance is the same or different. Also repeat the exercise while maintaining eye contact. Do you feel more comfortable with people of the same sex or those of the opposite sex? This will tell you a lot about your reactions to other people, how you relate to them and how comfortable you feel about extending yourself into the 'village' where you live, at work or among friends.

Top Tips for Nest-Building

- If, initially, you don't have the time or energy for a complete revamp of your home, make at least one area a haven for relaxation. Any room will do – sitting room, bedroom, bathroom or kitchen – as long as you use it very regularly and really enjoy 'living' in it. It is not intended as a parlour reserved only for esteemed guests, but as a nest for yourselves.

- If the view from your nest is interrupted by loads of clutter, turn to Less Is More, page 32, and slowly work through the list. In the meantime, if you are desperate, you could put up a screen to hide, say, a cluttered work area or wardrobe, but be warned that out of sight is out of mind. If you have to look at it, you may be more likely to do something about it.

- For a gradual approach to making a 'nest' of your home, start by redirecting your thinking towards the idea of creating a retreat. Add small things that will enhance your enjoyment of a space. Scented flowers (changed regularly), framed photos of people you love, something fun to read in the loo, a well-placed light on a dimmer switch can all have the desired effect.

- Light is vital for energy and life. Draw curtains and blinds to let the light in. Get rid of dingy net curtains and replace with half-height translucent blinds.

- Keep your home well aired. Central heating in a hermetically sealed home can make you feel groggy and rob you of energy. Open a window by just a couple of inches at each end of your home to allow air, and energy, to flow through.

- Candlelight is extremely soothing and wonderful for creating a nest-like ambience while at the same time distracting you from any clutter around you.

Housework Realities

Some people love it, some people hate it. But it can't (usually) be avoided. We are talking about housework.

Q: *Housework is not my favourite activity. If there is a short-cut I'll take it, and usually I just let it build up until it becomes intolerable. Any ideas?*
A: If you want to minimize cleaning, try to have fewer places where dirt builds up or is noticeable. Hard flooring such as wood, tile or stone always wins out over carpet in this respect. White and light-coloured fabrics are only for masochists (unless they can be thrown in the washing machine and definitely won't shrink). Darker neutrals such as taupe work well with light walls, or go for petrol blue or brights. Pare down your possessions. If you have one treasured item highlighted on a sideboard, you can soon see when the dust builds up and you can then wipe it down. However, it is much more disheartening when that treasured item is surrounded by countless other less-valued objects and they stop you from having the energy to clean the area.

Tips for Keeping a Lid on Housework

- Instead of perpetually nagging your family members or flatmates to do their bit, have a calm, sit-down meeting with all of you present and bash out an agreement while being determined to stay calm (see Delegating, page 30).

- It is much easier to let the dust build up a bit if you make a point of spring-cleaning twice a year (technically spring- and autumn-cleaning). At the same time you can make a point of clearing your clutter (see Less Is More, page 32).

- If you can afford it, you might consider finding some home help. One way to help with the decision is to make an evaluation of your own time. If you figure out that an investment in some help for a few hours a week frees you up to be more financially productive, or less stressed, it could well be worth it. Go by word of mouth if you can, otherwise the stress of managing someone who is no good at the job might make the exercise counterproductive.

- A local teenager will probably be happy to earn a bit of pocket money by helping with the ironing and car-cleaning – all time-intensive jobs.

- If you are about to get a new pet, consider a short-haired breed to minimize the dirt and dust.

- The effect of housework on health and fitness has been studied, and it has been found that we don't need to go to the gym after all. If you really put some old-fashioned elbow grease into the job, you can find that you 'get fit as you shine as you clean'! It makes sense obviously – our grandparents did not have the time-saving devices we enjoy today, and as we have become more sedentary we have become less fit. The housewives of the early to mid-20th century apparently did the equivalent of running a marathon every week.

- Beware the effects of cleaning chemicals on your family's health. Because our homes are almost hermetically sealed environments these days, we are typically breathing in a cocktail of around 400 chemicals and this has been linked to allergies and other health problems. Levels of pollutants in the average home are around ten times higher than outside. Instead of using sprays, aerosols, room fresheners and antibacterial wipes, substitute old-fashioned cleaning techniques which use brushes and scourers along with soap, water, borax, bleach, white vinegar for cutting grease and mould, bicarbonate of soda for kitchen and bathroom surfaces and tea tree oil and grapefruit seed extract as natural antibacterials. For further information, see page 203.

Creating a Workplace in the Home

The last 20 years have seen more and more of us working from home. The age in which we live demands flexibility and cost effectiveness, and provides us with communication capabilities to capitalize on this new approach. This appears unlikely to change in the near future, which means that, willingly or unwillingly, many of us are having to learn new strategies for turning part of our home into a workplace. (For more advice on working at home, see page 30.)

Q: *When I worked in an office, I could leave my work behind, but working from home means it is always there reproaching me when I am not working.*

A: The greatest burden of working from home is that you may find you don't know when to stop. It can be too tempting to catch up by working late at night or sitting at your desk in your pyjamas at 6am. This is fine if you really enjoy what you do or need to meet the occasional deadline, but for most people it then becomes a vicious spiral of increased work, less productivity and more stress. Decide what your working hours are and stick to them. Not only is this the first step towards making a healthy division between work and home time, but it is more professional and you will be respected for it by your clients.

Q: *I'm just about to start working from home for the first time, instead of commuting into an office each day, and I need some advice on how to make it work best.*
A: Working from home can have many advantages. It cuts the need for expensive and time-consuming travel and, in theory, lends us these hours for increased productivity. It can allow us to combine child-rearing and a productive work life. You are your own boss and can prioritize your workday in any way you wish – time to be creative, time to get organized, time to meet deadlines. It also has some potential disadvantages including being distracted by domestic events and losing the camaraderie of workmates. Working from home suits some and not others. Many people embrace this discipline enthusiastically and yet months later return to the traditional workplace, desperate for office routine and the company of others. Whether you are working at home voluntarily or because it has been thrust upon you, there is a range of particular stresses engendered by this, which can be minimized or eliminated. The following tips will enable you to handle any strains more calmly, leaving you free to focus on the life-enhancing benefits of your situation.

Top Tips for Working at Home

- Don't jumble up your work with your domestic clutter – create a separate workspace. Ideally, set aside a room to work in, but if this is not possible, ensure that you at least have a desk plus sufficient bookshelves and a filing cabinet dedicated to your work needs, so that you can either literally or metaphorically shut the door on your work when you need to (see also pages 32 and 147).

- Avoid sharing your computer with others in the household if you can. In this way you can access what you need when you need it.

- If you can afford it, have a separate telephone line for work with an answering machine that clearly delineates when you are available for office calls. It is more professional and also stops work intruding on your personal life.

- Make it clear that your time 'in the office' is sacrosanct.

- The temptation to fiddle around with home life when working can seem overwhelming. But if you have decided that you need to be at work by 9am, stick to it. Do whatever domestic chores you can before you sit down at your desk, and then forget about them.

- Structured interruptions, on the other hand, can work for you, as they can be used to break up the day when you have no colleagues to chat with. Take regular breaks – at mid-morning, lunchtime and mid-afternoon. Decide what you are going to do with them. A short walk can provide an invigorating change of scenery. Use breaks constructively to make a couple of personal calls or take something out of the freezer and chop some vegetables for the evening meal.

- If you are able to do so, answer calls when they come in. If you always have to reply to a long list of messages, it takes twice as long, and costs more in phone bills. Communicate by e-mail whenever possible (but see page 25 for how to use this efficiently).

- Use an answering machine to screen calls when you have a piece of work that requires absolute concentration or you are trying to meet a deadline.

- In the traditional office the chances are that you would attend regular meetings of one sort or another. While businesses often hold more meetings than they need, they are useful for taking stock from time to time. A lesson can be learned from this by the home-worker – put in your diary regular planning sessions and then stick to them. This will enhance your confidence in your own efficiency by preventing you from just responding to incoming events and feeling 'not in control'.

- Schedule your workload realistically. The common cry of the self employed is that they are terrified of saying no to a project because they don't know where the next offer will come from. Get this into perspective and recognize that you can only do so much.

- We all need human contact in our working lives. Make a point of joining an association linked to your work in some way and attend events. Keep up with old colleagues in your line of business. There may also be a local group of home-workers in a variety of occupations, who meet up principally for the social contact.

- Make your home/work environment a pleasing one. Take some time to organize the space around your desk or work area. Put up a picture you like and pin some humour on your noticeboard. Make a point of having a vase of scented flowers or a plant on your desk along with a photo of a happy moment in your life. Ensure that your desk height, computer angle and chair are comfortable and ergonomically correct (see page 190).

- Take regular time out from work – try to avoid working late at night or on weekends, and put holidays into your diary well in advance. That way you can plan around them.

Leaving Home

Whether leaving home to go on to further education, to share a flat or to start a new job, this is a significant phase of life. Cutting that cord can seem very liberating, but also more than a little scary.

Q: *I'm moving away from home for the first time and it is a bit daunting. What do I need to know?*
A: You may have been aching to break free, but suddenly not having a parent to ask for advice can be daunting. Do not be afraid to call home whenever you need to – it is not a sign of weakness. Many young people avoid calling home because they do not want to worry their parents, but just imagine that you had a child of your own who had left home, and think whether you would want to know how things were going, good or bad. The answer is obvious.

Top Tips for Moving Away from Home

- This may be the first time you have had to manage your money, from receiving a pay packet (or student grant) to paying bills. It is so easy to get into debt, and getting to grips with your money is the first and most important thing to do.

- Going to university or starting your first job is an exciting time, with lots of possibilities and new challenges. However, if you are a little shy, it can take time to adapt to your new life and really get into the swing of things. Make full use of the various clubs and societies that will be available to you. You may find it easier to live in halls, rather than in digs, so that you can meet people. On the other hand it is all too easy to get sidetracked with all the fun and to forget about studying until the exams loom. Work at finding a balance, and pace yourself.

- Burning the candle at both ends can seem tempting and easy to do. In your late teens and early twenties you may just have the stamina to compensate for getting home in the early hours and then presenting yourself for work or study the next morning. And if it is difficult then you may be tempted to take a little chemical help – some extra-strong coffee or perhaps even illegal stimulants. You might be able to get by like this for a short while, but the reality is that it will inevitably catch up with you. You may start to feel unwell, your performance will suffer and you may get a nasty shock if you are dismissed because you are not doing as well as you thought you were.

- In your new job, you may be ready to set the world on fire. But it is often a bit of a comedown to realize that there are so many mundane things to do, office politics and departmental budgets to sort out, before you can get round to achieving your goals. Do not let this blunt your ambition but use planning (see page 22) and time-management skills (see page 24) and to make sense of what needs to be done.

- Avoid subsisting on sandwiches, junk food and take-aways. Because home cooking might no longer be an option, it can be tempting just to not bother, but it is much cheaper and you will feel a lot better if you brush up your cooking skills and eat properly. And don't forget fruit, whch is nutritious and doesn't require cooking.

Downsizing

There are many reasons why you might need to move to a smaller home. It could be because you are relocating for work or school purposes and properties cost more in the area you are moving to, meaning that you can afford less space. You might be separating from your partner. You might feel that your home is too big for you and you want to simplify your life. You could be retiring or have left your job.

Q: *I need to downsize my house and am finding the whole experience quite depressing. How can I change my outlook?*
A: Once the decision has been made to downsize, you need strategies to avoid feeling overwhelmed by the practicalities. If you are moving for unhappy reasons, the stress is likely to be greater. One way or the other, those who wear the change best are those who see it as a newly opening door and not as a closing door. Change your viewpoint and put a positive slant on the experience to move forwards.

Top Tips for Downsizing Your Home (or Your Life)

- If you are upset at the idea of giving up all that you value, focus on the idea that sometimes in life we have to take a step back to take two steps forwards. Nobody has a crystal ball, but if you stay positive about the move you can probably make more out of it than if you feel badly about it all the time.

- Look forwards, not backwards. The trick is not to hanker for what might have been, but to say to yourself, 'Next!' That one little word can change your whole attitude to life.

- List all the benefits that this move will have for you: you are ditching that neighbour from hell; you are near a really good library and can start to read all the latest novels; you don't have a spare room for guests any more but will have a nook for your computer so you can finally write that novel.

- Instead of trying to cram all your old belongings into your new, smaller home, why not be radical and sell the lot, then reinvest the proceeds in new, good-quality modern classics? After all, a mattress should be replaced every ten years, a new sofa bed could be more versatile than your existing sofa and a well-designed work-desk might be the most efficient use of a small space.

- A smaller home might benefit from a unified approach to decoration, so keep one theme and colour palette throughout. An attractive setting will make you feel great.

- On your first day in your new home, make a point of buying two or three large bunches of flowers to brighten up your day.

The Boomerang Generation

A newly coined term, the boomerang generation, refers to adults who return to live with their parents after many years. The most frequent cause is divorce accompanied by financial problems. A recent census found that 17 per cent of people over the age of 65 had an adult son or daughter who had moved back in with them. The only way to deal with this situation is to recognize sources of potential strain and to discuss them, hopefully planning for the change in advance. The following are the most likely sources of stress in this situation:

- One parent may suggest that an adult child move back in but the other parent may not be equally welcoming, especially if they see this as a time for themselves.

- It may be a burden on parental finances.

- The returnee may expect more in the way of 'services' such as meals and laundry than the parents are willing to provide.

- The adult child may bring with them all sorts of stresses, such as depression, relating to any marriage break-up or job loss they may have been through, and the parents may not be able to deal with this.

- The person moving in may bring with them a grandchild or two, and the grandparents may not be used to the hurly-burly of the permanent presence of children.

- The parents may treat their adult offspring like a child and want to know where they are at all times and set curfews for returning home in the evening.

The Once-and-for-All Clutter-Busting Guide

There is no avoiding it: if you want a calm and clear environment in which to live, you (and those you live with) have to roll up your sleeves and work methodically through your home to sort things out.

Kitchen
- Go through your cupboards and get rid of all kitchen equipment you have not used for two years. You don't need four strainers and if you haven't used the ice-cream maker in the last two years, you probably aren't going to.

- Go through your food cupboard and systematically chuck out all items past their sell-by date and all the impulse purchases that have not translated into meals yet.
- It is common to have a drawer where items that have no other home are dumped: take-away menus, screwdrivers, pencils, notepads, broken handles to be fixed and so on. Clear this out and put pencils in a jar, mount a notepad on the wall next to the phone, and put menus in a plastic folder.
- A fridge containing healthy food with lots of stress-busting nutrients will include at least a third vegetables and fruit.
- A cluttered noticeboard diminishes the usefulness of the information, or the visibility of any photo, cartoon or joke pinned to it, so sort this out.
- Mend broken lids, handles and drawers, or get someone to do it for you.
- Clear out odds and ends of unwanted and broken cutlery and china.

Hall

- Halls are notorious for becoming dumping grounds. If you want to have a coat rack, umbrella stand, outdoor-shoe spot and small table for the post, that is fine if the hall is uncluttered. But boxes of things on their way to the dump, bags left unpacked from the supermarket, a sports kit that is used only once a week, trainers and other items that build up will only make you feel bad each time you walk in the door.
- If there are several members in your household, the build-up of coats and other kit can become overwhelming. If each person has their own coat peg, then it is up to them to decide what they want to keep on it, but they can't hijack everyone else's coat pegs.
- If you always leave stuff on the stairs to take up or down when you are passing by, clear it away and use the opportunity of moving the items to get some exercise.

Living Rooms

- Your living room and dining area are the most likely to be seen by visitors, so take some time to see these areas as they see them when they first walk in. Are they welcoming or an assault course? Make a plan if the latter applies.
- Dining tables are notorious for attracting items that don't have a home elsewhere. If your table is a mess, consign newspapers to a magazine rack or recycle old ones, sweep the children's toys up into boxes in their rooms, put their homework projects into neat folders to be put away and taken out as needed, do the same for your pile of correspondence and deal with unopened post (see page 33). Firmly put a bowl of fruit or some flowers on the table to remind everyone to stop the clutter from building up again, and perhaps lay out a jigsaw puzzle that everyone can contribute to each time they go by.
- CDs, cassettes, DVDs and videos all need proper homes. Invest in some stacking racks, turn over a drawer or two in a dresser to store them or use a crate.
- If you've been meaning to put up those bookshelves for ages, now is the time to do so. Alcoves next to fireplaces are crying out for them.

- Trailing wires for TVs, sound systems and computers can be dangerous and are unattractive. Spend some time tacking them down and ideally hiding them – or reorganize the position of your equipment.

Bedrooms

- Go through all wardrobes and give to charity or recycle anything that you have not worn for a couple of years. Get rid of anything that does not fit and mend any clothes that need it.
- Organize your clothes by colour. You will discover several new outfits in this way.
- Praise be to whoever invented duvets. They are so easy to shake out and make up, or to turn back so as to air the bed.
- Invest in several large, brightly coloured stacking boxes for the children's bedrooms, and at the very least get them to throw in their toys at the end of the day. If you are feeling energetic you could segregate the types of toys into different boxes (dolls, train sets, building bricks). This will encourage them to play with toys more effectively as they can find all the 'bits' for each.
- Bedrooms are places in which to wind down and rest, so make sure that the lighting can be dimmed when needed.

Bathrooms

- Clear out your bathroom cabinet of all the tubes with dregs of dried-up potions in them and put them in the bin.
- Invest in several inexpensive small wicker baskets and divide between them your collected grooming items – one for nail varnishes, one for make-up, one for moisturizers.
- Keep your vitamins by your toothbrush so you can remember to take them at the same time.
- Stack towels neatly on open shelves so that they enhance the room rather than detracting from it.
- Put a rack of hooks up high at the side of the bath for scrubbing brushes on ropes and shower caps. More hooks arranged along the opposite wall are good for the family's bathrobes and towels and prevent the hook on the back of the door from being piled up too high.

Garden

- If you just don't have the time to do any gardening, it might make sense to replace part of the lawn with decking, gravel or flagstones.
- Spend just one day putting up loads of hooks and shelves around your garden shed to clear all the small clutter off the floor. This will leave room for big items such as deckchairs – and allow you to get to them quickly and really enjoy your garden when the weather is fine.
- Get broken lawnmowers, strimmers and other equipment fixed, or throw out what is beyond repair.

Step 10

Energize Your Life

KEY MESSAGE:

Treat your Body and Brain with Respect

Investing in your health is a profound way of ensuring you have the necessary reserves when you find yourself in stressful situations. A holistic, balanced approach using nutrition, fitness and relaxation pays the best long-term dividends.

Your physical health is one of the first things that will suffer when you are feeling stressed. Tense muscles, disturbed digestion, sleepless nights, headaches and susceptibility to frequent colds and flu can all conspire to drag you down. Stress also places a heavy demand on your nutritional resources. The basic stress reaction is a physical one, and the long-term effects shut down efficient digestion, wear out body tissues and imbalance brain chemicals.

Changing habits while in a stressed frame of mind may seem difficult and even seem to be an added burden and source of stress. But as the rewards can often be felt fairly quickly, you might find that dealing with physical symptoms lightens the burden and inspires and motivates you to tackle other areas of your life.

This chapter starts with the basics of healthy eating, which apply to most people most of the time. Get these five easy steps under your belt and many things will start to improve. Nevertheless, for some there will be other hurdles that interfere with maximizing energy, reducing stress and capitalizing on the best that life has to offer. The most important of these, such as boosting immunity, improving sleep and dealing with addictions, are dealt with later in the chapter.

Healthy Eating: Five Stress-Free Goals

The food we eat determines our health at the most fundamental level – you are indeed what you eat. The modern diet, filled with processed ready meals and junk food, is a proven factor in the escalating numbers of people affected by illnesses such as tooth decay, diabetes, arthritis and bowel and heart disease, among others. The terms 'healthy eating' and 'balanced diet' are bandied about, but many people are not really sure what these terms mean or how they can achieve these ideals.

It is monumentally off-putting and threatening to be given a long list of what not to do. Being told to give up salt and saturated fats, cut down on the booze and avoid sugar can seem a daunting list of injunctions because they get to the very core of our dietary addictions and poor eating habits. Changes can be stressful if they lead to feelings of deprivation – a negative approach that does not give people the tools they need to make necessary changes. So here is a different approach.

Make sure that you eat positively by consuming more of the foods your body needs to carry out its normal functions and repair itself, and, of course, protect you from stress. The habits that serve us less well are then automatically crowded out. That cream cake and coffee will not kill you. What will make you feel progressively worse is if you have them day in, day out. So moderation is important, as is variety, which is an important mainstay of excellent nutrition. If you eat the same foods all the time, you will be getting only the nutrients (vitamins and minerals) that those foods give you. However, if you eat a range of foods you will consume a wider choice of nutrients.

Goal 1: Eat loads of fruits and vegetables

- We are advised to eat at least five portions of fruits and vegetables daily. (This does not include potatoes, which are mostly starch.) A portion means:
  — one apple, banana, orange or pear
  — a couple of kiwis, tomatoes or plums
  — a large slice of melon or pineapple
  — a small bunch of grapes or a handful of berries
  — a wineglass of fruit, tomato or other vegetable juice
  — a cup of loosely packed chopped vegetables
  — a small side salad
- Fruits and vegetables are our principal sources of antioxidants, such as the vitamins A, C and E, which are protective against a variety of degenerative diseases. The role of antioxidants is to neutralize damaging molecules called free radicals, which oxidize our body tissues – in the same way that iron rusts or an apple turns brown when exposed to air. An antioxidant-rich diet can reduce the onslaught of time, protect our body tissues against stress-induced damage, help keep skin in good condition and protect against eye damage. Ideally, eat and prepare fresh or frozen fruits and vegetables, and if you occasionally have canned produce make sure that you rinse off salty water and avoid sugars and syrups.
- To get five portions, eat at least one serving with each meal (for instance, chopped fruit on cereal or a glass of juice at breakfast, a side salad or a couple of tomatoes at lunchtime, a portion of vegetables or pulses in the evening) and snack on fruit, or dried fruit, between meals mid-morning and mid-afternoon. By snacking on health-giving fruits, you will reduce the desire to have biscuits, chocolates or crisps.

- Remember, if five portions of fruit and veg are good, more is even better. Ideally go for seven to ten portions. As a minimum this just means one extra vegetable at lunch and with your evening meal.
- Finally, fruit is excellent as a sweet-tasting substitute for sugary foods, and a mashed banana on toast, or chopped dried apricots in cereal or yogurt, can go a long way to satisfying a sweet tooth and so cutting dependency on sugar. Sugar is a nutritional void with no nutrients to recommend it. (No, you do not need sugar for energy – quite the opposite, in fact, as in the long run excess sugar leads to depleted energy.)

Goal 2: Eat foods that are sources of healthy fats

- Low-fat, no-fat, trans-fats, cholesterol… don't let this confusing array of fats scare you. The first thing is to realize that cutting out all fats is unhealthy. We all need a certain amount of fat, and problems only arise when we eat too much of the wrong sort, such as the saturated fats found in meat and dairy products. Certain fats, such as the omega-3 and omega-6 EFAs (essential fatty acids), are needed for vital body functions, including building all the cells in our bodies, sex-hormone and stress-hormone production, brain cells and nerve insulation.
- An important source of beneficial unsaturated fats is oily fish such as mackerel, sardines, sprats, anchovies, salmon and tuna (not canned tuna). The omega-3 fats found in these are particularly important for brain and eye function but are also needed for other purposes, such as making anti-inflammatory prostaglandins and anti-coagulation substances. This is why fish oils are so useful for helping to treat conditions such as arthritis, eczema and high blood pressure.
- Other vital fats, the omega-6s and some omega-3s, are found in all fresh nuts and fresh seeds. These can be chopped or ground and added to yogurt, cereal and casseroles, or just eaten as satisfying snacks with some fruit. Seeds you might like to experiment with include sunflower seeds, pumpkin seeds, linseeds and pine nuts (which are not nuts but seeds of the stone pine).
- Other healthy fats can be found in naturally fatty foods such as avocados, olives and coconut. Olive oil is probably the best oil to cook with, particularly if you use extra virgin oil, because it is more heat-stable than other oils and is a good source of antioxidants. This lends itself to all the wonderful Mediterranean dishes that you will want to create as you experiment with eating more vegetables, which help protect against heart disease and cancer.
- The two main types of fat to cut back on are excessive saturated fats and hydrogenated fats (see page 164). If you replace three or four meat-based meals with fish and vegetarian dishes (using pulses) each week, you will automatically cut back on your intake of saturated fats. Easy choices would be to order a chickpea curry instead of a lamb curry, to make a lentil patty instead of a beefburger, to stuff pitta bread with hummus instead of ham, or even just serve good old baked beans on wholemeal toast. The rest of the time, eat lean cuts of meat such as chicken breast, turkey breast or game meat such as pheasant.

- You can reduce your consumption of saturated fats derived from dairy produce with delicious half-fat or low-fat milk and yogurt or experiment with soya milk and other products. Get into the habit of using plain yogurt instead of cream on desserts and in cooking, as well as in salad dressings.
- If you have already started following the advice on pages 162–163 about snacking on fruits or nuts, or low-fat yogurts, you will automatically be reducing the main sources of hydrogenated fats, which tend to lurk in processed snack foods such as crisps, cakes and biscuits. Some margarines are also sources of hydrogenated fats. Marketed as 'healthy', these alternative spreads have been linked to the rise of some cancers. In fact, a little scrape of butter or a drizzle of olive oil is a better option than these margarines.

Goal 3: Eat more fibre-rich foods

- Fibre is the indigestible portion of plant foods which we need to regulate our digestive system. Eating fibre-rich foods encourages the growth of beneficial bacteria in our bowels, keeping digestive disturbances, irritable bowel syndrome (IBS) and even bowel cancer at bay. Fibre is also needed to slow down the absorption of carbohydrates, which are our main source of energy, ensuring more sustained energy levels throughout the day as our blood-sugar level is kept in balance. This process is also thought to protect against diabetes, as well as hormonal imbalances that lead to premenstrual syndrome/premenstrual tension (PMS/PMT) and menopausal problems.
- Some of the most valuable and also versatile fibre-rich foods are pulses, beans and lentils. Enjoy all sorts of dishes, from familiar baked beans and peas to lentil soup, Mexican refried beans, black-eyed beans with rice, flageolet beans (traditional in France) and others. Add them to soups, stews, casseroles and salads. They are versatile, low in fat, nutritious, satisfying and delicious.
- Choose wholemeal versions of grains whenever you can. In the refining process, much of the fibre is removed from bread and rice to make the white varieties. At the same time, they lose many of the vitamins and minerals, and while some are put back into flour (iron, B vitamins and calcium), many are not. The antioxidant vitamin E and minerals such as selenium and chromium are lost when the wheatgerm is removed from flour. Any grain eaten whole is better than its refined relative. This means choosing wholemeal bread over white bread, brown rice over white rice, whole porridge oats over instant oats. Potatoes are a starchy food, and jacket potatoes, boiled potatoes, or potato wedges with their skins on are to be preferred over peeled potatoes.
- If you find that adding more fibre into your diet means that you suffer more bowel problems, instead of less, you will need to increase your fibre levels more slowly by easing into eating wholegrains over a period of a few weeks. In the short term you may also find that you are reacting badly to having more wheat in your diet, in which case concentrate on other grains such as oats, rye, barley, rice, buckwheat, millet or amaranth.

Goal 4: Enjoy drinks that are hydrating

- Our bodies are 70 per cent water, and dehydration contributes to a wide variety of problems including overeating, joint pain and headaches. Part of the problem is that instead of drinking hydrating liquids such as water and diluted fresh fruit juices, we have dehydrating drinks such as coffee, colas, strong tea and alcohol.
- Weak tea is OK, or try Rooibos or green tea. Make yourself a large jug of fruit tea, add slices of orange and lemon and sprigs of mint and keep it chilled as a refreshing drink. Alternatively, keep a large bottle of water by your desk and drink it all each day.
- If you like the ritual of putting on the kettle, have hot water and lemon with a teaspoon of honey.
- All of these will keep you hydrated but remember that, if you find you are thirsty, you have let it go on too long – you are already dehydrated. Make sure that you get 1.5–2 litres of water a day (not 1.5–2 litres of coffee!).

Goal 5: Use healthy flavourings

- Herbs are amazingly hardy and grow successfully in pots even if you don't lavish as much love on them as you ought. A few snipped fresh herbs (such as chives, thyme, mint, coriander, basil or tarragon) or a sprinkling of dried herbs or spices such as turmeric, chilli or cinnamon not only makes the simplest dishes and salads more delicious, but more importantly helps to cut back on salt levels.
- You can also add flavour with a squeeze of lemon or a dash of vinegar or balsamic vinegar.
- Add garlic to everything you can as it is a delicious flavouring and has many health properties.
- We eat about twice as much salt as we need, a lot of it in the form of ready meals and snacks, and by cutting back on processed foods and using more herbs and spices you should be able to reduce your salt intake to a healthy level. Excess salt consumption (which, in this country, averages 10–12g per person, against the recommended maximum of 6g daily) is linked to high blood pressure and heart disease as well as water retention.
- Get out of the habit of reaching for the salt cellar when you are cooking. If this is difficult, use a potassium-based salt (see page 203), which is also a source of valuable trace minerals.
- Another ideal alternative is to replace the salt in your grinder with seaweed granules (available from health food shops or see page 203). These have a mildly salty taste but are also rich in many other minerals such as iodine.
- Avoid automatically reaching for the salt shaker or grinder when you sit down to a meal. Not only will holding back on the salt stop you from inadvertently over-seasoning dishes, but you will gradually train your palate to prefer less salt.
- You will quickly find that a diet such as this, with its fresh, varied ingredients and cleaner taste, will lead you to cut back on salty, sugary and processed foods. Over time many convenience foods will taste greasy and unpalatable.

Making Easy Changes

- Concentrate on adding healthy habits to your life. Don't worry right now over what you need to be giving up and avoiding. Instead, enjoy the satisfaction of making small, but important, positive changes to your diet.

- Don't allow yourself to feel deprived. If and when you do decide to wean yourself off particular foods (junk food, fatty dishes, foods that do not agree with you), take the time to work out what you really enjoy eating and which foods you find most satisfying. If you want to indulge occasionally, let yourself.

- Get organized. When you come back from work and all you have in the fridge is a bit of mouldy cheese and half a jar of jam, it is no surprise that the next move is to the phone to call the take-away. Stock up on some of these basics for your store cupboard:
  — tins of tuna, salmon, anchovies and sardines
  — jars of sun-dried tomatoes, olives and gherkins
  — varieties of delicious pastas, couscous, quinoa, rice and buckwheat grains (kasha)
  — cans of tomatoes and peas
  — packets of dried fruit (such as raisins, apricots, cranberries)
  — pesto sauce, tapenade dips
  — tortilla wraps
  — packets of unsalted nuts and seeds (such as pine nuts, walnuts, almonds, sunflower seeds)

- Shop twice a week for fresh fruits and vegetables. Make sure at least one-third of the food in your fridge is fresh produce.

- Cook at weekends in triple quantities and make use of your freezer. Pack serving-size portions you can take out in the morning before you go to work.

- Make a plan each week, taking a few minutes to see what is missing from your larder. Plan a main meal or two and work out how it can do for left-overs in the next couple of days (say, roast chicken followed by cold chicken with salad, followed by chicken soup). This approach also saves money.

- Experiment once a week, or once every second week, with one new recipe or one new ingredient you have not tried before. This way you can broaden your repertoire and the variety of nutrients you eat.

- If you think you can benefit from a more in-depth approach to managing nutritional changes, you might find it helpful to consult a nutritionist.

Disordered Eating

If you want to make the best of the foregoing advice, you need to think about whether this section applies to you. Disordered eating covers a range of factors that are familiar to those with eating disorders including bingeing and stress eating, but could also be as simple as just not being organized or knowledgeable enough about food. Disordered eating is often a result of busy lives where take-away food is eaten on the run (see Let's Do Lunch, page 170). Extreme faddiness about food and a lack of attention paid to eating in a balanced way, for whatever reason, come under this heading. If your eating habits are disordered, here are some tips to help you bring order back to them:

- Eat with family or friends where possible.
- Make the table and each plate look inviting.
- Make your food attractive even if you are at work.
- Take time to savour the food.
- Never eat on the run or fridge-graze. Sit down and make eating an event.

The Role of Stress

Stress plays a big part in disordered eating. Many people just forget to eat, or to eat properly, when they are under duress, sometimes for days at a time. If this is you, make a point of observing mealtimes, even if you don't actually eat very much. Take time out to consciously nurture yourself by eating healthily.

Stress also causes some people to hoover up anything they can lay their hands. This is invariably about anaesthetizing pain. The foods we crave, particularly carbohydrates and sugary foods, trigger endorphins and serotonin which make us feel better in the short term. Just knowing this can make you more aware of the process, helping you to resist that afternoon chocolate bar. Choose healthy options such as nuts and seeds, vegetable sticks or fruit as a snack.

Avoiding Junk Food

In Italy, a 'Slow Food' movement was started in which people were encouraged to choose a proper, preferably home-cooked meal instead of a burger. Initially this was a slightly tongue-in-cheek offensive against fast food, but it grew to have significant impact. We can all learn from this.

You might eat reasonably healthily at home, but find that when it comes to take-aways you are a junk-food addict. Take-aways tend to be higher in fat and calories than home-prepared food, so concentrate on making healthier choices at every opportunity, as in the following examples:

- Grilled or steamed rather than deep-fried foods
- Tomato and herb-based rather than cream-based sauces
- Lemon, balsamic vinegar or mustard rather than mayonnaise
- Leaner add-ons such as seafood and tomato on pizzas rather than double cheese and salami
- Tandoori and plain rice rather than masala and pilau

- Stir-fried vegetables and seafood with plain rice rather than spring rolls, fried prawn balls and fried rice
- Ask for salad dressings on the side and measure out the minimum amount you need to flavour the dish.

Resistance Tactics

Bingeing usually involves switching off the conscious brain until after the binge has taken place. A sort of numbness takes over as you go to the shop and consume what you buy soon after, cook a meal sufficient for two or three people to eat on your own at a sitting, or raid the freezer and tuck in. Become aware of this and at least observe the process. This is the first step towards doing something about it.

If you overeat habitually, observe the amount of food eaten by other people (those who do not overeat) when you are out or at friends' houses, or when you have visitors, and emulate them. If you overeat only when you are on your own, make a conscious decision to eat as if others were with you.

Bingeing often takes place in the car. There are not many places where you can eat and not be seen, and the car fits the bill for two-thirds of those with eating disorders (against a fifth of those without eating disorders). Make a rule of no food in the car.

If you tend to overeat, clean your teeth or chew gum to change the taste in your mouth at the critical moment when you want to add second helpings to your meal. Some people find that simply pausing before diving in for second helpings can diminish the desire for more food.

If you feel you have a real eating disorder, see page 203.

Problems with Self-Esteem

So much about food and eating is tied up with self-esteem (see page 38). Feeling unattractive, overweight, uninteresting or weak-willed is a great way to send yourself straight to the biscuit jar. Replace such thoughts with something positive, like 'My hair is looking terrific today' or 'I have a lovely smile'. (People remember a stunning smile more than a flat tummy anyway.)

Self-Deprivation

The newly coined term 'orthorexia' has been used to describe people who are over-fanatical about eating health foods. If you feel that you are on the slippery slope of cutting out too many foods from your diet and can't even eat out for fear that foods might have chemicals in them or be processed in a way that you don't know about, then this could be you. It might even be a first step towards anorexia. Those who are overly worried about healthy eating usually end up not actually enjoying food. It is important to seek some sort of balance.

If you are permanently dieting, this is likely to be another source of stress. If dieting is a source of worry, then it is likely to rebound and not be successful in the long term. Concentrate on healthy eating and making more fundamental changes in eating habits for a long-term result.

Feeling deprived is really not the point about changing eating habits. Instead of giving yourself a long list of foods you 'ought not' to be eating, concentrate on foods that you *can* eat and that you enjoy.

Another way to avoid feelings of deprivation is to treat yourself to non-food rewards, such as a glossy magazine, a video rental, a new accessory, a book or a theatre ticket.

Nutrition to Help Resolve Disordered Eating

- Make a point of eating three meals a day – not one meal a day, and not six meals a day.
- Include fresh fruit and vegetables whenever you can. The ideal plate consists of one-third protein (fish, eggs, meat, pulses), one-third complex carbohydrates (bread, pasta, potatoes) and one-third vegetables.
- Carbohydrates have the worst reputation for perpetuating the bingeing cycle. (Have you noticed that 'stressed' is 'desserts' spelled backwards?) If you head for starches and sugars all the time, greatly moderate your intake of bread, rice, pasta, biscuits, sugar and other carbohydrate sources. Concentrate on eating lots of fresh vegetables, fruit and protein and see if this makes a difference.
- Don't cut out fats from your diet – you need them for brain function and hormones. Low levels contribute to depression and eating disorders. See page 163 for more information.
- It is thought that one reason we crave fats is that we are deficient in essential fatty acids. Making sure you get enough in your diet – the best source for this is flax oil, 1tbsp daily – might help to reduce fat cravings.
- Take a healthy-eating cookery course to develop your understanding of how to prepare delicious and healthy food.
- Get more involved in other areas of food health, such as how it is grown and distributed. You can visit your local farmers' markets and talk to the traders about how their food is produced. You could grow vegetables in your garden (or if you have only a windowsill, some herbs, lettuces and radishes), go hunting for edible mushrooms or go blackberrying in the countryside in the autumn. You could even gather (unsprayed) nettles in town for nettle soup!

Supplements to Help Resolve Disordered Eating

- The mineral chromium helps to balance blood-sugar levels. Take 200–500mcg daily. It works best if you take a B-complex alongside it.
- Zinc has a good track record in helping people with eating disorders, especially severe under-eaters. Zinc is needed for brain health and may help to normalize thinking patterns. Take 25mg daily.
- Liquorice root helps to normalize blood-sugar levels. (Do not take it if you have raised blood pressure.)
- If you are terrified of calories, in the first instance at least make sure you get sufficient nutrients. Take a multi-vitamin and multi-mineral supplement and a free-form amino acid mixture (a protein supplement usually sold for athletes).

These have very few, if any, calories and can help to normalize brain chemistry, which helps if you are receiving counselling for an eating disorder. You cannot subsist on them but they will help if you are seriously under-eating.

Let's Do Lunch

Sometimes everything seems to conspire against eating healthily at work. Business-lunch menus are tempting. Sandwiches are gobbled up hurriedly at desks, afternoon sugar-boosts are craved and meals are often skipped when under pressure. Forty per cent of calories are consumed out of the home these days, and the meals we eat at work form a large part of these. Because take-away foods tend to be higher in fat and calories than the foods we eat at home, it is a great idea to brush up on the skill of making healthy fast-food choices. For more ideas on how to choose healthy take-away options see page 167. With a little forethought and planning, healthy eating at the office can be quite easy. As a result, you will improve your energy levels and ability to concentrate and feed your body the nutrients it needs to deal with workday stresses.

Breakfast at Home: It all starts with breakfast, and if you are always running to get to the office on time, you might well be tempted to skip this vital meal. If you habitually grab a coffee and Danish pastry on the way in, you are just giving yourself an adrenalin hit (which perpetuates stress) and a meal of empty calories (ie, plenty of calories but virtually no nutrients). Ideally, allow an extra 15 minutes each morning to eat a bowl of muesli cereal and a piece of fruit, or a couple of slices of wholegrain toast and a glass of juice. If you are convinced that breakfast is not your thing, you could be wrong. Not feeling hungry until mid-morning is a classic sign of blood-sugar imbalance – and, of course, this perpetuates the disordered blood-sugar cycle. Quite often, hunger signals will be suppressed by several cups of coffee. You really need to make yourself eat something and keep it up for about four weeks to retrain yourself. You will then see how much better you feel, and you'll feel worse if you skip breakfast after that.

Breakfast on the Run: If you can't break the habit of eating on the run, grab some of the following healthy options: a banana or other piece of fruit, a bio-yogurt, a few oatcakes, some rye crackers spread with nut butter, or a toasted bagel with cheese and a cup of tea from a sandwich shop. Any of these will sustain you for a longer time and will be gentler on your body than the caffeine- and sugar-laden coffee and Danish.

Snacks: Snacking helps to keep energy levels up and keep you alert. But a chocolate bar will just aggravate your stress levels and lead to energy dips later by perpetuating the blood-sugar imbalance. A couple of cubes of chocolate or one biscuit is really not the point – it is when you are inexplicably drawn to eating the whole packet and feeling exhausted soon after that you know it is draining you. In your desk drawer, keep some muesli bars (you can find healthy choices among all the sugar-laden ones), packets of mini-ricecakes or oatcakes and nuts and raisins. You can keep an attractive fruit bowl on your desk to munch from. If you snack healthily, there is a greater chance that you will avoid the post-lunch energy slump that so many people suffer from.

Take-aways: If you haven't made your own lunch, then seek out the healthy take-away lunch options. Enjoy a baked potato stuffed with baked beans or tuna, sushi boxes, sandwiches made with wholemeal bread, salad boxes (avoid those drowned in mayonnaise) and tortilla wraps with healthy ingredients.

Home-Packed Lunches: There is a wide range of healthy home-packed lunches that are simple and quick to make. Make sandwiches from wholemeal or pumpernickel bread, using tomato salsa, hummus or pickle to moisten the sandwiches instead of butter or mayonnaise. Take vegetable soup or left-over casseroles in a flask. Make your own salad box, adding, for example, chickpeas, sunflower seeds, strips of lean meat, grilled peppers, sun-dried tomatoes – a trawl through the left-overs in your fridge will often dictate which extra ingredients you can add to the basic salad. Keep a packet of rye crackers at the office and then eat them with whatever is easy to hand as you rush out the door: a can of sardines and a couple of tomatoes, a boiled egg, tinned tuna, hummus. Pitta bread and crudités (chopped fresh vegetables) are easy and are also good with hummus, tzatziki and guacamole.

Restaurants: Choose the healthier options in restaurants at lunchtime. Order a salad with the dressing on the side or vegetable soup. Healthy meals include baked fish or chicken with a selection of vegetables or a side salad, pasta with a low-fat sauce such as tomato, tandoori chicken or chickpea curry with plain rice. Favour fresh-fruit salad topped with yogurt or with a little ice cream for dessert.

Canteens: If you have a works canteen and are unhappy with the choice, get together with a few like-minded colleagues to press for change and give them suggestions for what they could offer.

Tired All the Time

Many people actually believe it is normal to feel washed out most of the time. They rationalize that with their frenetic pace of life, burnout is inevitable and exhaustion is just something they have to put up with. But it is not normal to feel this way and there is a lot that can be done about it. Of course, it helps not to burn all your candles at both ends all the time, but you can also shore up your body's reserves to help you cope with a busy life. If you are feeling exhausted, take this as a wake-up call to look after your health. Don't ignore extreme tiredness, or you may find that it becomes serious depression or chronic fatigue as a result of a little push from a stressful event such as moving house or changing jobs.

Ideally, you need to take a multi-disciplinary approach when dealing with exhaustion. The best results are achieved by using a combination of diet, nutritional supplements, stress management or counselling, physiotherapy, massage or gentle exercise, and perhaps another discipline such as homeopathy or acupuncture.

Lifestyle Factors

Eat three meals a day and make sure you are making healthy choices (see Healthy Eating, page 161). You would not expect your car to perform without the right fuel, so do not expect this of your body.

A nutritionist can look for various 'loads' placed upon the immune system – for instance, pollution, toxins, allergies or food intolerances can have an effect – and can advise on measures to take to reduce these.

If you are staying up late to catch up on domestic or work-related jobs, or are out clubbing into the early hours, and then getting up early to go to the office or to deal with family needs, and pushing yourself between times, you really need to take a long, hard look at your lifestyle.

Exercise can seem impossible if you are exhausted. Nevertheless, it is important for wellness to keep moving, no matter how gently. Find a programme that works for you. Slow walking, yoga, moderate swimming and gentle stretches are all ways gradually to get yourself moving again.

Medical Factors

If you are feeling chronically burned out over a period of time, it is important to rule out possible causes, such as anaemia, glandular fever or diabetes, with your doctor. It might be a good idea to ask your doctor for a blood test to rule out such physiological conditions as an underactive thyroid.

More doctors are becoming aware of the diagnosis of chronic fatigue (also variously called ME, post-viral fatigue and adrenal syndrome, depending on the symptoms). Chronic fatigue involves a diagnosis of symptoms lasting at least six months, including excessive fatigue that is worsened by physical or mental exertion, and possibly also muscle weakness, painful lymph nodes, depression, sleep disturbance, memory and concentration problems or digestive problems. For support organizations see pages 203–204.

Another possible cause of tiredness is an overgrowth of an opportunistic yeast organism called *Candida albicans* which is normally resident in the bowels. But if the immune system of the person is weakened, there is a greater chance of candida spreading. Most commonly this manifests itself as thrush, which leads to a white discharge and itchiness in the vagina or anal area. Thrush of the mouth, eyes, under the nails or other areas is also quite common. Occasionally, however, the candida manages to invade higher up the digestive tract, in the small intestine and other body tissues. This can cause the sufferer to feel quite debilitated, with energy problems being one of the most severe effects. There are often a host of other related problems such as food allergies, sensitivities to moulds and damp environments, and headaches and migraines. For advice on dietary treatment for candida, see page 174 and 198.

The Road to Recovery

The greatest mistake that many people make when they are on the road to recovery and begin to feel better is to do too much, too soon. If you have been exhausted or ill for a while, it takes time to build up your reserves again, so take it slowly in order to avoid another setback.

Increasing Enjoyment

If you are not inspired by what you are doing and find your life a bit of a drudge, that can be as tiring as having too much to do. Use mind-mapping techniques (see page 16) to find out what it is you really want to be doing with your time. People who enjoy what they do are less likely to feel tired.

Stay Healthy while Exercising

- Take a yin-yang approach to your exercise – find a balance between aerobic exercise, such as fast walking (rapid enough to build up a sweat without making you so breathless that you can't hold a conversation) and anaerobic exercise, such as weight-training sufficient to sculpt and define muscles. Find a balance between fast-and-exciting and smooth-and-calm.

- Hydration is vital to fully benefit from exercise. Keep a bottle of water handy to sip as you need it, and drink a large glass of water just before and just after exercise. Carrying a water bottle with you at the gym is also a good idea.

- Exercising on a full stomach is not a good thing for digestion, but exercising on an empty stomach can trigger migraines and low-blood-sugar attacks. Just before you exercise, eat a small complex-carbohydrate snack such as a banana sandwich or a couple of oatcakes spread with nut butter. You'll enjoy a larger meal at least half an hour after exercising.

- While exercise is obviously beneficial, especially when we are stressed out, it does cause a degree of wear and tear on body tissues as well as on ligaments and joints. A daily antioxidant supplement that includes vitamins A, C and E as well as selenium and zinc helps to protect body tissues and reduce inflammation of joints. If the supplement also has bioflavonoids and beta-carotene, so much the better.

Nutrition to Help Boost Energy

A healthy diet is essential to improve energy levels and promote recovery from either constant tiredness or illness, and this is covered in detail at the beginning of this chapter. Here are some key aspects of this:

- As stressed throughout this book, eat plenty of high-energy foods such as fruits, vegetables, lentils, pulses, brown rice, oats, barley and fresh fish, and drink 1.5–2 litres of water daily for hydration and cleansing of your body tissues and organs.

- Favour oils that provide you with healthy EFAs (essential fatty acids), such as cold-pressed, linseed and walnut oils. Completely avoid hydrogenated fats, which are found in margarines and in packaged foods such as crisps, biscuits and pies. (Vegetarian packaged foods are also often sources of hydrogenated fats.)
- Eat to balance blood-sugar levels. Eating five small meals/snacks daily will reduce the energy taken to digest large meals.
- Avoid all sources of caffeine and alcohol. You may want to reduce coffee gradually over a couple of weeks to prevent a rebound reaction and headaches.
- Keep sources of sweetness to fruits, a little honey, a little fructose or FOS (see page 204), a sweet-tasting fibre in powder form to use as a sugar substitute. Because FOS is actually a fibre it helps bowel health.
- Sprinkle cracked linseeds or psyllium husks on your cereal or include them in drinks daily in order to improve digestive function and to help the elimination of toxins from the body.
- Food sensitivities can be a particular problem for people who seem to be perpetually exhausted, especially if there does not seem to be any other obvious cause of their fatigue. It often pays dividends to follow a wheat-free diet for a few weeks. You could also possibly investigate other sensitivities, such as dairy products.
- A typical Western diet means we generally eat twice as much salt as we need, with all the linked problems of high blood pressure and water retention. However, if you have been on a salt-restricted diet for a long time and have very low blood pressure, which can lead to exhaustion, you may actually need temporarily to increase the salt in your diet. Do not do this if you have been on a 'normal' diet.
- The main dietary advice for getting rid of candida (see page 172) is to avoid all sources of sugar rigorously because the yeast feeds on sugar. In addition to cutting out sugar, fast-releasing carbohydrates (which turn into sugar quickly) and alcohol, it may also mean cutting back on over-ripe fruit and sticking to fruit such as green apples and pears.
- The other main dietary treatment for candida is to avoid all yeasts. These include bread (apart from breads and crackers that do not use yeast, such as soda bread and oatcakes), alcohol (again), most cheeses (cottage cheese is OK) and in extreme cases mushrooms, Quorn and vinegar. It is also necessary to avoid stimulants and any foods to which you may be sensitive or allergic.

Supplements to Help Boost Energy

- The most important nutrients to combat energy depletion are the B-group of vitamins, which are involved in all aspects of energy production in the cells. Take either a 50mg B-complex or some brewer's yeast daily (but not if your problem is candida – see above).
- Other important energy-producing nutrients are magnesium, vitamin C and iodine; iodine helps to produce the thyroid hormone which regulates metabolism and so is important for energy. Maintain healthy iodine levels by taking 150mcg of kelp daily.

- Liquorice root can help to stabilize blood sugar and also improve low blood pressure, which can be linked to tiredness. In order to elevate your blood pressure you need to use liquorice that contains glycyrrhizin rather than the DGL (deglycyrrhized) version. You can also find compounds that combine liquorice and Siberian ginseng (see next tip). Do not take liquorice root if you have high blood pressure.
- Herbal adaptogens are used to help the body adapt to stress and have even been used on space programmes to help cosmonauts adapt to the stress of being in space. The ginsengs (Siberian, Korean and American) are the best-known adaptogens for improving energy and reducing the harmful effects of stress. Ginseng should not be overused as it can lead to overstimulation and insomnia, and this is particularly a risk if it is taken with sources of caffeine. It should not be used by those with high blood pressure.
- Another useful adaptogen is rhodiola (see page 204).
- Taking a probiotic supplement, which includes lactobacillus acidophilus and bifidobacteria, is helpful if you are dealing with candida.

Giving Up Smoking

Many people smoke to relieve their stress, and even the idea of giving up smoking, which is one of the most potent addictions we know, can be incredibly stressful. But you have decided to quit, so how can you help yourself through the process?

There are around 4,000 toxic chemicals in cigarettes, and the average smoker gets through 5,500 cigarettes each year. But all the health warnings in the world are not going to make you give up unless you really want to do so. A multi-faceted approach taking behavioural, nutritional and herbal methods into account is probably the most effective way forward. (For organizations that can help you, see page 204.)

How to Go about It

Just cutting back will usually simply lead to increasing the amount you smoke later on. Better to go cold turkey and give up totally.

Women in particular link giving up smoking with putting on weight, and this can interfere with their resolve. Studies show that those women who had counselling for this fear while giving up smoking not only were significantly more likely to be successful in kicking the habit but also were less likely to put on weight.

Aids to Quitting

Avoid situations that trigger the craving for a cigarette – particularly having an alcoholic drink or a coffee. Drink tonic with lime and Angostura bitters, tomato juice or green or herbal teas instead.

You may find that keeping your mouth and hands busy helps. Chew gum (with xylitol in it for healthy teeth) and take up fiddling with a squeezy stress ball or worry beads.

Imagine what it is like to kiss a dirty ashtray. Really imagine this in full detail – go as far as rubbing your nose in a real dirty ashtray. This sounds disgusting (don't do it in public or everyone will think you have gone crazy) but it is a graphic way of bringing your other senses into the process, and it helps with sensory memory.

Some people find that acupuncture or hypnotism is highly effective at reducing cravings for nicotine.

Nutrition to Help Stop Smoking

- The desire to smoke is usually worsened by poor blood-sugar control. Smoking is often just one prop among many – including coffee, alcohol, sugar and carbohydrates. The yo-yo assault on blood sugar is a reason why so many ex-smokers exchange one fix, tobacco, for another, such as sweets or crisps. By eating a diet based on lean meats, beans, lentils, chickpeas and other pulses, nuts and seeds, wholegrains, vegetables and fruit, blood-sugar balance can be improved and the desire to smoke reduced.
- When you give up smoking there is often an outpouring of mucus as your body finally has the chance to throw off years of accumulated toxins. This can be exacerbated by a diet high in milk and cheese, so during this time it may be best to significantly or reduce these.
- A diet rich in antioxidants is vital to counteract the damage that smoking can do. Eat seven to ten portions of fruits and vegetables daily. For instance, you can have one piece of fruit and a glass of fresh juice for breakfast, a couple of tomatoes and a piece of fruit at lunchtime, a bowl of vegetable soup and a portion of broccoli with your evening meal, and a couple of pieces of fruit as snacks mid-morning and mid-afternoon. It isn't too difficult.

Supplements to Help Stop Smoking

- Each cigarette robs the body of about 25mg of vitamin C, so a diet rich in this nutrient from fruits and vegetables is vital. Taking at least 500mg daily can help to counteract some of this loss.
- The herb wild oats, *Avena sativa*, has a calming effect on the mind, helping to reduce the craving for a cigarette. The herb *Acorus calamus* was once used by miners to keep their lungs clear, though it should not be taken for more than a couple of months. Another herb, which should be used only under the supervision of a herbalist, is lobelia, which has a similar chemical structure to nicotine and helps to wean a person off cigarettes. (To obtain more information on lobelia, see page 204.) Levels of the brain chemicals serotonin and dopamine fall when someone is giving up cigarettes, and the herb St John's wort will help to ease the resulting depression and low moods.
- The mineral chromium, at 200mcg daily, can reduce cravings by helping to balance blood-sugar levels.

Sleep Quality

Sleep deprivation is known to be one of the most effective torture methods, and yet one-third of people suffer this ghastly imposition on daily life at some time or other. Lack of sleep destroys coordination and affects concentration. But it is not just the absence of sleep that affects us – the actual quality of sleep is important, too. When we sleep we repair our bodies and make up for the stresses of the day. Sleep improves immune function and relaxes digestion. Dreams are thought to play an important beneficial psychological role.

People's sleeping patterns are affected in various ways by different forms of stress. Some may find they become depressed and tend to want to sleep all the time though the quality of the sleep is poor, frequently with early waking, and leaving them still feeling tired. Others find that worry keeps them tossing and turning all night and unable to get to the deep level of sleep needed to feel refreshed and raring to go in the morning. Some people are not consciously feeling stressed but because of irregular habits – such as working shifts, burning the candle at both ends or simply consuming the wrong foods – find that their sleep quality is poor.

Sleep is governed by cycles, and going through all the stages of sleep from the lightest (stage 1) through to the deepest (stage 4 and the so-called REM sleep, when dreaming takes place) is necessary. Rising levels of the hormone melatonin, released by the pineal gland, together with lowering levels of the stress hormones cortisol and adrenalin, govern when we feel sleepy, while the opposite pattern, triggered in part by daylight in the morning, wakes us up.

The Bedroom

Check that your bedroom is well ventilated, though not draughty. Change your bedding according to the season to avoid becoming too hot or too cold. Darkness is needed to raise melatonin levels, so consider having interlined curtains or a blackout blind.

Sleep Routines

Your circadian rhythms (body cycles), controlled by hormones, govern when you sleep. Establish regular routines to allow these rhythms to work properly. If, for example, you work shifts, keep the pattern going at weekends if you can and talk to your bosses about always working the same shifts instead of altering them frequently. It's in their interest, too, for you to function efficiently.

If you have got out of a routine of going to bed at the same time, avoid having a lie-in in the morning even if you feel the need to catch up. You can't always control when you fall asleep but you can control when you wake up. If you always wake at the same time (even at weekends), the time you go to bed should sort itself out.

If you occasionally miss a full night of sleep to have fun, that is one thing. But if you regularly miss out on sleep to meet work deadlines, you will cheat your health in the long run – you probably need to work on time management (see page 24), by imposing working hours and sticking to them or learning to say no to too much work.

Before Bedtime

Avoid television late at night. If there's something you really want to watch, set your DVD or video recorder. Give yourself time to wind down. Save vigorous exercise for earlier in the day, as exercising within three or four hours of bedtime will boost your metabolism and make it difficult to sleep. Try stretching and relaxing exercises instead, followed by a warm bath. Take a book to bed (but not a high-tension one).

Wakefulness

Keep a pen and paper on your bedside table. If worry is keeping you from falling asleep, write down the worry and some quick thoughts about solutions, and then lie down again. By transferring the worry to paper, you can banish it from your mind and have something positive to work with in the morning.

Some medications such as decongestants or asthma treatments can stop you getting to sleep. Check with your doctor about any possible side effects to drugs you are taking. (Do not stop prescribed medication without consulting your doctor first.)

If you find yourself counting the minutes and hours, you will find it even harder to sleep. Stop any chiming clocks and remove your alarm clock to a place where you can't see it. It can be better to get up and do something low-key, such as reading, in a chair – if you do this in bed, it can become a reminder of not being able to sleep.

If you regularly wake up worrying about irrelevancies such as shopping lists and whether you changed the cat litter, set aside time earlier in the day to make lists of these things to get rid of the need in the middle of the night.

Daytime Napping

There are two schools of thought on the question of daytime napping. Some say that a ten-minute nap is refreshing and a useful stress-buster, while others say that getting into the habit of napping is counterproductive. Experiment to see which might help you. Certainly, if you are unable to nap, a period of quiet repose and possibly meditation can be beneficial. Some famous nappers were highly productive people, such as Sir Winston Churchill, John F Kennedy and Napoleon Bonaparte. To obtain more information about napping, see page 204.

Snoring

Snoring can wake up both the snorer and their partner during the night. (The loudest snore on record peaked at an astounding 93 decibels – louder than a passing Tube train.) It is a sign of partially blocked airways and may be associated with sleep apnoea. (In this, breathing is repeatedly suspended for ten seconds or more during sleep, most often as a result of over-relaxation of the muscles of the soft palate in the throat, which obstructs breathing. Medical treatment is available for sleep apnoea.)

Snoring may be exacerbated by obesity, alcohol or smoking. Several sprays, based on mint-flavoured natural oils that lubricate the palate and back of the mouth, are available, as is a product containing enzymes that help to break down mucus and also contains decongestant herbs (see page 204). Changing your diet may also help (see page 180).

Sleep Diary

If you are finding it difficult to solve your sleep problems, keep a sleep diary, noting what happens and when, including what you eat and do during the night. Include what food/medication you consume. You will get a truer picture if you keep the diary for a period of three or four weeks, as you will be able to see common threads and recurring behaviours that can be modified to break bad sleep patterns.

Nutrition to Help Improve Sleep

- Eating late at night stimulates digestion and metabolism and can keep you awake, particularly if the meal is heavy or fatty. Normally metabolism drops by around 20 per cent, and eating late prevents this initially.
- Caffeine is a strong stimulant which can keep some hypersensitive people awake even if they drink only one cup a day. Even decaffeinated coffee has similar stimulants, theobromine and theophyline, which may cause sleep problems. Caffeine is found in coffee, tea, colas, chocolate, painkillers, cold remedies, the herb guarana and some 'energy' supplements. Substitute decaffeinated tea, herb or fruit teas, hot oat drinks and hot toddies made with a little cordial.
- Avoid alcohol, especially late at night, as it can interfere with the ability to reach deep, restful sleep, even if it initially induces sleepiness. The result is fitful and restless sleep. Nicotine can also interfere with sleep.
- Low levels of the brain chemical serotonin are linked to sleeplessness. An amino acid (protein link) called tryptophan is made into 5HTP, which in turn makes serotonin. Tryptophan-rich foods include fish, turkey, chicken, cottage cheese, beef, eggs, bananas, oats, avocados, milk, cheese, nuts, peanuts and soya, but eating carbohydrates helps to selectively take up the tryptophan. Vitamin B6 is also needed to help this process. Eating protein-based meals earlier in the day and carbohydrate-rich meals based on rice, bread, pasta and potatoes at night is likely to help to induce sleep. Oats are particularly soporific so a small bowl of porridge might do the trick.
- A nightcap of a sleep-inducing herb drink can help enormously. Camomile, vervain, peppermint, lemon balm, hops, rose hips, dill and fennel – either used singly or in blends – have a calming effect.
- Calcium is a sleep-inducer, which is why a glass of warm milk at night helps some people. Combine the milk (or calcium-enriched soya milk) with oats and you have the classic night-time drink. It can also help if you take any daily calcium supplement you are using at night-time. Magnesium helps calcium to work more effectively and it is also a relaxant. Take a supplement that combines the two with your evening meal – at a ratio of two parts calcium to one part magnesium (eg, 500mg calcium to 250mg magnesium). You might think that as milk is a good source of calcium, cheese would also do, but the compound tyramine in cheese is thought to be behind its nightmare-inducing propensity.
- Blood-sugar lows in the middle of the night can wake you up and make it difficult to get back to sleep. Combat this by eating mainly complex carbohydrates during

the daytime, such as brown rice, wholemeal bread, rye bread and whole porridge oats, and keeping a small snack such as a banana or a couple of oatcakes on your bedside table to nibble on just before you drop off.

- Snoring is more likely if you are bunged up with mucus, and avoiding milk or all dairy products may help to reduce the amount your body produces. Although using soya products instead will help quite a lot of dairy-intolerant people, soya can also increase mucus levels in others, so it is question of experimenting with all the options. Goat or sheep products might work, as could rice milk or coconut milk.

Supplements to Help Improve Sleep

- Natural sleep is always preferable to drug-induced sleep. Even with herbal sleep-inducers it is best to view them as a short-term measure, while you establish a healthy sleeping routine.
- Hops, lemon balm, valerian, passiflora, wild lettuce, skullcap and other sleep-inducing herbs are readily available in different combinations. Buy them from a reputable company and follow the instructions. You could take one capsule of the herb valerian half an hour before bedtime to help promote deeper sleep in the long term, but be patient as it does take a month or so to kick in.
- Early waking in which you cannot get back to sleep again can be a sign of depression, in which case seek counselling (see also Cognitive Thinking, page 66). Your doctor may prescribe a short course of antidepressants, which can help your sleeping cycle as well. For mild to moderate depression the herb St John's wort is as effective as an antidepressant but without similar side effects. St John's wort is fine used on its own, or with complementary herbs, but must not be used alongside other prescribed medication, including the contraceptive pill, without checking with your doctor or a medical herbalist.

Concentration and Memory

The stress of having too many things to do really plays havoc with your ability to focus. Stress has a lot to do with reduced concentration. Often, lack of concentration in children is attributed to laziness and in the elderly is put down to reduced mental capability, when stress may be the actual culprit. Sometimes lack of concentration is quite simply a bad habit which can be worked on. It can be dispiriting and at times embarrassing to forget things, and it can also affect self-esteem.

If you are concerned about your memory power, you could arrange to have a series of memory tests to set your mind at rest (see page 204).

Avoiding Distractions

If you need to concentrate – say, to finish some revision or to meet a work deadline – you will find it hard to concentrate if surrounded by hustle and bustle. Find a quiet place where you can hide away for as long as you need to.

If you are doing research for a project, beware of getting sidetracked. It is all too easy to go off on a tangent when sitting in the library, browsing the Internet or interviewing people. To a degree this will keep you absorbed and might lead to other interesting avenues. However, if it gets out of hand, you need to pull yourself back and decide to concentrate on the job in hand. Keep a piece of paper next to you and note down any extraneous thoughts.

Increasing Interest

If you are not really interested in what you are doing, concentration will not come easily. This may be a hint that you need to change your study course, job or activity. Alternatively, fall back on your inner resources and find something interesting about the 'dull' activity. It may be that you respond better to a different medium. For instance, some people are better at listening to tapes, while others prefer to read books or watch a video, and still others will be better off copying down text or browsing the Internet. Many people improve their powers of concentration by mixing some of these media.

Lifestyle Factors

Sometimes a person's ability to concentrate is seriously impaired by blood-sugar swings, as their brain simply does not have the fuel to keep focused. This is particularly the case when mid-afternoon energy slumps are the problem. See the diet tips on page 173.

Get a good night's sleep if you know you need to concentrate the next day.

Cannabis and other recreational drugs definitely impair concentration and memory if used regularly.

Tricks for Improving Memory

If you always have trouble remembering the names of people to whom you have been introduced, this is likely to be related to lack of concentration at the time, rather than failing memory. Get into the habit of really paying attention, and not worrying about other things, such as what they think of you or whom you are going to talk to next. Make a memory link, such as imagining Mary with a lamb under her arm ('Mary had a little lamb'), or repeating their name a couple of times when you speak to them.

The same goes for misplaced items. If you are not consciously aware when you put your keys down or put your wallet in a drawer, you could spend many fruitless hours looking for them. Aim to get into the habit of noting where you put things down. Or have a place where you always put something, such as a hook in the hall for keys.

Transfer lists to paper rather than keeping them in your mind. A cluttered brain can slow you down as much as a cluttered desk can.

Use it or lose it. If you want to remember something, practise, practise, practise.

If you need to remember a long list, break it down into memorable 'chunks'. Memorizing a shopping list of ten random items is more difficult than remembering a few items from each shop – so break the list down into, say, three items from the baker, two from the butcher and five from the grocer. Similarly, a series of numbers, such as 392503557, might be difficult to remember, but 392-503-557 is much easier.

If you know that you generally find it easier to concentrate at a particular time, then plan your day accordingly. Try to arrange your activities so that you can undertake the more demanding tasks at the best time for you.

Mental Workouts

Give your brain a workout with mental gymnastics. By breaking normal thinking and concentration patterns, you can exercise your brain and improve brain functioning. Challenge your normal patterns by, for instance, eating breakfast with chopsticks, brushing your teeth using the wrong hand or reading a book upside down. This may sound crazy but it can help. You can also exercise your mental faculties by doing crosswords, word games like Scrabble, and jigsaw puzzles (or see page 204).

Memory Problems in Pregnancy

Pregnancy can certainly make you more fuzzy-brained than normal – it isn't just a myth. First of all, you may be doing more than usual and your sleeping patterns may change, both of which can affect memory. Also, the pregnancy hormone progesterone has a relaxing effect. But brain size actually shrinks slightly during pregnancy and then recovers about six months after the birth. No one is absolutely sure why this is but it is believed that the developing baby is literally using for its own development the fats that make up the brain. It could therefore help to eat lots of oily fish, fresh nuts and seeds, and take a GLA and EPA fatty acid supplement.

Retirement Years

Stay interested in life. Those with the sharpest mental acuity in retirement years are people who never give up learning. An active life is the best way to preserve brain health for the future. People of retirement age who have interests and hobbies and are physically active not only live longer but also hang on to their mental faculties for longer.

Nutrition to Help Improve Concentration and Memory

- If you know you need to concentrate at a particular time of the day or evening, make sure you avoid alcohol, which would play havoc with your resolve.
- Blood-sugar swings lead to drowsiness, often just when you need to concentrate and particularly mid-afternoon. If this is the case, make sure you eat wholefoods and wholegrains and avoid sugary snacks. Nibble instead on fruit or vegetable sticks with a little yogurt or cottage cheese for protein, or a small handful of nuts or seeds.
- While coffee may keep you alert in the short term, if you regularly drink too much of it (more than two cups a day) you are likely to find that it has the opposite effect on your brain functioning. Substitute alternative coffees such as dandelion, chicory, barley or acorn coffee – there are many different types available at health-food shops.
- Antioxidants are vital for brain health and are thought possibly to slow down age-related degeneration of brain tissues. Eating a diet rich in fruit and veg will boost your antioxidant level, and an antioxidant supplement might be a good insurance.

Supplements to Help Concentration and Memory

- Ginkgo biloba can be useful when you need to make sure your concentration is at a peak, say for an exam, interview, presentation or difficult meeting. Take 60–300mg two hours beforehand.
- As ever, B-vitamins are vital for brain health and concentration. Take 100mg daily. (Do not worry about your urine turning bright yellow, which results from high doses of B2.)
- Phosphatidyl serine is used by the body as a building material for brain tissue. Take 100–300mg daily.
- Lecithin contains a high amount of choline which is used to make an important neurotransmitter (a brain chemical involved in neural activity). Take 1 tablespoon of lecithin daily (in yogurt or straight off the spoon) or a choline supplement of 300–600mg daily.

Dealing with Addictions

Addictions are a chicken-and-egg situation as far as stress is concerned. Chemical dependency – whether it be to drugs, nicotine, alcohol or food – is vastly exacerbated by stress, and the addiction itself is a serious source of stress, both mental and physical.

All addictions share the common feature that a 'high' becomes harder and harder to achieve, requiring more and more 'hits' and leading further and further into addictive behaviour patterns. Much time is spent thinking about how to get the next 'fix', and it will often involve subterfuge. The pointers in this section are designed to be of use for those who find that they have the mild to moderate forms of addiction, which are sufficient to impact on daily life and be a source of anxiety.

The information can also be used in conjunction with other therapies for more serious addictions, but should never be used as an alternative to professional and medical advice. Anyone who has a serious addiction should seek the advice of their doctor and the relevant support organizations (see page 204). To be addicted to any substance is to be in a lonely situation, and it is vital to realize that you need all the help you can get. There are plenty of people out there who can help you through the experience and who understand what is involved – you just need to seek them out.

Understanding the Problem

There is a biochemical aspect to all addictions. Even a thrill from something that does not have an obvious chemical aspect to it, such as gambling or shopping, results in a type of electrochemical activity in the brain that is typical of addiction. What this means is that all types of addiction have both behavioural and chemical effects, and both elements have to be addressed in order to beat the habit. Diet can often help with the biochemical aspects (see page 185). Relief from the behavioural effects can be gained by following the advice in this section and also, possibly, seeking out one of the listening therapies such as counselling.

Some people are able to make that quantum leap from being a person who has a habit to being someone who doesn't. The process by which they arrive at that point is one of self-discovery and understanding the problem, even though the actual moment of making that irrevocable decision appears to happen in an instant. You can accelerate this process just by knowing this and actively looking for the one motivating factor that might make the difference to you personally. The first step in dealing with any addictive habit is to recognize it exists. The second step is to have a genuine desire to overcome it.

Making Progress

Be kind to yourself and congratulate yourself on every small achievement. You can support yourself through the journey you are on and feel a lot better about the process if you are not always being self-critical.

If at first you don't succeed, don't let it put you off. You are not a failure, you just need to do it again until you achieve the results you want. If you do not get the results you want, treat it as a learning experience to apply the next time around.

Make a plan by using the techniques covered in Setting Goals (see page 8). Describe in detail what your goal is, how you are going to get there, what will help you and what might hinder you.

You may find it helpful to make a 'contract' with a friend who is in the same boat as you and has an addictive problem. Meet regularly, once or twice a week, and agree between you the measures you are going to take this time around. Discuss any successes or failures since your last meeting. Talk about what worked and what went wrong. Sharing the experience makes you realize that you are not alone.

Keep a private journal in which you can write down your wins, what has helped and what has not. Be honest with yourself, but also remember to keep your sense of humour. Put in an entry every day, even if it is just one word.

Some people need to hit rock bottom with their addiction before they can move towards recovery. Because they are caught up in self-deception, they need to see themselves as others see them. Such clarity of vision usually eludes those who can't kick a habit. Awareness can help an addict turn towards recovery, before it is forced upon them by circumstances.

Positive Action

Addiction is a form of compulsive behaviour. In this case you might be able to substitute another, non-damaging intense activity for the damaging compulsion. You might take a serious interest in a particular hobby or sport, which will distract you from your compulsion. Staying active helps to deflect your focus from seeking out another 'hit'.

Nurture yourself through the process of getting off your addiction by applying the principles of mindfulness discussed in Meditation (see page 141). Concentrate on nurturing activities. For instance, make delicious fresh juices to drink and really enjoy the process of making them, as well as the final juice to drink, and feel great about treating yourself well. The same goes for writing a letter to a friend, taking a relaxing bath, enjoying a meal or a walk. You can change your mental emphasis from self-abusing to self-nurturing.

Nutrition to Help Beat Addictions

Dietary adaptations are not just for those with dietary addictions. By dealing with diet you can influence the balance of brain chemicals that govern addictive tendencies. This section is for everyone who has a habit they want to give up.

- Having some protein with each meal and snack can reduce the impact that carbohydrates have on brain-chemical imbalances. Protein sources are eggs, lean meats, fish, lentils, beans and other pulses, soya, yogurt, cottage cheese and other cheeses, nuts and seeds.

- Blood-sugar imbalance is one of the main dietary contributors to addictions. You may not be aware of this tendency but it could be appropriate if you exist on coffee, strong teas, colas, sugary snacks, cigarettes and even foods that you might consider healthy but that have a dramatic effect on blood sugar – for instance, lots of dried fruit, large glasses of orange juice, large bowls of pasta or rice. You will probably suffer from accompanying drowsiness which makes you feel like you need an energy boost, which you resolve with yet another coffee or some chocolate. Make sure that all the carbs you eat are complex carbohydrates, such as wholemeal bread, brown rice, porridge oats and quinoa, and avoid stimulants such as coffee and sugar.

- Alcohol lowers the resolve to avoid whatever it is you are addicted to. It might be best, while you are on the journey to kick your habit, to also avoid alcohol.

- The brain needs very specific fats for optimal functioning. It is particularly important to consume the healthy omega-3 and omega-6 essential fatty acids (EFAs) found in oily fish, soya, walnuts, linseeds and pumpkin seeds. These help to normalize the functioning of the brain chemical serotonin.

- Antioxidants in the diet are vital to help your liver through the process of detoxifying any substances to which you have been addicted. Eat plenty of fruits and vegetables – at least five portions daily and preferably more.

- If you are a chocoholic but are worried about 'death by chocolate', take heart – it is not all bad. The unhealthy stuff is the typical chocolate that is sold at most confectionery counters. Instead, find good-quality 60–70 per cent cocoa-mass dark chocolate, and enjoy this in moderation. Cocoa in chocolate is actually a perfectly good food and is very rich in antioxidants, but it is the high sugar levels that are the real problem. However, remember that chocolate with a high cocoa-solid content is also relatively high in caffeine compounds.

- If you are attracted to colas, energy drinks or the herb guarana, these are really just caffeine and/or sugar in another form. Caffeine is the most widely consumed drug; in high amounts, or if the person is sensitive, it perpetuates other addictions. Substitute non-caffeine drinks such as dandelion coffee, fruit or herbal teas or fruit juices diluted with sparkling water.

Supplements to Help Beat Addictions

- All addictive substances, including alcohol, nicotine, sugars and over-the-counter and illicit drugs, deplete the body of certain important nutrients. The most vulnerable are the B-vitamins, vitamin C, magnesium and chromium. If you have not yet kicked your particular habit, it is certainly a good idea to take a good daily multi-vitamin and multi-mineral supplement.

- B-vitamins are vital for all aspects of mental health and are most often depleted when someone has been taking any addictive substance for a while. Take a 100mg supplement daily (don't worry about your urine turning bright yellow – this is just the B2 part of the supplement).
- L-glutamine is helpful to reduce cravings. Take 3–5g twice a day. It is easiest and cheapest to take in powdered form, mixed into water or juice. Avoid it if you have liver or kidney damage.
- If you don't like to eat oily fish, it is advisable to take 1–2g of fish-oil supplements every day.

Beating Infections and Boosting Immunity

If you dread the coming of winter because you always seem to catch every bug going, you can prepare a couple of months ahead by tuning up your immune system. The immune system is easily depressed by stress. This is quite apparent when we become ill at just the time when we need all our resources – when moving house triggers the flu, a promotion brings a heavier workload along with chronic fatigue syndrome and students develop glandular fever around exam time (a very common phenomenon). By supporting your immune health you give it the resources it needs to fight off infections.

Your Surroundings
A polluted environment can reduce immune health. At work avoid standing or sitting near the photocopier too much (see Healthy Office, page 190). Avoid smoky atmospheres and at home cut back on the number of chemicals used around the house (see Housework Realities, page 152).

Mind and Body
Laughter is one of the best immune stimulants. Retain your sense of humour.

Keep moving. Moderate exercise improves immune health. It also improves the flow of lymph throughout the body. The lymph system can be thought of as the body's waste disposal system and helps to excrete immune-dampening toxins.

Smoking is guaranteed to bring immune health to its knees. Give it up (see Giving Up Smoking, page 175). If you continue to smoke, then take at least 500mg of vitamin C a day to partially compensate, and eat loads of antioxidant-rich fruits and vegetables (see pages 162 and 176).

If you have had two or more pregnancies close together, your immune health might well be suffering. Follow the dietary advice on the next page even more closely and make sure you get at least two full nights' sleep (without crying babies) each week.

When Illness Strikes

If you feel ill, don't fight it, but operate at a level at which you feel comfortable. If necessary, take to your bed for complete rest. If you ignore the warning signs and try to work through it, you do not allow your body to mount the necessary immune response as energy is diverted into other activities. One or two days at home or in bed might be a good trade-off against several days of bed-rest when you are finally incapacitated.

Excessive use of antibiotics (more than once or twice a year) ultimately suppresses immune function. Taking acidophilus and bifidobacteria (also found in live yogurt, see page 188) can help to redress the bacterial balance of the bowel, which in turn supports immune health.

Nutrition to Help Boost Immunity

- As you will already have gathered by now, there is no substitute for eating at least five portions of a variety of fruits and vegetables daily. The body uses the antioxidants in these to improve immune health. Vitamin C-rich foods, which are probably the most important, include citrus fruit, blackcurrants, kiwis, dark green leafy vegetables such as cabbage and broccoli, and potatoes and sweet potatoes in their jackets.
- Aim to include at least one portion of dark berries in your diet daily – autumn and winter options, to help protect against colds and flu, include blackberries, blueberries (frozen or canned are fine), cranberries and elderberries. Sambucol (available from health food stores) is a tonic made from elderberries, and a teaspoon once or twice a day is a delicious way to keep infections at bay. Biona make a cranberry juice sweetened with apple juice instead of sugar.
- If you are low in zinc, not only are you more likely to get an infection but the illness is likely to last longer. Zinc-rich foods include lean red meat, shellfish, wholegrains, seeds and nuts.
- A clove of garlic a day, added to food, is a painless way to improve immune health. It is antiviral, antibacterial and anti-parasitic. Garlic has even been shown to prevent the growth of antibiotic-resistant MRSA (*Streptococcus aureus*), which kills many hospital patients. The immune-enhancing effects of the allicin it contains have been well studied. If you find it easier you could take garlic supplements, which are virtually odourless.
- Fresh ginger root is known to enhance immunity. Together with garlic, ginger is an essential ingredient for Chinese-style chicken broths and healthy vegetable stir-fries. Grated with lemon and honey, ginger makes a comforting drink, useful for promoting sweating to lower body temperature when you have the flu.
- Making fruit and vegetable juices is a delicious way to support immune health and get a boost of antioxidants. Aim to make three or four fresh juices each week. The quercitin in apple is particularly useful for lung health, and the beta-carotene in carrots keeps mucus membranes functioning well. A healthy gut also promotes overall immune health, and eating pineapple and papaya helps to maintain the health of the digestive tract.

- Eat one live yogurt each day. The beneficial bacteria will help to keep your bowel health optimal, which in turn boosts immunity. Alternatively, take a beneficial bowel-bacteria supplement daily.
- Oriental mushrooms such as maitake, shitake and reishi contain powerful immune-stimulating polysaccharides. You can buy them dried (see page 205) and add a couple a day to soups and stews. Or make an immune-supporting, delicious and very warming broth by adding them to some miso boiled up with chopped onion and garlic.
- Seaweeds are rich sources of minerals, and the alginic acid they contain helps to clear out toxins. Fill a pepper grinder with seaweed granules (see page 203) and add to savoury dishes for a mildly salty taste.

Supplements to Help Boost Immunity

- A good-quality antioxidant supplement once a day during autumn and winter is an excellent investment.
- The immune-boosting herbs echinacea and astragalus can be taken as tinctures (use about 30–50 drops of each in water) or as capsules (take one of each daily). One good formulation for winter ills combines echinacea with eucalyptus (an antiseptic to clear sinuses), liquorice root and aniseed (expectorants), peppermint and cloves (to soothe ticklish throats) and fennel (a natural stimulant).
- Cat's claw, a Peruvian herb, is drunk as a tea and provides strong antioxidant protection to boost immunity.
- Tickles in the throat should respond to zinc and echinacea (see page 205) and Propolis lozenges.

Muscle Tension

Frequently, we hold tensions in our body as an alternative to voicing our stresses. We may also find ourselves hunched over desks or computers for hours at a time, leading to tight or painful neck and shoulder muscles. Working on muscle tension, whether short- or long-term, can have profound effects on relieving stress and improving overall health.

Postural Factors

To see if posture may be at the root of your tension problems, strip to your underwear and stand in front of a full-length mirror with legs together and your hands hanging loosely by your side. Look carefully to see if one shoulder is higher than the other and if your hip alignment is out. If so (and it is the case in many people), you will probably benefit from a discipline such as Alexander Technique, yoga or Pilates.

If you are worried and are holding tension in your neck and back as a result, work on the source of your concerns (see Anxiety, page 55, and Problem Solving, page 35).

Posture is a very good indicator of our internal emotional state. If we are depressed, we round our shoulders; if we are anxious, we tense our shoulders; and if we are happy, we tend to throw back our shoulders and look the world in the eye. Try this experiment: throw back your shoulders, walk briskly and look ahead while you are smiling. It is actually quite difficult to feel low and depressed when you adopt this posture. Now you know what to do when you are feeling fed-up.

Releasing Tension

Heat treatments can relax muscles and relieve pain. These simple treatments can be done at home. A warm shower, followed by a cream containing essential oils of lavender and rosemary rubbed into the affected area, is warming and relaxing. A hot-water bottle wrapped in a fluffy towel may also bring relief.

There is nothing quite like massage for relieving muscle tension, and it is even more effective if you have a massage after a heat treatment such as a sauna. For very bad muscle tension make sure that you go to a properly trained remedial-massage therapist.

A well-trained kinesiology practitioner can pinpoint the reason for muscle tensions and use a form of acupressure to rebalance the tautness of muscles so that they work in better balance.

Holding tension in the jaw is common, as is teeth-grinding at night. Your dentist may be able to give you advice about this, or a kinesiologist (see above) who is familiar with temporomandibular joint (TMJ) work can help to sort it out.

Nutrition to Help Relieve Tension

- Dehydration is a common reason for muscle tension. Low back pain is often particularly related to dehydration, which affects the strength of the muscles. Drinking 1.5–2 litres of water daily, while cutting back on dehydrating caffeine and alcohol, can make all the difference.
- Magnesium is vital to help muscles relax. Food sources include green leafy vegetables and wholegrains.

Supplements to Help Relieve Tension

- The minerals magnesium and calcium help to relax muscles, which can be involved in back spasm and other muscle tensions. While both minerals are important, the bias is often towards using magnesium (at around 400mg daily) to reduce muscle tension. It has a marked effect on cramped leg muscles, can be effective at treating back pain and is very useful for migraines.
- Another useful anti-spasmodic and muscle relaxant is the herb cramp bark, which can be taken as a tea or in capsule form.
- Devil's claw, a southern African herb, can provide fairly fast-acting relief for muscle tension through its muscle-relaxant action.
- The herb butterbur (Petasites) is a useful anti-spasmodic supplement for muscle tension. It can relieve tension-related migraine, menstrual cramps and muscle spasms. In about half to two-thirds of people it is fairly fast-acting (having an effect within about half an hour). Take 50mg twice daily for chronic muscle tension (see page 205).

Healthy Office

We spend a third of our day in the office, yet often give little thought to how our environment affects our health and stress levels. Think about the following factors in order to make your office a healthier and more pleasant place in which to spend your working day.

- If you are sitting at a desk all day, you may be storing up postural problems. Back and neck ache, repetitive strain injury (RSI) and tension headaches can all result. Check the following:
  — Your chair should give good back support and allow you to sit comfortably with the computer screen just below eye level.
  — Sit with your hips and back roughly at right angles to the chair, with both feet resting on the floor or on a footrest.
  — When typing, your upper arms should be vertical and your forearms parallel to the floor. The keyboard may need to be at a lower height than the desktop (for example, on a pull-out keyboard shelf) to achieve this.
  — Avoid cradling your phone under your chin or against your shoulder.
  — Change positions and get up and move around frequently.

- Many items of office equipment give off ozone, a hazardous gas that can worsen asthma and allergic attacks for many people. Even non-allergic people might be adversely affected by ozone emissions and might experience headaches, tiredness and itchy eyes. Photocopiers, printers, fax machines and computers are all to blame. Keeping green plants nearby can help to mop up some of these gases – ferns and spider plants are particularly good at this. If your exposure is high, and you experience adverse symptoms, you might consider a relatively inexpensive desk-top vaporizer to reduce ozone levels (see page 205).

- Keep a 1.5 litre bottle of water on your desk and keep topping up your drinking glass until you get through the bottle each day. Staying hydrated will help to keep dry skin, dry eyes, headaches and muscle aches at bay.

- Also have a bowl of fruit on your desk and nibble your way through this when you feel like a snack. Fruit, being watery, will keep you hydrated while providing power-packed nutrients.

- If your office does not yet have a no-smoking policy, lobby your managers to implement one. Most large offices have a no-smoking policy, but you may work in a small office with a chain-smoking colleague.

- In an ideal world, companies would always provide facilities to allow employees to unwind when necessary. A staff room that can be used for eating meals and taking rest periods away from your desk, with a water fountain and herbal teas alongside the usual tea and coffee, can all make your work life more pleasant. If you feel you lack such facilities, get together with colleagues to lobby for them. Alternatively, make your own workstation as pleasant as possible with plants, photographs and other pictures. See also page 134 for ways to unwind at work.

• Office strip-lighting does not provide the full-spectrum light needed for optimal functioning. The people who are most likely to suffer as a result of this are those who are prone to Seasonal Affective Disorder or SAD (see page 194). However, everyone can benefit from a half-hour stroll outside in full light, even in winter.

Pain Relief

Even though many people will simply try to suppress pain by taking analgesics, most will recognize that pain can be thought of as a messenger. The pain from a sprained ankle tells you not to put weight on that foot. Your toothache is a warning that a visit to the dentist cannot be delayed. That arthritic twinge is telling you to find out what might be causing the inflammation. But what many people do not realize is that stress can worsen pain. And, of course, pain is in itself a major anxiety in people's lives and is sometimes, in the case of injury or arthritis, a source of long-term stress.

Painkiller Options

In the UK we spend more than £270 million on painkillers each year. But not everyone can take over-the-counter (OTC) painkillers. Aspirin can cause gastritis or ulcers, and if you are asthmatic, aspirin can trigger an attack. A recent study concluded that those who take paracetamol once a week increase their risk of developing asthma by 80 per cent. Painkillers have also been found to induce 'rebound' headaches when more than 12 doses are taken weekly. Long-term use of prescription steroids, which suppress inflammation, can have far-reaching consequences, including osteoporosis. It is far better to treat the source of the pain if at all possible and to use painkillers that are free of side effects whenever you can (but do not stop taking prescribed medication without first consulting your physician).

Pain should never be ignored as a sign of stress. It is often the case that, subconsciously, people will feel it is OK to admit to physical pain, but will not find it easy to admit that they feel frightened, anxious or depressed. The psychological pain they are feeling may well be showing up as physical pain.

Drug-Free Pain Relief

Acupuncture is a proven method of pain relief in the short term. It is also a treatment that can eventually restore harmony and balance to your whole system, eliminating or vastly reducing pain. Consider osteopathy or chiropractic help to resolve back pain. (See page 205 for details of organizations.)

A transcutaneous electrical nerve stimulation (TENS) machine is another way to help block pain in a drug-free way. It is available from large pharmacies, or you can rent one. Best known for use during childbirth, it is employed for all sorts of pain management.

Many people find that copper bracelets offer relief from arthritic pain.

Magnets (see page 205) placed on the affected joint have been found to relieve pain. Magnetism is thought to increase the blood flow, thereby increasing oxygen and resulting in relief from pain. You can buy mattresses and pillows containing magnets or, more economically, buy plasters and straps that are designed for specific parts of the body, such as the elbow or knee.

A powerful healing meditation is the 'mountaintop meditation'. Visualize yourself at the top of a mountain, where the air is clean, you are surrounded by blue sky and there is a breeze and the warmth of the sun on your face. You are surrounded by other mountains covered with forests and with ribbons of rivers and pools of lakes in the valleys. Concentrating on your breathing, see a bright white channel of light and energy flowing from the sky into the top of your head (your crown chakra). The light flows through your body and limbs, energizing you and flowing through your feet into the mountain, connecting you to both the sky and the earth. Let the light channel healing energy from the sky and the earth as it flows through your body.

Prevention and Cure

So much pain and discomfort, particularly that of the joints and back, is related to poor posture and inappropriate footwear. As a first step, visit a qualified podiatrist to check for foot alignment and to find out if you have fallen arches. To improve all aspects of posture, consider Alexander Technique classes or one-to-one sessions with a qualified practitioner. Also, check your bed and mattress to make sure they are not contributing to the problem; a properly supportive mattress is always a worthwhile investment.

Nutrition to Help Relieve Pain

- Hormone-like chemicals produced in the body called leukotrienes and prostaglandins regulate inflammation. Changing the type of fats that a person eats is usually the first step in a nutritional programme aimed at pain relief. Saturated fats, found in meat, butter, eggs, cheese and full- and half-fat milk, are rich in a substance called arachadonic acid, which produces leukotrienes and these promote inflammation. Conversely, unsaturated fats found in oily fish, fresh nuts and seeds – for example walnuts, almonds, pecans, pumpkin seeds, sunflower seeds and evening primrose oil – are rich in omega-3 and omega-6 fats, which promote anti-inflammatory prostaglandins. Fish oil switches off the COX-2 enzyme that kills joint pain. Aspirin also does this but with the unwelcome effect of also inhibiting COX-1, which triggers gastrointestinal upset.
- Some people find that inflammation is worsened by certain foods to which they are sensitive, such as wheat, dairy products, citrus fruit, coffee, sugar and alcohol. Food sensitivities have been associated with arthritic pain in a significant number of cases.
- Histamine is the chemical involved in inflammation and allergies. The ever-popular vitamin C has a mild histamine-reducing effect and also appears to help stabilize the structure of cartilage. Another antioxidant substance, quercitin, found in apples

and onions (and also available in capsule form), blocks histamine release as well as stopping the release of leukotrienes, and is often used alongside vitamin C for pain relief. Ginger has a long history as an anti-inflammatory compound (but do not use it if you have stomach or duodenal ulcers) and also acts as an antihistamine.

- Substance P is a neurotransmitter (chemical messenger in the brain) responsible for the pain message. Elements that can block that message include curcumin (the active agent in turmeric), a potent antioxidant which gives the spice its dark yellow colour and is said to work as well as the steroid cortisone in relieving acute inflammation. Chillies are another powerful blocker of substance P, but if you can't take the heat there are capsicum supplements available.

- Some specific foods might be helpful. One study found that 20 cherries contained 12–25mg of anthocyanins, with more potent painkilling capability than an aspirin tablet, and this has to be one of the more pleasant pain-relief options.

Supplements to Help Relieve Pain

- The enzymes bromelain (found in pineapple) and papain (from papayas) are known to break up a substance called fibrin that collects in areas of inflammation and is one cause of painful swelling. Available in capsule form, these substances are proteolytic enzymes (which digest proteins), high doses of which have been used successfully to treat back problems and acute strains. Capsules are normally taken with meals to aid digestion but, when taken between meals, it is believed that they remove waste products and fibrin in the area of the injury, helping speed up the healing process. Bromelain also seems to block the formation of inflammatory prostaglandins. Do not take enzymes if you have ulcers or gastritis.

- Curcumin and ginger also promote the breakdown of fibrin, and as well as adding them liberally to your diet (see above), you can take supplements (but avoid ginger if you have stomach or duodenal ulcers).

- 600mg of Boswellic acid (Indian frankincense) can help with arthritis pain. You can also get it in a cream for localized inflammation, strains and back pain.

- Borage oil is a more potent source of GLA (gamma-linolenic acid) than evening primrose oil and is a potent anti-inflammatory agent. Take 300mg of GLA daily.

- White willow is really herbal aspirin, but it contains the full spectrum of complementary (synergistic) compounds and is therefore less likely to cause gastrointestinal upset.

- Nettle tea is particularly helpful for rheumatic pain. Drink three cups of it daily or take a supplement.

- Devil's claw is a powerful anti-inflammatory for pain relief and is suitable for long-term use.

- Knotgrass breaks down painful deposits in joints. It needs to be taken for at least four months for any benefit to be gained.

Seasonal Affective Disorder (SAD)

As the winter months draw in and daylight hours eventually dwindle from around 18 hours to half that, many people feel that their moods, their energy levels and, in fact, their whole metabolism are adversely affected. In some people, instead of this being an almost natural adjustment to the seasons, the changes interfere quite dramatically with their everyday lives at home and at work and are a significant source of stress.

If your energy levels are noticeably lower in the winter months it is always possible that you are experiencing Seasonal Affective Disorder (SAD). SAD can be distinguished from other conditions, such as chronic fatigue or depression, because its symptoms are only present in autumn and winter, and go away completely in the spring and summer. It is estimated that around five per cent of people in the northern hemisphere are affected by SAD, though many more than this may complain of feeling 'out of sorts' in the winter months and may have a milder form. In countries that are below the equator, few incidences of SAD are found.

There are four major symptoms experienced by those afflicted with SAD. These are an increased desire to sleep, extreme lethargy, depression and an increased appetite (which often leads to weight gain). It is fairly common for the need to withdraw to become quite incapacitating. Other secondary symptoms might accompany these, including loss of libido, mood swings, phobias and an inability to cope with stress. The most useful time to start measures to combat this effect is in early autumn before the days have shortened too much.

Light Therapy

Light therapy during winter months, using a special light-box (see page 205) for up to a couple of hours a day is a tried and tested way of helping to relieve SAD, improving the situation for around 70 per cent of sufferers. The light which is needed to offset SAD is full-spectrum light, sufficiently strong for us to manufacture vitamin D in our skin (half an hour's sun exposure a day in the spring or summer for a light-skinned person and a bit longer for darker skins). Indoor lighting at home and in offices does not accomplish this. Full-spectrum light affects the hormone melatonin, which is made in the pineal gland in the brain and is responsible for setting a person's 'body-clock'. Insufficient activity of the pineal gland in winter is thought to contribute to SAD.

Other Treatment

Being cooped up indoors throughout winter will make the symptoms worse. Take every opportunity to get out, even in the thinnest winter sunshine. Brisk walking will boost endorphin levels and improve symptoms.

A factor that seems to be important in understanding SAD is low levels of the brain chemical serotonin. This is often called our 'satisfaction' brain chemical, and low levels are linked to depression and overeating. In people with SAD, levels may plummet with shorter days. Antidepressants that affect serotonin levels are sometimes prescribed, but foods can also have an impact (see page 195).

If you are able to, take your holidays in the winter when you need them most, and find a sunny location you can afford to go to.

Nutrition to Help Relieve SAD

- Protein foods, including meat, fish, eggs, cheese, milk, yogurt, nuts and pulses such as peas, beans and lentils, seem to have a positive effect on serotonin levels. Particularly good sources are turkey, cottage cheese, pheasant and partridge.
- In winter, those with SAD tend to eat more and their food choices may change. Often food is being used to seek comfort from tension and fatigue. Satisfying the need for comfort foods by eating thick bean soups or home-made casseroles helps to avoid the perceived need to eat refined carbohydrates, such as white bread, white rice and sugary foods, which are followed by dips in serotonin levels soon afterwards. Be aware that cravings for coffee, alcohol, sugar and chocolates are also triggered by lowered serotonin levels and can make the urge to binge worse.
- Many people find relief by following a 'food-combining' programme to discover which foods make their SAD better. Principally, food-combining involves making sure that you do not eat protein foods (such as meat, fish, eggs, cheese, milk) at the same meal as carbohydrate foods (bread, rice, pasta, potatoes). This means having a meal of, say, chicken with salad and vegetables, or a baked potato with salad and vegetables, but not chicken *and* baked potato.
- Eat protein-based meals on one day, and carbohydrate-based meals on another. Alternate the two types, keeping this up for a week. At the same time, keep a detailed diary of what you eat, why you are eating (hunger, energy boosters, mood enhancers), when you are eating and what your energy levels were at the time of eating, as well as an hour or so after the meals. Meals may make you feel alert, relaxed, calm, refreshed, energetic, able to concentrate and enthusiastic or lethargic, 'woolly brained', agitated, anxious, tired, depressed and tearful.
- At the end of the week you will have a much clearer idea of how foods make you feel. You can then use this to your advantage. For example, you could eat protein-based meals in the daytime when you need to feel more lively, and carbohydrate meals in the evening to bring on a soporific state ready for bedtime.
- Eating lots of fruits and vegetables, which are rich in antioxidants, has been shown to improve melatonin levels. You can simulate a summer diet, and prepare for winter by freezing large quantities of berries, using autumnal blackberries, blackcurrants and elderberries in recipes, or buying frozen or canned berries (in their natural juice). They are high in phytonutrients called proanthocyanidins, which are strong antioxidants.

Supplements to Help Relieve SAD

Do not use all the following supplements at the same time, but find out which one works best for you.

- Natural supplements that help to normalize serotonin levels are the herb rhodiola and a plant extract called 5-HTP (5-hydroxy-tryptophan). 50–100mg of 5-HTP is usually enough for most people (but more can lead to sleep disturbance resulting from too much serotonin). See page 204 for details of availability of rhodiola.

• Herbal help can also be found by taking St John's wort which is an effective antidepressant for mild to moderate depression, with fewer side effects than the pharmaceutical antidepressant options. Avoid using this herb with a light-box as it can increase photosensitivity. The SAD Association has recently conducted a study among its members regarding St John's wort and has chosen not to endorse it as they feel that light-box therapy is more likely to be of use and they should not be used together. However, of the respondents to their survey, 40 per cent found the herb helpful, 60 per cent would use it again and 30 per cent had some adverse effects, though a percentage of these had used it with the light-boxes or with antidepressants, both of which are contraindicated.

Digestive Stress

Nervous tummy, butterflies in the stomach, collywobbles – we all know that stress affects digestion faster than anything else. Stress is linked to heartburn, indigestion, bloating, stomach ulcers, irritable bowel syndrome (IBS) and wind, among other problems of the digestive tract.

When we experience stress one of the first symptoms is a tight, fluttering feeling in the stomach. This happens because the blood supply is shunted away from the digestive tract towards the skeletal frame, a response that evolved to help humans escape from danger in prehistoric times. But in this day and age, stress is more likely to be triggered by a late train or a row with the kids. Stress also has the effect of encouraging the breakdown of the tissues lining the digestive tract. This reduces absorption of nutrients from food and creates a vicious circle in which we don't have an adequate supply of the nutrients needed to combat the effects of stress on the body. Additionally, acute stress can encourage painful spasms of the gut wall, one of the effects of irritable bowel syndrome. Stress also lowers immunity and stomach acidity, allowing the bacteria *Helicobacter pylori* to get a foothold which encourages ulcers.

Obviously the best way to reduce the impact that stress has on digestion is to reduce your stress load. However, much can also be done to use diet to compensate for the worst effects of stress on the digestive tract.

Relaxed Eating

Make a point of eating in a relaxed, non-stressful environment. Eat slowly, chewing food properly and concentrate on enjoying your meal. Do this even if you are just having a snack, and especially if you are eating at work. If you are prone to not eating when nervous, make sure that you at least have a small, healthy snack, such as a banana, to keep you going. Your digestive tract mostly feeds directly from the contents of the tract, rather than from its blood supply, and needs to be kept nourished to function well. Eating a series of small, healthy snacks throughout the day helps to alleviate nervousness.

Relaxed Digestion

Relaxation or yoga classes can improve digestion if you apply yourself over time. Use visualization techniques (see page 142) during quiet moments to imagine your digestive tract functioning normally. Imagine the food going through, being broken down thoroughly, and the nutrients being absorbed across the healthy mucus membranes lining your tract. Now visualize a stressful situation and see what effect it has on your digestion in your mind's eye. Work out a visual way in which the stress 'bounces' off your digestive tract and does not interfere. Imagine a healing light coursing through your digestive tract and restoring normal function.

Autogenic training (see page 136), which is a form of intense relaxation, focuses on different parts of the body and can help to calm stressed digestion.

Nutrition to Help Relieve Digestive Stress

- Wheat is the food that most commonly stresses the digestive tract, which may find it hard to break down a protein called gluten contained in wheat, among other cereals. In Western diets, wheat is commonly eaten several times a day and can lead to bloating, stomach cramps and irritable bowel syndrome (IBS). Alternatives to wheat include rye, oats, barley, rice, buckwheat, corn and quinoa. Good health-food shops, and increasingly supermarkets, stock many standard foods, such as bread and pasta, made from these grains.
- Food-combining (see page 195) has been found to help many people to normalize nervous digestion, as it is said to work *with* the efficient process of digestion rather than against it. So a meal might consist of *either* meat/cheese with salad and vegetables *or* pasta/bread with salad and vegetables, but not the meat/cheese and pasta/bread together. Fruit such as melon is eaten either as a first course, with 20–30 minutes allowed to pass before eating the main meal, or as snacks between meals.
- If you have irritable bowel syndrome, make sure you keep your water intake up by drinking two litres daily. It will help to reduce constipation and will replace liquids lost as a result of loose bowel movements.
- Peppermint tea drunk after meals – four to five times a day is ideal – is a great normalizer of digestive function and reduces gassy bloating.
- Essential fats are needed to repair the digestive tract; good concentrated sources are nuts, seeds and oily fish.
- Coffee, tea and alcohol interfere with the absorption of nutrients, particularly minerals and B-vitamins. Coffee also raises stress-hormone levels, making digestive problems worse.

Supplements to Help Relieve Digestive Stress

- All bowel problems will benefit from taking one or two teaspoons daily of psyllium husks, available from good health food shops, to normalize bowel movements. This gentle fibre provides a great 'workout' for the muscles of the digestive tract. Mix it with water, pinch your nose and swallow it down – it tastes like sawdust.

However, if you mix it with apple juice and let it swell up for five minutes, it takes on the consistency of apple sauce and is really quite pleasant. Follow it with another glass of water.

- Take a good antioxidant supplement containing vitamins A and C and the mineral zinc to encourage healing of the digestive tract.
- Digestive enzymes taken with each meal can ensure that you actually absorb nutrients from your meal if your digestion is disturbed. Take between one and four capsules with each meal depending on the size of the meal. To test if the supplement you are taking is working properly, put one in half a cup of warm porridge, and it should turn it to liquid in 15 minutes or so. Digestive enzymes will not reduce your digestive capability but will allow you to absorb nutrients to improve your own digestive-enzyme output.
- An excessive growth of candida, a yeast that occurs naturally in the gut and other areas of the body, can also cause bloating and constipation. Taking acidophilus and bifidobacteria supplements can normalize the bacterial balance in the bowels, replacing the healthy, yeast-eating bacteria which are depleted by stress.
- Aloe vera is a potent healer of the digestive tract. Buy a good brand and take 20ml before meals.
- Slippery elm is also a proven digestive-tract healer. It protects against ulcers and is a soothing drink for after meals.
- The amino acid L-glutamine is used by the digestive tract directly as fuel and helps to heal stomach ulcers. Take 5–10g daily. As this is a large amount, it is easiest to take as a powder mixed in water in two doses, 5g in the morning and 5g in the afternoon (not too late or it might interfere with sleep).

Supplements

Nutritional Supplements

There are many brands of nutritional supplement on the shelves. The consumer is bombarded with so many varieties of multi-vitamins and minerals, or of single nutrients, that a trip to the health-food shop can feel overwhelming. In addition to this there are many 'ancillary' nutritional aids available. It is difficult to tell, just by looking at a label, if the contents of the bottle are going to be any good or not. If you are a nutritionist, you can get some basic information from the label, such as what form of a particular nutrient is in the formula, what the balance of quantities is between various nutrients and if there are any complementary (synergistic) compounds. Even for the trained nutritionist, however, there is little to tell you about the quality of the ingredients and how absorbable they are. And in some cases the contents simply do not match what is put on the label, which can only be uncovered by a testing laboratory.

For all these reasons, I list on page 200 supplement companies in whose products I have confidence. These are the ones that I have used effectively with my clients or that I know have stood up to testing procedures. This does not mean there are not other excellent products that are not in this list, and omission does not imply that other products are necessarily not of a suitable quality. By and large, you get what you pay for in nutritional supplements, and those that are of a good quality (in other words, absorbable) will usually be a little more expensive.

If you prefer not to swallow capsules or pills, you can get many supplements in liquid or powder form, though you may need to do a little detective work with different companies. Alternatively, you can get a pill-crusher from Health Plus (see page 200).

Be aware that, if you are planning a pregnancy or are pregnant or breastfeeding, you must take only specially formulated antenatal products. This is to protect you from taking too high a dose of some nutrients, such as vitamin A, or consuming ingredients unsuitable for pregnancy, such as many herbs.

If you are on medication, you need to consult a qualified nutritionist or doctor to find out if the medicine is known to clash with your supplements, or vice versa.

BIOCARE 0121 433 3727 or www.biocare.co.uk
   An excellent range of products from an innovative company, available via mail
   order direct from the company and from selected good health-food shops.
BIOFORCE 01294 277344 or www.bioforce.co.uk
   Herbal tinctures and supplements made from freshly prepared organic ingredients.
BLACKMORES 020 8842 3956 or www.blackmores.com.au
   A full range of herbal supplements.
GNC (General Nutrition Company) 0845 601 3248 or www.gnc.co.uk
   A number of stores around the country supplying a full range of products.
HEALTH AND DIET COMPANY 0845 076 5358
   A wide range of products at a number of stores throughout the country. FSC
   supplements are stocked by them and by other companies.
HEALTH PLUS 01323 737374 or www.healthplus.co.uk
   A range of useful supplements packaged for particular conditions in one-a-day
   pouches.
HEALTHY DIRECT 01481 710117 or www.healthydirect.co.uk
   A wide range of supplements available by mail order from their catalogue or on
   line.
HIGHER NATURE Nutrition line 01435 882964 (for advice), 01435 882880 (order line) or
www.highernature.co.uk
   A wide range of products including some helpful products brought in from
   overseas and not generally seen in other ranges. Available by mail order.
LICHTWER PHARMA 01803 528668 or www.lichtwer.co.uk
   Herbal preparations under the Lichtwer and Kira brands formulated to give
   standard doses of active compounds as used in many clinical trials.
NAPIERS HERBALISTS 0131 343 6683 or 0906 802 0117 (chargeable advice line)
   A full range of herbals including some very good specific formulations. Available by
   mail order. The herbal advice line is staffed by four-year qualified herbalists.
NATURE'S STORE 01782 794300 or www.naturesstore.co.uk
   Suppliers of a wide range of natural products and supplements. Nature's Store Ltd
   is the UK's largest independent wholesaler and distributor of wholefoods and
   natural products.
NUTRI CENTRE 020 7436 0422 or www.nutricentre.com
   A drop-in centre with an extensive range of high-quality products and books, as
   well as a mail order service.
REVITAL 0800 252875 or www.revital.com
   A comprehensive selection of supplements, books and natural healthcare products.
SOLGAR 01442 890355 or www.solgar.com
   An excellent range of supplements from a reliable company and available widely
   through independent health food shops.

Herbal Preparations

Herbal preparations complement the benefits of a nutritional programme. In particular we use many culinary herbs that are known to have soothing, stimulating or healing qualities, and that also add delicious variety to meals and make satisfying drinks.

However, it must also be recognized that herbs have the potential to be powerful medicines, and indeed a vast number of modern pharmaceutical medicines are drawn from this natural pharmacopoeia. Because they are 'natural' does not necessarily mean that they are benign, but they can be highly effective if used properly. Here are some pointers to be aware of when taking herbs:

- There are a limited number of herbs which are safe to take during pregnancy and breastfeeding – see my book *Eating for a Perfect Pregnancy* (Simon & Schuster) – but apart from these, all herbal preparations need to be avoided at this time.
- If you experience any adverse effects from taking a herbal preparation, stop immediately.
- Herbal preparations will usually take a bit of time for you to notice an effect. Some are effective within an hour or so, but more commonly you need to take a herbal preparation for a month or two to notice a radical change in symptoms. They usually have a more subtle effect than medications as they have a full spectrum of complementary compounds found within the plant. Even an extract that has a certain amount of the 'active compound' will still have other beneficial synergistic compounds in it.
- Combinations of herbs are often more effective than single herbs and mean that you can take smaller amounts. For this reason some products are formulated with several synergistic herbs, and herbalists might recommend herbs that support each other.
- Herbs have a medicinal effect and so it is not surprising that there are known interactions with medicines. For example, ginkgo biloba has blood-thinning effects and should be used cautiously by anyone on blood-thinning medication such as Warfarin. (The same is true of vitamin E, garlic capsules and fish-oil capsules.) Sedative herbs such as valerian and kava kava should be avoided if you are taking other sleep medications. St John's wort needs to be avoided if you are taking prescribed antidepressants. It also speeds up the clearance of drugs through the liver and so can reduce the effectiveness of some medication such as migraine medication, the contraceptive pill, asthma, blood-thinning (heart) and AIDS medications. It is impossible to give all possible interactions here, so the best advice is, if you are on any medication, check with a medical herbalist.
- Follow dosage guidelines given and do not fall into the trap of thinking that 'if a little is good, then more is better'.

Further Information

Sources for and information about many of the products mentioned in the book are given below. For information about Suzannah Olivier and her books, visit her website, www.healthandnutrition.co.uk.

Step 1
For more about mind-mapping, read the definitive book on the subject, *The Mind Map Book*, by Tony Buzan (BBC Books). Also look up www.mapyourmind.com.

Step 3
For more information about NLP, contact the Association for Neuro-Linguistic Programming (ANLP), 0870 870 4970 or www.anlp.org. You will find a stack of books about NLP in your bookshop. Useful ones include *Unlimited Power* and *Awaken the Giant Within* by Anthony Robbins (Simon & Schuster).

Step 4
For more information about dealing with panic attacks, contact HOPE (Help Overcome Panic Effects), www.support4hope.com.

For help with depression, organizations that will assist with specific problems include Relate (www.relate.org.uk) for marital problems or Compassionate Friends (www.compassionatefriends.org) and Cruse (www.crusebereavementcare.org.uk) for bereavement. Other helpful organizations include MIND (www.mind.org.uk), Depression Alliance (www.depressionalliance.org) and The Samaritans (www.samaritans.org.uk).

If you want to find out more about cognitive thinking, read *Feeling Good, The New Mood Therapy* by David D Burns, MD (Quill, Harper Collins).

Step 6
For help with a range of problems that come about as a result of marital discord and broken or complex family arrangements, contact National Family Mediation, 020 7383 5993 or www.nfm.u-net.com. Alternatively, look up the Institute of Family Therapy, www.instituteoffamilytherapy.org.uk.

For information about bedwetting, contact the Enuresis Resource and Information Centre, 0117 926 4920 or www.gnfc.org.uk/bedwetg.html.

Information about dealing with bullying can be found at www.pupiline.net or from Childline, www.childline.org.uk.

Helplines and professional help for a range of problems include Childline (see above) and the Institute of Family Therapy (see above).

For help in dealing with eating disorders, contact the Eating Disorders Association, www.edauk.com.

Information leaflets about solvent abuse are available from Re-Solv, www.re-solv.org.

For marriage counselling, contact Relate, 01788 573241 or www.relate.org.uk.

For organizations that will help with sexual problems or provide psychosexual counselling, contact The British Association for Sexual and Marital Therapy, PO Box 13686, London SW20 9ZH; The British Association for Counselling, www.bacp.co.uk; The Institute for Psychosexual Medicine, www.ipm.org.uk; The Impotence Association, www.impotence.org.uk (for factsheets about diverse conditions including premature ejaculation, prostate problems, male impotence, sexual difficulties for gay men and female sexual dysfunction); or The European Sexual Dysfunction Alliance, www.esda.eu.com, for a variety of support groups.

Step 7
For help with phobias, contact Triumph Over Phobia, www.triumphoverphobia.com or the National Phobics Society, www.phobics-society.org.uk.

Step 8
For information about ADD/ADHD, contact the Hyperactive Children's Support Group, www.hacsg.org.uk – the information is useful for adults as well as for children.

For details of training courses in meditation, *The Good Retreat Guide* by Stafford Whiteaker (Rider) lists secular and non-denominational centres as well as those allied to Christian and other faiths.

Step 9
For a list of products that are free of various harmful chemicals, see www.greenpeace.org.

Step 10
For salt substitutes, try the potassium-based salt Solo (www.soloseasalt.com) or seaweed granules (www.seagreens.com).

For inspiration and advice about disordered eating, look at www.comfortqueen.com. If you feel you have an eating disorder, contact the National Centre for Eating Disorders, www.eating-disorders.org.uk, or Overeaters Anonymous, www.oagb.org.uk.

If you think you might be affected by chronic fatigue (ME), you can find support from the ME Association, www.meassociation.org.uk, or the Association of Youth with ME, www.ayme org. uk.

The sugar substitute FOS is available from Biocare and Higher Nature (see page 200) and other health-food suppliers.

Rhodiola is available from Solgar (see page 200).

For help in giving up smoking, contact www.quit.org.uk and www.ash.org.uk. For information about the herb lobelia and its use in giving up smoking, contact the National Institute of Medical Herbalists, www.nimh.org.

Products designed to reduce snoring include NeverSnore from Higher Nature (see page 200), which contains enzymes and decongestant herbs, and the natural oil Snorenz (www.passionforlife.com).

For more information and the latest research on daytime naps see www.napping.com.

Good ideas for exercising your brain can be gained from Brain Gym, www.braingym.org.

For a simple set of memory tests, contact Neurologica, www.neurologica.co.uk, who will refer you for specialist advice if necessary.

L-glutamine in powdered form is available from Higher Nature (see page 200).

Organizations that will help in combating addictions:
Addiction Today, 020 7233 5333 or www.addictiontoday.co.uk
Alcohol Concern, 020 7928 7377 or www.alcoholconcern.org.uk
Alcohol Recovery Project, 020 7403 3369 or www.arp-uk.org
Alcoholics Anonymous, 01904 644026 or www.alcoholics-anonymous.org.uk
Debtors Anonymous, 020 7644 5070
Gamblers Anonymous, www.gamblersanonymous.co.uk
Narcotics Anonymous, 020 7251 4007 or www.ukna.org
National Drugs Helpline, 0800 776600 or www.ndh.org.uk
See above for organizations to help give up disordered eating or smoking.

The East West Herb Shop, www.ewhs.co.uk, sells mushroom-based supplements.

For tickles in the throat, try zinc and echinacea from Bioforce (see page 200).

The herb butterbur, for treating muscle tension, is available as Petaforce from Bioforce (see page 200).

A desk-top vaporizer that reduces ozone levels is Nozone (www.atmospherics.co.uk), available from larger Boots and other chemists.

For foot problems such as foot alignment and fallen arches, contact Dr Scholls, www.drscholls.com.

For information on pain-relief magnets, try www.homediscsuk.com. Patients with chronic pain can be referred by their doctor to the Walton Centre for Pain Relief, NHS Trust (www.wcnn.co.uk). Other organizations concerned with pain relief include The British Chiropractic Association, www.chiropractic-uk.co.uk; The McTimoney Chiropractic Association, www.mctimoney-chiropractic.org; The General Council and Register of Osteopaths, www.osteopathy.org.uk; The National Back Pain Association, http:/homepages.nildram.co.uk/~backtalk.

Helpful books about pain relief include *Foods That Fight Pain* by Neal Barnard (Bantam Books) and *The Back Pain Bible* by Anthony J Cichoke (Keats), an American book available on www.amazon.co.uk.

Details of light-boxes for SAD-sufferers are available from the SAD Association, www.sada.org.uk. You can rent before you buy.

For wheat-free products available by mail order, try www.allergyfreedirect.co.uk.

For more advice on digestive problems, read my book *Banish Bloating* (Simon & Schuster).

Index